Distant Allies

Distant Allies

Canada and the Anglo-Japanese Alliance, 1900 - 1923

PETER W. NOONAN

MAGISTRALIS
OTTAWA, CANADA

Copyright © 2021 by Peter W. Noonan

All Rights Reserved

Cataloguing in Publication Data for this book can be obtained from:

Library and Archives Canada
395 Wellington Street
Ottawa, ON K1A 0N4
CANADA

ISBN 978-0-9683534-9-3 (hardcover)

ISBN 978-0-9683534-8-6 (softcover)

Published by Magistralis, Ottawa, Canada

Contents

	Abbreviations	vii
	Introduction	1
1.	The Pacific World at the Turn of the Century	5
2.	The End of Splendid Isolation	20
3.	Triumph at Tsushima	38
4.	The Second Alliance	50
5.	The Anglo-German Naval Race and the Birth of the Royal Canadian Navy	65
6.	The North Pacific on the Eve of the World War	78
7.	The Outbreak of World War One and a West Coast Panic	100
8.	The German Raider Threat	126
9.	The Japanese North American Squadron	142
10.	The Cruise of the German East Asiatic Squadron	151
11.	The South Pacific 1914-15	172
12.	Conquering the German Pacific Empire	178
13.	The Strains in a Wartime Alliance	205
14.	The Zimmermann Telegram	219
15.	The Last Years of the War and the Siberian Intervention	231
16.	The Versailles Settlement	244
17.	The Anglo-Japanese Alliance in the Balance	258
18.	Canada's Opposition to the Japanese Alliance	267
19.	Arthur Meighen	283

20.	The Imperial Conference of 1921	295
21.	The End of the Alliance	316
22.	The Reckoning of History	325
	SOURCES	333
	SHIP INDEX	341
	GENERAL INDEX	345

Abbreviations

ANZAC – Australian and New Zealand Army Corps

BC – British Columbia

FS – French Ship

CP – Canadian Pacific steamships

CPR – Canadian Pacific Railway

CSEF – Canadian Siberian Expeditionary Force

HIJMS – His Imperial Japanese Majesty's Ship

HIRMS – His Imperial Russian Majesty's Ship

HMAS – His Majesty's Australian Ship

HMCS – His Majesty's Canadian Ship

HMCHS – His Majesty's Canadian Hospital Ship

HMD – His Majesty's Dockyard

HMS – His Majesty's Ship

IJN – Imperial Japanese Navy

KGS – Kaiserliches Governments Schiff – His Majesty's Government Ship – a prefix used for the German New Guinea Governor's yacht

KM – Kaiserliche Marine – Imperial German Navy

k.u.k. KM – kaiserliche und königliche Kriegsmarine – Imperial and Royal Navy of Austria-Hungary

NSHQ – Naval Service Headquarters – command function of the Royal Canadian Navy

RAN – Royal Australian Navy

RCN – Royal Canadian Navy

RMS – Royal Mail Ship

RN – Royal Navy

SMS – Seiner Majestät Schiff – His Majesty's Ship – a prefix used by the Imperial German Navy, and by the Imperial and Royal Austro-Hungarian Navy

SMY – Seiner Majestät Yacht – His Majesty's Yacht – a prefix used by the Imperial German Emperor's yacht

SS – Steam Ship

US – United States

USN – United States Navy

USS – United States Ship

Introduction

It has been a century since Canadian diplomacy at the Imperial Conference of 1921 precipitated the termination of the Anglo-Japanese Alliance, a historic relationship between the countries of the British Empire and Japan that served Canada and the British Empire well during World War One. Canadian naval historians have long known that when World War One broke out in the summer of 1914, and German Admiral Maximilian von Spee's powerful German Pacific naval squadron posed a significant risk to Canada's west coast it was not the practically moribund Royal Canadian Navy, nor the Royal Navy, or even the United States Navy that offered vital protection to Canada's vulnerable west coast. Rather, it was the Imperial Japanese Navy that acted quickly to ensure the protection of Canada from the potential depredations of the German fleet, or from attacks by individual German cruisers on wartime missions against the British Empire.[1] Thereafter, in the war years that followed, Japan employed its navy to ensure allied control over the North Pacific Ocean, as well as contributing substantially to allied naval control in Australasian waters, and in the waters of the Indian Ocean. Without the assistance of Japan, the allied naval control of the Pacific Ocean during World War One might have been jeopardized.

Despite its loyal service to the common cause, Canada pressed hard at the Imperial Conference in 1921, the forerunner of today's Commonwealth Prime Minister's Meetings, for the British Empire to abandon its alliance with Japan. Canada was concerned that the Japanese alliance was potentially prejudicial to Canada's relations with the United States.

In the short run, the placation of the United States may have avoided some friction in Canada – US relations but in the larger context, it was a miscalculation to abandon the alliance with Japan.

Japan was left feeling spurned and isolated. Over time, the isolation of Japan in international affairs, and the weaknesses displayed by the parliamentary governments of Japan in the twenties and thirties, provided Japanese militarists with an opening to increase their influence in the Japanese cabinets until the whole of government was largely in their possession. From 1937 onward Japan's militarist leaders embarked upon a policy of large scale conquest, first in China, and then subsequently in the entire Asia – Pacific region, imperilling the southern dominions of Australia, and New Zealand, as well as the extensive territories of the British Empire in the Far East.

Can one say whether the ravages of the war in the Pacific between 1937 and 1945 might have been avoided if the alliance relationship with Japan had been maintained? Perhaps not. But it is certainly possible that a continuing alliance of Japan with the British Commonwealth and Empire might have offered a means to restrain Japanese aggressiveness in Asia, and it might have also possibly strengthened the hand of the faltering Japanese parliamentary governments in the years preceding World War Two by avoiding Japan's international isolation. While the harshness of the Peace of Versailles was always likely to lead to a future revanchist war with Germany,[2] Japan had been an ally of the West in World War One, and, in 1921, when the alliance failed, there was no cause to think that a war with Japan was inevitable. It was shortsighted to abandon the alliance and Great Britain did so only under great pressure from Canada, whose Prime Minister, Arthur Meighen, proved intractable on the subject of renewing the alliance. In fairness, Canadian opposition was not the only factor that led to the end of the alliance but it was Canadian obduracy on the question of renewing the alliance that operated as the catalyst for jettisoning the alliance relationship.[3]

In writing about this chapter in Canadian history I was interested in how the alliance had been developed and managed by the British and Japanese empires in both peace and in war. Thus, it was necessary to start at the beginning, before the alliance was even contemplated, in order to examine the changes occurring in British foreign policy at the start of the twentieth century, and how it became desirable for two such different empires to align their interests in the Orient.

The original alliance, which was little more than an insurance policy against the Dual Alliance, was subsequently transformed into an active alliance with a broader Asia – Pacific regional scope in the years leading up to World War One. At the same time, important developments were occurring in Canada, as the naval debates thrust Canada forward on a more nationalistic path, and as successive governments sought to maintain Canada's restrictive immigration policies while avoiding offence to the British Empire's alliance partner on the far side of the Pacific Ocean.

In the aftermath of the war, the substantial naval and other support that Japan gave to the British Empire in the Asia-Pacific region during World War One was soon overlooked by Canada, as Canada became transfixed by the visible proof of America's enormous power and the realization that through a diplomatic realignment American power could also serve Canada's own national security interests. The result was a strong continentalist focus in Canadian foreign policy, as Canada slowly began a historic shift away from its integration with Britain's foreign and security policies, towards a new Canadian security relationship with the United States. The Anglo – Japanese Alliance was seen as an impediment to Canada – US relations and therefore Canada deemed it necessary to dispense with it. Canada's policy on the alliance was the earliest example of Canada asserting its independence from Britain in foreign policy, although that result was partially obscured by the limited public disclosure of the inner workings of the Imperial Conference of 1921. Unfortunately, however, this first example of Canadian foreign policy independence would ultimately have serious consequences for the maintenance of peace in the Asia-Pacific region.

NOTES

[1] Barry M Gough, *The Royal Navy and the Northwest Coast of North America, 1810 - 1914*, University of British Columbia Press, Vancouver, 1974, 238, fn75

[2] The allied commander-in-chief in the west, Marshal Foch, famously referred to the Treaty of Versailles as an armistice for twenty years.

[3] Ian H Nish, *Alliance in Decline: A Study In Anglo-Japanese Relations 1908 - 1923*, University of London/The Athlone Press, London, 1972, 352

1. The Pacific World at the Turn of the Century

The Pacific Ocean is an immense body of water covering one-third of the total area of the Earth. It is so vast that all of the lands on Earth would fit within the boundaries of the Pacific Ocean. The deepest place on Earth is in the Mariana Trench within the Pacific Ocean, and the highest mountain on the planet, as measured from its footings, is Mauna Kea in the Hawaiian Islands. As a geographical feature, the Pacific Ocean was unknown to Europeans before the Age of Discovery, although early travellers to China must have been aware of it. The Spanish explorer Balboa glimpsed the Pacific Ocean from the western shores of Central America in 1513, but it was not until the great expedition of Ferdinand Magellan in 1519, that this huge body of water was crossed by Europeans for the first time.

In the ensuing centuries trade routes across the Pacific were devised by intrepid western explorers and traders. The littoral areas of the Pacific were colonized by the West where local resistance was limited. Where littoral states were too strong to be colonized, such as China and Japan, trading posts were established to facilitate international commerce. For the most part, the interior islands were left to govern themselves by the western countries until well into the Age of Imperialism in the nineteenth century. With few exceptions, however, initial western indifference did not mean that the isolated islands were considered to be part of the community of nations recognized by western powers. In fact, only Hawaii and Tonga, both with indigenous monarchical forms of government, managed to enter into foreign treaties with western powers, and only the Kingdom of Hawaii maintained active foreign relations with western states.

For a great part of the nineteenth century, the European powers embarked on imperial expansion in Asia and Africa, where a frenzy of occupations and colonisations reached its apex in the eighteen seventies and eighties. Although France established control over the Society Islands before mid-century it was only in the last years of the nineteenth century that western (and Japanese) control was firmly established over the majority of the isolated Pacific Islands.

Canada had emerged from a confederation of British North American colonies in 1867, and subsequently established itself on the Pacific coast with the entry of British Columbia into the Dominion of Canada in 1871. As an inducement to the entry of British Columbia into the confederation, the Canadian Government promised to construct a transcontinental railway, which was finally accomplished in 1885, when the Canadian Pacific Railway reached Vancouver. By the turn of the century, the province of British Columbia was prospering, and in the last years of the nineteenth-century, the Klondike gold rush in the territories north of British Columbia led to a surge in prospectors and miners travelling north to the goldfields. The sudden surge in the north-western population led the Federal Government to carve out a new territory, the Yukon Territory, from the larger Northwest Territories. The new territory lacked direct access to the Pacific Ocean however, and ambiguity over the exact location of the international border with the United States resulted in a major territorial dispute that would subsequently have consequences for the development of Canada's international relations, by leading to the creation of the Department of External Affairs, a nascent foreign ministry for the new country.

Farther south, in the United States of America, the Americans had consolidated the occupation of their own western lands. After the eleventh American census in 1890, the US census superintendent stated that the American western frontier had closed, bringing to an end the continental project of Manifest Destiny. The United States had rapidly industrialized in the decades following the conclusion of the Civil War, and by the mid-1890's the United States had crossed the urban-rural divide, now having a majority of its population contained in cities and towns.[1] The crossing of the urban-rural divide marked the emergence of the United States as one of the world's great industrial powers, and like other major industrial powers, it began to develop important interests abroad.

One of the most important interests of the United States concerned the Kingdom of Hawaii, an independent state in the mid-north Pacific Ocean that lay astride the trade routes to the Orient from North America. The United States had long claimed an interest in the Hawaiian Islands, and a three or four-cornered standoff occurred in the nineteenth century between the United States, Great Britain, France, and Russia, over the future of the Hawaiian Islands, which allowed the indigenous population to maintain their sovereignty, albeit under the guidance of the European and American settlers who initially came to Hawaii to spread Christianity.

The introduction of foreign diseases contributed to a major demographic decline in the indigenous Hawaiian population, however, which even affected the viability of the Royal House founded by King Kamehameha I, who had united the islands under his crown in 1795. When the last monarch of the Kamehameha dynasty died in 1872 without a direct heir, the country was forced into elections to fill the throne. A cousin of the late King secured the throne but he reigned for only one year and then subsequently a new candidate, David Kalakaua, defeated the consort of an earlier King to claim the throne, sparking serious riots which resulted in the landing of foreign troops from offshore warships in a bid to restore order. The elective processes revealed deep cleavages in public opinion and boded ill for the future of the kingdom.

King Kalakaua however proved himself to be a striking figure in Hawaiian history. Known colloquially as the Merry Monarch he strove to reinforce the sovereignty of his kingdom. Some of his mostly western advisors, particularly the British-born and

Canadian-raised Premier Walter Murray Gibson, were at odds however with the increasingly powerful American expatriate community, which exercised a vise-like grip on a Hawaiian economy that was based on the production of sugar. Sugar production required considerable manual labour, which the declining indigenous Hawaiian population was unable to provide. That led the local American and European sugar magnates to lobby the Hawaiian government for the immigration of foreign manual labourers, especially from Japan, China, and Portugal into Hawaii. The substantial influx of immigrants in the late nineteenth century contributed to the ongoing demographic and economic marginalization of the indigenous Hawaiian population. Consternation at the King's spendthrift ways and anger at their lack of political authority to match their economic power led to an armed rebellion by western expatriates (primarily American, but also including some Europeans, and even one or two Canadians[2]). The revolution of 1887 greatly circumscribed the powers of the Hawaiian monarchy.

Following the death of the King in 1891, the throne passed to his strong-willed sister, Queen Liliuokalani, who plotted to restore the primacy of the indigenous Crown in Hawaiian governance. At the same time, certain members of the expatriate community had formed themselves into a secret society with the avowed intention of procuring the annexation of the Kingdom of Hawaii by the United States. They were motivated in that endeavour by the erection of new US tariff barriers applicable to sugar in the early nineties that were intended to protect sugar producers in the southern United States but which also had a devastating impact on the Hawaiian economy. The administration of President Benjamin Harrison (in office 1889-93) encouraged the American expatriate community in Hawaii to promote annexation to the United States. A pro-annexation American diplomat maintained active contacts with the local annexationists.

In early 1893, Queen Liliuokalani attempted to promulgate a new constitution, bypassing the existing mechanisms for amending the constitution. That led to a *coup d'état* with the encouragement of the American Minister. US Marines and sailors were landed in Honolulu, and a Provisional Government seized power and abolished the monarchy. After an interim period of rule by a white minority government, the US annexed Hawaii in 1898 during the Spanish-American war, recognizing its strategic position in the Pacific Ocean.

The Spanish-American War was fought not only in the Caribbean but also in the North Pacific, where Spain held important possessions. The war in the Pacific underscored how important military installations in Hawaii could be for the projection of American military force in the Pacific Ocean, and the administration of President William McKinley (in office 1897-1901) had moved rapidly to annex the islands. American commerce favoured the annexation, and those views were strengthened by Russian and German acquisitions of new territories in China following China's defeat by Japan in the Sino-Japanese War of 1895.[3] In Hawaii, the United States acquired its first major overseas colonial possession.

Hawaii, however, was not the only colonial possession that the United States would acquire from the Spanish-American War. Commodore George Dewey and his US Asiatic Squadron based in Hong Kong descended upon the Spanish-owned Philippines shortly after hostilities commenced and destroyed the Spanish Asiatic Fleet in an afternoon engagement. The US subsequently landed troops in the Philippines, and the archipelago surrendered to the American invaders on August 14, 1898. Cuba and Puerto Rico in the Caribbean also fell to the Americans, as did the island of Guam, east of the Philippines, in the Pacific Ocean.

At a stroke the United States became a substantial imperial power in the North Pacific through its acquisition of the Philippine archipelago, Guam, and Wake Island, to complement its annexation of the Hawaiian Islands. But the Philippines desired to chart its own destiny and a vicious guerrilla war began between the indigenous population and their new American masters that would take several years, and several thousand lives, to resolve in America's favour. Spain, now defeated, and demoralized, elected to withdraw from the Pacific and sold its remaining colonies (the Caroline and Mariana Islands) to Germany, which took possession of them in 1899. Germany's acquisition of the Spanish islands in the Pacific complemented its earlier acquisition of the Marshall Islands, which lay east of the Caroline Islands in the North Pacific Ocean.

While the United States was undertaking its great Pacific expansion, farther west there was a significant development in the relations between the two main Oriental states, Japan and China. Japan had emerged from isolation in 1853, with the forced opening of the country by Commodore Matthew Perry of the United States. Subsequently, after the Meiji Restoration in 1868, and the fall of the Tokugawa shogunate, Japan rapidly modernized and began flexing its power as a major state.

However, Japan's main foreign ambition in the late nineteenth century was to be admitted to the community of nations as an equal of the western powers. Consequently, the first objective of the Japanese Government was to renegotiate certain unequal treaties that the western powers had imposed upon it when Japan was first opened up to the west. Japan's quest for equal status began in 1893, with Great Britain, when it sought to negotiate a new commercial treaty with Europe's most important power.[4] Japan was successful in that endeavour, and in 1894 a new commercial treaty with Great Britain came into force which abolished the British consular court system in Japan. It was agreed that other unequal provisions under the previous treaty with Great Britain would be sunset in 1899. Soon, other major powers followed suit and negotiated new commercial arrangements with the rising power in the Far East.[5]

The rising power of Japan was reflected in its line of interest, which extended beyond its home islands into the nearby Pacific. Japan began its expansion into the Pacific by taking the Bonin Islands in 1878, the Ryukyu Islands in 1879, and Marcus Island in 1899, the beginnings of an oceanic advance that would lead to the creation a great island empire before Japan's collision with the United States in World War II destroyed its overseas empire.

But in the 1890's the main foreign concerns of Japan were the two decrepit monarchies on the Asian mainland, China and Korea. For Japan, the Korean peninsula was an area of primary strategic interest. Japanese strategists perceived the Korean peninsula as a drawn dagger pointed across the Sea of Japan at the Japanese home island chain.

Although Korea was an independent country, the Chinese Empire had historically exercised a substantial degree of suzerainty over Korea. The rising power of Japan, however, led both China and Japan to enter into a treaty to regulate their spheres of interest in Korea. In the 1885 Convention of Tientsin a prominent late Manchu Empire statesman, Hung-Chang Li, agreed with his Japanese counterpart that neither China nor Japan would introduce troops into Korea without first consulting the other party to their treaty.

By 1894 however, the continuing decrepitude of the Korean state, as witnessed by its failure to suppress a rural rebellion, provided Hung-Chang Li and his proconsul in Korea, Yüan Shih-k'ai, with an opportunity to reinvigorate the suzerainty of the Manchu Empire over Korea by sending an army to suppress the rural revolt. Japan countered the Chinese initiative by sending its own military expedition to Korea pursuant to the terms of the Convention of Tientsin. A tense standoff ensued but the Japanese government, under considerable pressure from its military commanders took steps to portray China as an aggressor in Korea. In Tokyo, Foreign Minister Count Mutsu Munemitsu despatched a diplomatic note suggesting that the future domination of Korea by Japan would be desirable as a means to modernize the country. Hung-Chang Li quite correctly perceived that the Japanese intention was to wrest

Korea from China's orbit and he sent reinforcements to the Chinese army in Korea. Japan responded by sinking a Chinese troopship on July 24th, and capturing the Korean Royal Family in their palace in Seoul. On August 1, 1894, war was declared by Japan on China.

On September 17, 1894, the Japanese and Chinese fleets met in the Battle of the Yellow Sea (also called the Battle of the Yalu River). Both navies were equipped with modern steam-propelled armoured warships firing explosive shells. However, the Imperial Japanese Navy (IJN) had received excellent training from Great Britain's Royal Navy (RN), the dominant and most professional navy in the world at the time, and its superior training was telling against the Chinese fleet. Admiral Juchang Ting, the commander of the Chinese fleet, lost five of his ships, in part due to the lack of anti-fire control procedures. Nevertheless, he escaped at night into the harbour at Weihaiwei with the remainder of his squadron, leaving Japanese Admiral Ito Sukeyuki in command of the sea. Although the Japanese flagship was severely damaged, Admiral Ito's squadron was otherwise intact. The Battle of the Yellow Sea was the first significant engagement by modern warships, and it illustrated how destructive modern naval technology had become.

The Japanese army also succeeded on land against the Imperial Chinese Army, defeating the Chinese at the Battle of Pyongyang, after which the Japanese army crossed into Manchuria, which was part of China proper, and the native territory of the ruling Manchu Imperial House. An amphibious assault on the Liaotung Peninsula resulted in the capture by Japan of strategic Port Arthur. Faced with defeat, the Manchu Empire sued for peace, resulting in the Treaty of Shimonoseki under which China ceded to Japan the island of Formosa (modern Taiwan), the Pescadores Islands, and the Liaotung Peninsula, with its strategic port of Port Arthur.

The European powers were alarmed at Japan's success, which was quite unexpected, and Russia, France, and Germany together pressured Japan to give up some of its gains. In particular, the

Europeans pressured Japan to give up the strategic port of Port Arthur, which Russia coveted. Japanese Foreign Minister Mutsu was compelled to attend an international conference and to agree to return the Liaotung Peninsula to China although he managed to retain Formosa and the Pescadores. This effort by the European powers, known in Japanese history as the Triple Intervention, humiliated the Japanese government. Cynically, after forcing Japan to disgorge some of its territorial gains the European powers immediately carved out portions of China for their own benefit, with the Germans taking Tsingtao and its environs, the French taking concessions in southern China, and the Russians taking the Liaotung Peninsula and Port Arthur, as well as certain concessions in Manchuria. Thoroughly humiliated, Japan's leaders never forgot the Triple Intervention.

Although Great Britain was not part of the formal remonstrance made to Japan over the Liaotung Peninsula, it secured Weihaiwei, across from the Liaotung Peninsula.[6] Nevertheless, Anglo-Japanese relations were not affected by the British acquisition of Weihaiwei from China. In Japan, more store was placed on the fact that Great Britain had declined to participate in the Triple Intervention although it had been invited to do so by the other European powers. In hindsight, Great Britain's decision not to participate in the humiliation of the Japanese government through the Triple Intervention was one of the most important diplomatic decisions made by Britain in the late nineteenth and early twentieth centuries.[7] Its reluctance to humiliate Japan made it possible for Great Britain to subsequently arrange an alliance with Japan.

Although the outcome of the Sino-Japanese War established Japan as a major power in the Orient, the inability of the Japanese government to prevent the European powers from forcing Japan to disgorge the territorial gains it had made in the Treaty of Shimonoseki made a deep impression on the country, especially after the Europeans made their own territorial acquisitions at the expense of China (and Japan). Japan would not soon forget the perfidy of Russia and Germany.

For China, however, its defeat in the Sino-Japanese War was a further agony in the long decline of the Manchu Empire. The Qing Dynasty, the last of the Chinese Imperial dynasties, had ruled China since 1636, when the leaders of the Manchu minority emerged from northeast China to wrest control away from a preceding Han dynasty. Now long past its zenith, the Qing dynasty was approaching its nadir. Bested by Japan in the late war, China desperately needed to modernize. The Guangxu Emperor, whose exercise of sovereign powers was subject to the paramount authority of his former regent, the Dowager Empress Cixi, embarked upon a sweeping set of modernizing reforms, aided by modernizing officials. His One Hundred Days of Reform campaign sought to put China on the same course as Japan by adopting western innovations to improve the efficiency of the state. However, reactionary officials, fearing their loss of power, appealed to the Dowager Empress who mounted a successful military *coup d'état* that effectively removed the Guangxu Emperor from political control, although he was retained as a figurehead. The process of reform stopped, and anti-foreign antipathy increased in China.

In the north, a public backlash against the encroachments of foreign powers following China's defeat in the Sino-Japanese War developed into a hatred of all foreigners among Chinese martial arts clubs, who became known as the Boxers, after the form of Chinese boxing that they practised. The Boxer movement grew in strength and professed allegiance to the dynasty but called for the expulsion, or killing, of all foreigners in China and the suppression of Christianity throughout the empire. The Boxer movement grew rapidly in strength and received the imperial imprimatur when Empress Cixi threw her support behind it. The Boxers entered Peking (modern Beijing) and put the foreign quarter, where the foreign diplomatic legations were located, under siege, after first assassinating the German Minister. The siege of the foreign legations in Peking led to a rare international spirit of cooperation among the European, American, and Japanese governments, and an international relief force was raised and sent to China to rescue the besieged foreign missions. The foreign legations were relieved by the international force in August, 1900, and the Boxer War ended in a humiliating defeat for the Imperial Court and the Boxers. Foreign influence, particularly Russian and Japanese influence, began to increase in China with the Russians taking the opportunity afforded by the Boxer War to occupy Manchuria.

The outcome of the Boxer War brought further consternation to those Chinese intellectuals and others who despaired of the ability of the Qing dynasty to reverse the empire's continuing decline. Many young Chinese began studying in Japan and their knowledge of that country, together with the very prominent role played by the Japanese Army in relieving the besieged legations in Peking served as an example to Chinese modernizers and contributed to increased Japanese influence in China.

Farther north, in the Russian Empire, the great empire of the Tsar was undergoing far-reaching social and political change. For a long period of time, its great eastern possessions had been remote from European Russia but in the last years of the nineteenth century, the Russian Empire embarked on a great transcontinental railway project to connect European Russia with its Pacific Coast. In February, 1891, Tsar Alexander III announced the construction of the Trans-Siberian Railway, and he issued a decree on March 29, 1891, addressed to his heir, the Tsarevich Nicholas, directing him to lay the foundation stone of the Great Siberian Railway upon his arrival in Russia from Japan at the conclusion of a round the world tour that Tsarevich had embarked upon.

While in Japan, Nicholas was almost assassinated by a fanatic who struck him with a sword. The assassin would have killed Nicholas but for the quick action of his cousin, Prince George of Greece, who parried a second blow of the assassin's sword with his walking stick. The assassination attempt would forever colour Nicholas' opinion of Japan and the Japanese, and he would often refer to the Japanese as 'monkeys'. On May 23, 1891, the youthful Tsarevich disembarked at Vladivostok after touring Japan.[8] On May 31st the cornerstone of the Pacific Station of the Great Railway was laid by Nicholas, and the massive construction project was underway.[9] Although the Tsarevich was nominally in charge of the project it was actually overseen by the Imperial Minister of Finance, Sergius Witte, a capable technocrat, who oversaw the day-to-day work of the project, and who was the driving force behind its construction.

The Russian encroachments on Manchuria that followed the Triple Intervention afforded the Russian Empire the option to construct a less costly route to the Pacific through Manchuria to reach the Russian Pacific port of Vladivostok. On November 3, 1901, the Trans-Siberian and Chinese Eastern Railway, all under Russian suzerainty, was provisionally opened and then subsequently opened for regular traffic in February, 1903.[10] A section around Lake Baikal still remained to be built, however, and it was not until September 25, 1904, during the Russo-Japanese War, that the difficult section around Lake Baikal was completed.[11] Later, after the conclusion of the Russo-Japanese War, the Russians would commence construction of the more difficult section north of the Amur River in Siberia proper, extending from Lake Baikal to connect to Vladivostok through an all-Russian route. That leg of the Trans-Siberian Railway would not be completed until 1916, during World War I, when the Khabarovsk Bridge was finally finished.[12]

While the building of the Trans-Siberian Railway was a great feat of engineering, it also raised the stakes in the gamesmanship between Japan and Russia for the control of northern China. After the Boxer War, the Japanese seethed at the Russian control of Manchuria, and when Russia began encroaching on Korea there was genuine alarm in Tokyo. Efforts were quickly undertaken to effect a diplomatic solution to the challenge posed to Japan by Russian encroachments in northeast Asia.

In the South Pacific, the western powers had largely taken control of the scattered paradisaical islands by the turn of the century. France was well established in Tahiti by mid-century, and later it extended its control to the Marquesas, and the Tuamotu Archipelago, by the 1880's. France had also taken the Loyalty Islands, including New Caledonia, in 1864. New Guinea had been divided three ways by 1901, with the Netherlands taking the western half of the island while Britain and Germany divided the eastern half between them in 1899. The British and the Germans also divided the Solomon Islands between themselves, and Britain and France established a joint condominium over the New Hebrides after the turn of the century. The British were well established in Fiji from 1874, and Britain also took the Ellice Islands in 1892, and the Gilbert Islands in 1899. Finally, the Kingdom of Tonga, the last independent Polynesian monarchy after the fall of the Kingdom of Hawaii, was declared to be a British protectorate in 1899, the same year that the troubled Samoan Islands were divided between Germany and the United States.

Farther south, the great British settler colonies of Australia and New Zealand marched forward to join Canada in the status of self-governing dominions under the British Crown. The Commonwealth of Australia was established in 1901, with a federal parliament that took responsibility for most domestic matters, and New Zealand, which already possessed a parliament and a responsible ministry, was proclaimed a dominion in 1907.

As the nineteenth century merged into the twentieth century, the relations between countries in the Pacific region were in flux. British settler dominions such as Canada, Australia, and New Zealand, were slowly emerging from colonial status to join the community of nations as separate countries. The United States had burst its continental boundaries by reaching out into the Pacific to take the Hawaiian Islands, and the Philippine Islands, making it an important imperial power in the North Pacific Ocean. The Spanish Empire was in terminal decline and was forced to withdraw from the Pacific, while a robust Germany now appeared on the scene and acquired territories in both the North and the South Pacific, leaving Britain and France to further consolidate their initial footholds among the Pacific Islands. Japan emerged as the most powerful Oriental power, while China continued its long slow decline, leaving Russia as the sole littoral power on the eastern shores of the Pacific that could challenge Japan for supremacy in the Northwest Pacific.

NOTES

[1] Walter A McDougall, *Let the Sea Make a Noise, A History of the North Pacific from Magellan to MacArthur*, Basic Books, New York, 1993, 390

[2] In particular, the brothers Volney and Clarence Ashford, both of whom were prominent in the Honolulu Rifles, a militia established and largely manned by the expatriate community in Hawaii, were Canadian. Clarence Ashford subsequently served as the Attorney General of the Kingdom

[3] Merze Tate, *The United States and the Hawaiian Kingdom, A Political History*, Yale University Press, New Haven (CT) 1965, 286-87

[4] The very first country to renegotiate an unequal treaty with Japan was, however, Hawaii, under Hawaii's Provisional Government in 1894.

[5] Richard Storrey, *Japan and the Decline of the West in Asia, 1894 – 1945*, The Macmillan Press, London, 1979, 22.

[6] McDougall, 387

[7] Storrey, 28

[8] Robert Massie, *Nicholas and Alexandra*, Dell Publishing, New York, 1967, 22

[9] Harmon Tupper, *To the Great Ocean, Siberia and the Trans-Siberian Railway*, Little, Brown & Company, Boston and Toronto, 1965, 82

[10] Tupper, 332-35

[11] Tupper, 339

[12] Tupper, 371

2. The End of Splendid Isolation

Throughout the nineteenth century, Great Britain and its empire reigned supreme across the world. It was the nineteenth-century version of a modern superpower whose strength came from its rapid industrialization following the defeat of Napoleonic France at the beginning of the nineteenth century. Guarded by the might of the Royal Navy, which was technologically superior to the naval forces of all other countries, Great Britain became a centre of industry, commerce, and finance. The Royal Navy gave Britain the ability to extend its reach to any part of the globe, and to enforce peaceful commercial relations between states. It also gave Great Britain the ability to conquer, or acquire, many important foreign bases, or territories, which ultimately gave to Great Britain the largest globe-girdling empire in history, exceeding in importance even the ancient empire of Rome in its impact on world-wide affairs.

However, Great Britain could not prevent other countries from following in its path and rapidly industrializing. By the end of the nineteenth century France had recovered from its defeat, and from the political instability that had followed the Napoleonic Era, and it had also acquired an empire spanning the globe. Prussia had slowly consolidated its position in central Europe and then burst forth in the 1860's in three victorious wars against Denmark, Austria-Hungary, and finally, France, which allowed Prussia to wrest control of the Germanic states away from Austria. The Germanic states were consolidated into a new German Reich that was proclaimed at the Palace of Versailles outside of Paris in 1871, following Germany's victory over France in 1870. Rapid industrialization made Germany a leading, if not the leading, industrial power in Europe by the end of the nineteenth century. In North America, the United States recovered from the terrible civil war that it fought in the 1860's, and it expanded its control over its western hinterland. Thereafter the US rapidly industrialized and grew demographically through mass immigration from Europe. By the 1890's, the US was a major industrial power, whose immense strength was yet only imperfectly perceived by the major European powers.

Hitherto, Great Britain had refused to enter into any alliances or entanglements with foreign powers. Secure behind its water frontiers, and guarded by the might of the Royal Navy, the British Empire had remained in what Canadian Senator Sir George Eulas Foster called 'splendid isolation' from entering into alliances with other countries. However, during the 1890's, Britain faced a succession of foreign challenges that began to erode its commitment to splendid isolation.

The first direct challenge came from the burgeoning power of the United States. Great Britain faced a significant boundary dispute between British Guiana, a Crown colony in northern South America, and Venezuela, in 1895. A large part of British Guiana was claimed by Venezuela but Great Britain did not recognize the validity of that Venezuelan claim. An agent of the Venezuelan government lobbied in Washington for the application of the Monroe Doctrine[1] to the dispute, and the administration of President Cleveland responded sympathetically. The United States sided with Venezuela on the need for international arbitration of the dispute, and on the scope of that arbitration. Great Britain's refusal to accede to the US view on the scope of the arbitration was perceived as a provocation by the Cleveland Administration. A far-off diplomatic dispute quickly escalated when the United States decided that Great Britain did not recognize the predominant role of the United States in the affairs of the Americas. For a time, war between Great Britain and the United States was a real possibility. Urgent steps were taken in Canada to prepare for war, including decisions by the Federal government to arm the Canadian militia with newer and more modern rifles, and to permit the formation of naval reserve units on the Great Lakes as a precautionary measure.[2]

Ultimately, the crisis passed when Britain responded to the American pressure and agreed to submit the dispute to international arbitration, with the scope of the arbitration defined in a manner that was satisfactory to the United States. Nevertheless, the danger of war with the United States made it plain to Whitehall that Great Britain's commitment to defend Canada, which was, after all, a constituent part of the empire, was increasingly unrealistic where the United States was concerned. British officials began to reconsider both the imperial defence commitments to Canada, as well as the nature of Great Britain's relations with the United States, and Britain soon began to align its diplomacy in the Americas in a manner designed to ensure good relations with the United States.

The second challenge faced by Britain in the 1890's concerned its historic rivalry with France. In the late nineteenth century both of those imperial powers were racing to claim as much as possible of the remaining unclaimed territory[3] that existed on the globe. A crisis emerged in Africa, when the desire of Great Britain to claim contiguous territory to create an all-British Cape to Cairo corridor running the length of the continent from the south, at the Cape of Good Hope, north to Egypt (under British protection), conflicted with the French desire to extend its North African colonies east from the Atlantic Ocean to the Red Sea, across North Africa. Expeditions sponsored by each country eventually collided with each other at Fashoda, in the Sudan. One column, led by General Kitchener of Great Britain had fought and won the battle of Omdurman against the army of the Mahdist state, an entity in the Sudan led by a mystic known as the Mahdi, and had captured Khartoum, the Sudanese capital. Afterwards, word reached the British that French troops travelling overland from Senegal had occupied the old Mahdist fort at Fashoda. General Kitchener embarked troops on five small river transports (one of which was commanded by Lieutenant David Beatty – later to command the Royal Navy) and arrived at the fort, vastly outnumbering the French forces under a Captain Marchand.

Kitchener and his officers carefully appeared under the Egyptian flag and asserted sovereignty over Fashoda on behalf of the Khedive of Egypt – Egypt then being effectively a British protectorate, and thus attempted to avoid offending French sensibilities. Kitchener and Marchand negotiated a delicate standoff, which saw the French retaining the ruined fort while the British positioned themselves across Marchand's line of retreat. The matter was then laid before the governments of the two empires. Despite French protests, Great Britain held the superior position, both tactically on the ground at Fashoda, and strategically through its control of the seas. France was forced to back down and evacuate its forces from Fashoda, thus permitting Great Britain to consolidate its control of the Anglo-Egyptian Sudan.

While Great Britain had compelled France to withdraw, the threat of war that the Fashoda Crisis produced caused the British to reconsider its relations with France and after King Edward VII, a notable Francophile, succeeded to the throne in 1901, steps were taken to reach an understanding between Britain and France. That understanding, known to history as the Entente Cordiale, came to fruition in 1904, by resolving colonial disputes between the two powers as far afield as Africa and Newfoundland and led to a tentative level of political cooperation between the two states – the precursor to an alliance.

The third major challenge that came to the fore in the case of late-nineteenth-century British policy concerned the growing might of Germany and, in particular, the German Kaiser's ambition to create a blue-water fleet equal to the might of the Royal Navy. Kaiser Wilhelm II was a mercurial figure in the decades leading up to World War One. Although he was a member of the British Royal Family by virtue of his position as a grandson of Queen Victoria, he nursed the slights that he had received from some members of the family, other than the Queen whom the Kaiser revered. The Kaiser's enmity was particularly reserved for his uncle, Victoria's heir, King Edward VII. Seeking both validation from his British relatives, and to dominate them, Wilhelm sought to build a great naval fleet that would bring him both personal renown and the acknowledgement of the growing might and world-wide reach of the German Empire.

A naval race began between Germany and Britain that would take on added urgency after the British constructed the technologically superior HMS *Dreadnought* class of battleship shortly after the turn of the century. The Anglo-German naval race sparked by the Kaiser would continue right up to until the outbreak of the world war and although the naval race would ultimately be won by Great Britain, Britain's victory would only come at great financial cost.

In seeking naval parity with Great Britain Wilhelm and his advisors failed to understand, or to acknowledge, that the construction of a great blue water fleet by Germany would pose an existential threat to Great Britain. Although Britain's Royal Navy dominated the seas it was deployed at bases around the world, and therefore its total strength was never available at one place at any one time. Germany, on the other hand, had few naval ships stationed abroad and therefore its blue water fleet was concentrated in the North Sea. From its bases in the North Sea, the German fleet could quickly descend upon the coasts of Great Britain and possibly overwhelm Britain's naval defences in home waters. Thus, the naval policy of Imperial Germany carried with it a great risk of making Great Britain into an adversary of Germany.

The initial British response to the challenge posed by Germany was to consider an alliance with Germany. Three times during the years from 1898 to 1902, Great Britain approached Germany seeking an alliance between the two countries, and on all three occasions Britain was rebuffed. Both the Kaiser and his naval commander, Grand Admiral Tirpitz, were set upon creating a blue water fleet that could rival the strength of the Royal Navy. They both knew that an alliance with Britain could forestall their naval plans since the German Reichstag would be unlikely to vote financial appropriations for a great naval fleet if Germany was allied with the world's greatest naval power. The Foreign Secretary, Bernard von Bulow however, might have pointed out to the Kaiser that logic alone dictated that Germany should enter into an alliance with Great Britain since France and Russia were formally allied with each other, and both were opposed to German interests. However, von Bulow was restrained in giving such advice by his ambition to succeed to the Imperial Chancellorship, and he was further restrained by a dark *eminence grise* of the Imperial bureaucracy, Friedrich von Holstein. Holstein was an influential figure in the late nineteenth and early twentieth-century German Foreign Office bureaucracy who seethed with mistrust towards Britain and held a general paranoia towards the intentions of other countries. As a result, all of the feelers Great Britain put out to Germany seeking an understanding between the two countries fell upon deaf ears, and the possibility of an Anglo-German alliance came to naught.[4]

The one European power that was of most concern to Great Britain around the turn of the century was Russia. During the late nineteenth century, Russia expanded its empire in Asia by conquering Turkestan and then began to encroach upon Afghanistan and Tibet. Russian expansionism in Asia threatened India, the jewel in the Crown of the British Empire, and for many years a cold war rivalry existed between Russia and Great Britain as each vied for influence in Central Asia, a diplomatic *pas de deux* which became known as the Great Game.

With Russia pressing Great Britain in Asia, and the Germans building a fleet in the North Sea, the existing British foreign policy of splendid isolation began to appear misguided to the statesmen of the British Empire. Looking abroad, however, Britain found few potential partners for an alliance. France and Russia were allied in the Dual Alliance, and both presented challenges to the British Empire in Africa, and Asia, and might continue to do so. Germany was allied with both Austria-Hungary and Italy in the Triple Alliance, and Germany had rebuffed all of Great Britain's attempts to form an alliance between the two countries. The United States continued to remain aloof from European entanglements, and the US presented challenges to Great Britain in the Americas.

That left only Japan as a potential partner for Great Britain, as the Chinese Empire was clearly in terminal decline following the Boxer War. So began a diplomatic minuet between Great Britain and Japan to develop a political alliance between them. In Japan, consternation at the way Russia, France, and Germany had forced Japan to disgorge the gains it obtained in the Treaty of Shimonoseki had caused an acceleration in the development of Japan's military strength and created a desire to reinforce the country's defences against the possibility of further foreign interference with Japan's foreign policy ambitions.[5]

In 1899, Japan obtained a revision of the unequal foreign treaties that had been forced upon the country when it emerged from its centuries of isolation earlier in the nineteenth century. Cooperation between Japan and Great Britain began to emerge in the Boxer War, in which both countries played a prominent role, and that cooperation laid the groundwork for a future political alliance between the two countries.[6] Further impetus towards a new relationship between Japan and Great Britain arose as a result of the Russian naval rearmament program, which projected increasing Russian naval strength in the Pacific at Port Arthur, and at Vladivostok. The need for the Royal Navy to maintain sufficient strength on its China Station to counter new Russian naval forces meant that the resources the navy needed in Europe to maintain Britain's naval superiority in home waters would remain depleted.[7]

Faced with these problems, the Ministry of Prime Minister Lord Salisbury in London recalled its ambassador to Japan, Sir Claude MacDonald, for urgent consultations. MacDonald had conversations with the Prime Minister, the Foreign Secretary, and the King-Emperor, concerning Great Britain's relations with Japan, and MacDonald laid particular stress on the machinations of Germany in the Far East, as well as the threat of Russia to British interests in the region.[8] Assistant Under-Secretary of State for Foreign Affairs Francis Bertie was also concerned about Russian expansionism in Asia and he began to press forward memoranda respecting a possible understanding with Japan.[9] Bertie's views particularly informed the Foreign Secretary, Lord Lansdowne, when he met the Japanese Minister Baron Hayashi Tadasu, on July 31, 1901, to discuss the strategic situation in the Far East. Of particular concern to Britain was the naval balance of power, with the British Admiralty voicing the view that it was highly desirable for Great Britain to reduce its naval deployments on the China Station to the minimum that was necessary to protect its far eastern possessions.[10] The Japanese Ministry under Premier General Katsura, which was a ministry of technocrats, proved amenable to opening negotiations with Great Britain.

Serious negotiations between Britain and Japan began in London on October 16, 1901, with the conversations between Lord Lansdowne and Baron Hayashi, the Japanese Minister to Great Britain, representing Baron Komura, the Japanese Foreign Minister. Lord Lansdowne was well-equipped by experience to conduct these sensitive negotiations. He had served as Governor General of Canada between 1883 and 1888, where Prime Minister Sir John A Macdonald had said of him that Lansdowne was perhaps the ablest Governor General with whom Macdonald had served.[11] Subsequently, Lansdowne served as the Viceroy of India and then rose to hold the important Cabinet positions of Secretary of State for War, and Secretary of State for Foreign Affairs. The Japanese negotiator, Baron Hayashi was a skilled diplomat who had originally been a Tokugawa loyalist in the wars that led up to the Meiji Restoration in 1868. Although he had been loyal to the losing side in the upheaval the Imperial authorities perceived his ability and they were impressed by the foreign experience he had gained as one of the students sent abroad by the Tokugawa shogunate to Great Britain. He was taken into the Imperial civil service and received rapid promotions, serving successively as the Japanese diplomatic representative to the Imperial Chinese Court, the Imperial Russian Court, and finally to the Court of St. James in London. In London, he cut a notable figure, not least because of his wife, Gamo Misao, Baroness Hayashi, a strikingly attractive woman, who had captivated the London press. Her activities were closely followed in the social pages and her portrait was featured on a collectible cigarette card. After the negotiations over the alliance were successfully concluded the Emperor raised Baron Hayashi in the Japanese peerage and he and his wife became the Viscount and Viscountess Hayashi.

For Great Britain, the prize in the negotiations was to reach some kind of accommodation with Japan that would permit the redeployment of British naval assets from the Far East to European waters and to gain the assistance of Japan if Great Britain became involved in a war with some combination of two powers in the Far East. For Japan, it was essential to secure British acquiescence to Japan's predominant interests, political as well as commercial, in Korea. On that basis, the two governments came to an agreement, and a treaty was drafted and signed by Lord Lansdowne and Baron Hayashi on January 30, 1902. The treaty was subsequently publicized but the accompanying notes pertaining to naval forces in the Far East were maintained in secrecy. The treaty was limited to a term of five years and it applied only in the Far East. And it only applied if a war broke out between one of the signatories and another great power, and then only if an additional great power entered the war against the signatory to the alliance.

> "AGREEMENT BETWEEN THE UNITED KINGDOM AND JAPAN RELATIVE TO CHINA AND COREA. Signed at London, January 30, 1902.
>
> THE Governments of Great Britain and Japan, actuated solely by a desire to maintain the status quo and general peace in the extreme East, being moreover specially interested in maintaining the independence and territorial

integrity of the Empire of China and the Empire of Corea, and in securing equal opportunities in those countries for the commerce and industry of all nations, hereby agree as follows

ARTICLE 1

The High Contracting Parties having mutually recognized the independence of China and of Corea, declare themselves to be entirely uninfluenced by any aggressive tendencies in either country. Having in view, however, their special interests, of which those of Great Britain relate principally to China, while Japan, in addition to the interests which she possesses in China, is interested in a peculiar degree politically as well as commercially and industrially in Corea, the High Contracting Parties recognize that it will be admissible for either of them to take such measures as maybe indispensable in order to safeguard those interests if threatened either by the aggressive action of any other Power, or by disturbances arising in China or Corea, and necessitating the intervention of either of the High Contracting Parties for the protection of the lives and property of its subjects.

ARTICLE II

If either Great Britain or Japan, in the defence of their respective interests as above described, should be come involved in war with another Power, the other High Contracting Party will maintain a strict neutrality, and use its efforts to prevent other Powers from joining in hostilities against its ally.

ARTICLE III

If, in the above event, any other Power or Powers should join in hostilities against that ally, the other High Contracting

Party will come to its assistance, and will conduct the war in common, and make peace in mutual agreement with it.

ARTICLE IV

The High Contracting Parties agree that neither of them will, without consulting the other, enter into separate arrangements with another Power to the prejudice of the interests above described.

ARTICLE V

Whenever, in the opinion of either Great Britain or Japan, the above-mentioned interests are in jeopardy, the two Governments will communicate with one another fully and frankly.

ARTICLE VI

The present Agreement shall come into effect immediately after the date of its signature, and remain in force for five years from that date. In case neither of the High Contracting Parties should have notified twelve months before the expiration of the said five years the intention of terminating it, it shall remain binding until the expiration of one year from the day on which either of the High Contracting Parties shall have denounced it. But if, when the date fixed for its expiration arrives, either ally is actually engaged in war, the alliance shall, *ipso facto*, continue until peace is concluded. In faith where of the Undersigned, duly authorized by their respective Governments, have signed this Agreement and have affixed thereto their seals. Done in duplicate at London, the 30th day of January,1902.

(L.S.) (Signed) LANSDOWNE, His Britannic Majesty's Principal Secretary of State for Foreign Affairs

(L.S.) (Signed) HAYASHI, Envoy Extraordinary and Minister

Plenipotentiary of His Majesty the Emperor of Japan at the Court of St. James."[12]

The Anglo-Japanese Alliance was clearly directed against the Russian Empire, and the Russians immediately perceived that to be so. Its purpose was to engage an ally in the Far East if either Japan or Great Britain found themselves in a war with both of the Dual Alliance powers of Russia and France. Although Russia did obtain moral support from France following the publication of the treaty, France also made it clear to its ally that it would refuse to be drawn into a conflict in the Far East if the conflict was caused by Russian aggrandizement. Thus, the main purpose of the Anglo-Japanese alliance – the restriction of Russian expansion – was amply served by the treaty.[13]

There were other benefits for the signatories as well. Japan obtained recognition as a great power through its alliance with Great Britain and it gained some support from Great Britain for its designs on Korea. The alliance with Great Britain was subsequently accepted by succeeding Japanese governments as a cornerstone of Japanese foreign policy.[14] The alliance also opened the door to British finance for the Japanese government. Britain, in turn, gained an important naval ally, and Japanese naval bases in the Far East were now made available to the Royal Navy should they be needed.[15] It has been suggested that the alliance allowed Great Britain to essentially conduct a sort of alliance experiment to determine if alliances would be of diplomatic assistance to Great Britain in the world that was emerging at the beginning of the twentieth century.[16]

The Anglo-Japanese alliance surprised the other great powers in both Europe and America because it marked a very significant departure in British foreign policy. It was the end of Great Britain's splendid isolation. And it was an important indication of the increasing power of Japan, which was now contending to be the major power in the Far East.

Canada was automatically bound by the treaty because Canada was still a sub-sovereign part of the British Empire, albeit an internally autonomous part of the Empire. For Canada, the alliance with Japan brought new opportunities but also new diplomatic complications for the young country. Modern Japan and modern Canada were born around the same point in time. The Canadian confederation was created in 1867, although it was not until 1871 when the Pacific coast province of British Columbia joined the new country that Canada obtained a position on the Pacific Ocean. In Japan, 1868 marked the end of the shogunate and the Meiji Restoration, which marked the beginning of Japan's nineteenth-century national modernization project. Prior to the last years of the nineteenth century, there had been little intercourse between Canada and Japan and few Japanese immigrants were to be found in Canada. On the other hand, there was a sizeable contingent of settlers from China, many of whom had been imported into the country by the railway contractor, Andrew Onderdonk, to complete the Pacific portion of the Canadian Pacific Railway, the great national transportation project that occupied such a large part of Canada's nation-building efforts under Prime Minister Sir John A Macdonald. The influx and settlement of a large number of Asian immigrants in British Columbia did not always go smoothly and a vociferous group that was substantially motivated by prejudices began to agitate against Asian immigration. In one notable incident while the transcontinental railway was under construction, the Governor General of Canada, Lord Dufferin, who was the representative of the Crown in Canada, refused to allow his vice-regal carriage to pass through a ceremonial arch that was inscribed with the words 'Chinese Must Go' when visiting Victoria, British Columbia, in August, 1876.[17]

In the final years of the nineteenth century there was substantial growth in Japanese emigration to Canada. From around 1000 Japanese immigrants in 1896, the proportion of the British Columbia population that was of Japanese descent reached approximately

4500 by 1901. A Japanese consulate was established in Vancouver in 1889, to service the needs of Japanese subjects in British Columbia. In 1894, Great Britain entered into a treaty of commerce with Japan that prevented discriminatory measures from being applied to Japanese nationals anywhere in the British Empire. Some provincial legislation enacted in British Columbia that was discriminatory towards Japanese immigrants was subsequently disallowed by the Federal government under Canada's written constitution, the British North America Act of 1867.[18] Canadian employers subsequently found that Japanese immigrants made good employees, and their popularity with business employers, as well as the perception that they would work for lower wages than Caucasian workers, contributed to a growing resentment towards Japanese immigration to Canada from working-class Caucasian Canadians. However, many of the Japanese who came to Canada during this period did not emigrate from Japan but were actually emigrating from Hawaii, where they had previously worked in the sugar cane fields.

Public agitation against further immigration from Japan reached a head in Vancouver in 1907, when a race riot broke out in the Chinatown and Little Tokyo neighbourhoods, leading to several injuries, as well as property damage. The serious nature of those disturbances led the Laurier Ministry to establish a royal commission under William Lyon Mackenzie King, then Deputy Minister of Labour, to assess the damages from the riot, and to inquire into the subject of immigration to Canada from the Orient. The government eventually paid out approximately $9,000 to Japanese Canadians to satisfy claims arising from the riots, and Mackenzie King found that of the Japanese who had settled in Canada about twice as many of them had emigrated from the US territory of Hawaii than had come into Canada directly from Japan. To forestall further disturbances Laurier sent a Minister of the Crown, Rodolphe Lemieux, to Japan in 1907 as a special envoy to negotiate an arrangement with Japan concerning immigration to

Canada. Lemieux negotiated a so-called 'Gentleman's Agreement' with Count Hayashi, the Japanese Foreign Minister, in 1908, under which Japan agreed to limit emigration from Japan to Canada. Thereafter, in most years Japanese emigration to Canada was held to a number under 1000, with the exception of a single year between 1909 and 1919.[19]

By 1911 there was a burgeoning trade between the two countries. Starting from small beginnings in the 1870's export trade grew substantially in Canada's favour from approximately $1000 to eventually reach $7,732,514 by 1920, while imports from Japan grew from $311,000 to $13,637,287 over the same period.[20]

The completion of the Canadian Pacific Railway in 1885, led the managers of the country's first transcontinental railway to consider expanding the reach of their services to the Orient by creating a steamship service. Moving slowly at first, the CPR acquired three older ships to prove the feasibility of the service, the first of which, the SS *Abyssinia*, arrived on June 13, 1887, at the Port of Vancouver from Hong Kong with a stop in Yokohama, Japan, along the way. Once the feasibility of the service was shown the company obtained Crown mail contracts, and subsidies from both the Imperial government in London, as well as the Federal government in Ottawa.

Thereafter, the company let contracts for the construction in Scotland of three transpacific liners, subsequently named the *Empress of India*, *Empress of China*, and the *Empress of Japan*. The mail contracts established the routing for the CP liners between Hong Kong, Shanghai, Nagasaki, Kobe, Yokohama, Victoria, and Vancouver. By 1892 all three ships were in regular service across the Pacific from Vancouver or Victoria, carrying Imperial government officials, tourists, and, occasionally, as in the Spanish-America War, or the Boxer War, American and British troops. On eastbound voyages, it profitably carried immigrants to new lives in Canada and the United States.[21] CP developed a good reputation for their transpacific services and soon carried more than half of the passenger traffic across the North Pacific Ocean.

The completion of the Canadian Pacific Railway and the expansion of the Canadian Pacific Steamship services to the Orient facilitated travel between Japan and Canada, and it was often beneficial from a time perspective for Japanese travelling to Europe to cross the Pacific to Canada on a CP passenger liner and then travel by CPR trains across Canada to connect with a transatlantic passenger vessel to Europe at Montreal or New York, rather than to sail to Europe by way of the Straits of Malacca, and the Suez Canal. Many Canadians also travelled to the Orient, including contingents of Christian missionaries who settled in Japan or China.

As one century passed into another, the world-wide transformation in transportation and communications slowly, and fitfully began to make the globe seem a little smaller.

NOTES

[1] The Monroe Doctrine was articulated by President James Monroe (in office 1817-25) which purported to warn European powers that the United States would not tolerate European powers colonizing, or intervening, in the affairs of the newly-independent states in the Americas.

[2] Peter W. Noonan, *Peace on the Lakes, Canada and the Rush-Bagot Agreement*, Magistralis, Ottawa, 2016, 222.

[3] Unclaimed, that is, by European powers. The existing possession of so-called unclaimed lands by the indigenous inhabitants of those

lands was not a significant factor in the calculations of European imperialist governments.

[4] Virginia Cowles, *The Kaiser*, Harper & Row, New York, 1963, 82, 169-73.

[5] Ian H Nish, *The Anglo-Japanese Alliance: The Diplomacy of Two Island Empires 1894 – 1907*, University of London/The Athlone Press, London, 1966, 35 [afterwards: Nish, *Alliance*]

[6] Nish, *Alliance*, 91

[7] Nish, *Alliance*, 94

[8] Nish, *Alliance*, 145

[9] Nish, *Alliance*, 153

[10] Nish, *Alliance*, 174

[11] James Noonan, *Canada's Governors General at Play: Culture and Rideau Hall from Monck to Grey, With an Afterword on their Successors, Connaught to LeBlanc*, Borealis Book Publishers, Ottawa, 2002, 133

[12] UK Treaties Online, https://treaties.fco.gov.uk [accessed February 10, 2021] is the source for all versions of the Anglo-Japanese Alliance Treaty that are quoted in this book.

[13] Nish, *Alliance*, 238

[14] Nish, *Alliance*, 250

[15] Nish, *Alliance*, 251

[16] Margaret MacMillan, *The War That Ended Peace, The Road to 1914*, Allen Lane, Toronto, 2013, 55 [afterwards: MacMillan, *1914*]

[17] Pierre Berton, *The Great Railway, Illustrated*, McClelland & Stewart, Toronto, 1972, p. 77.

[18] Klaus H Pringsheim, *Neighbors Across the Pacific: The Development of Economic and Political Relations Between Canada and Japan*, Greenwood Press, Westport (CT), 1983, 8

[19] Pringsheim, 19

[20] Pringsheim, 24

[21] Peter Pigott, *Sailing Seven Seas, A History of the Canadian Pacific Line*, Dundurn Press, Toronto, 2010, 40-41

3. Triumph at Tsushima

Having concluded the treaty of alliance with Great Britain, Japan could now turn its attention to its (and Great Britain's) chief Asian rival, the Russian Empire. Then, as now, Russia was the country of greatest territorial extent, spreading across the northern hemisphere from its capital at St. Petersburg on the Baltic Sea eastward across European Russia and Siberia to reach the Pacific at Vladivostok. After Japan was ousted from Port Arthur as a result of the Triple Intervention Russia moved to take possession of that strategic port, thereby winning access to the warm waters of the Pacific in 1897. Russia continued to expand its influence in Manchuria by obtaining both Manchurian railway concessions and the right to station Russian troops in Manchuria to protect its railway investments. Japan was chagrined by those developments and increasingly viewed Russia as a significant threat to Japanese territorial ambitions in China, and in Korea.

Russia was now ruled by Tsar Nicholas II, still smarting from his near-assassination at the hands of a renegade Japanese police official during his world tour as Tsarevich. Nicholas was not a strong leader, and he was miscast as an autocrat, although his main biographer has portrayed him as a basically decent man who might have made a fine constitutional monarch.[1] But Russia was not a constitutional monarchy and all power in the Russian state was constitutionally vested in the Tsar. The character of the monarch was therefore essential to the workings of the state administration. Perhaps the aptest characterization of the way the Russian state administration worked under Nicholas II was provided by the British Ambassador to Russia in the early years of the twentieth century, Charles Hardinge, who reported to London that:

> "At a Court where the autocratic power still exists the personality of the reigning sovereign is naturally of high

importance and the character of the Emperor who rules over this Empire is of great interest. It is a subject on which I am diffident in expressing an opinion; as to estimate fairly and honestly the character of any individual, in whatever station of life he may be, a close personal acquaintance is necessary. In the present circumstances, I must limit myself to a few general observations. I have not heard the slightest doubt expressed as to the honesty, the high sense of duty, and devotion to his country which animate the Emperor in the discharge of his important functions. I do not imagine that any impartial man of whatever shade of politics could deny to His Majesty the possession of qualities which are admirable and exemplary. It would be affectation to assert that the Emperor is not exposed to criticism, and that he is universally regarded as a beneficent and capable monarch. There are many who consider that His Majesty is too much wedded to the autocratic power; there are others who think that the strength of his will is not commensurate with the sincerity of his intentions; and there are others who lament that passing and incidental influences carry to much weight when important decisions have to be taken."[2]

Nicholas' negative views of the Japanese were counterbalanced to some extent by his capable Finance Minister, Sergius Witte, who played a predominant role in the Imperial Russian cabinets of the early twentieth century. Witte was sensitive to the growing strength of Imperial Japan, and he wished to avoid an outright breach between Russia and Japan. However, Witte did favour cautiously expanding Russian borders in the Far East, along the route of the Trans-Siberian Railway, which neared completion in the early years of the twentieth century.[3] Japan did not wish to see Russia expand into China, but Japan could probably have lived with Russian expansion in China if the Russian Empire did not also begin to seriously threaten Japanese interests in Korea. Other, less cautious voices than Witte's, now whispered in the ear of the

Emperor about the prospective glories of Russian expansion in the Far East. Torn between the caution of Witte, and the bellicosity of less prudent men, Emperor Nicholas followed a disjointed policy that nevertheless generally favoured expanding the Russian Empire as far as possible in the Far East. Thus, the stage was increasingly set for a collision between the ancient Slavic empire of the Tsars, and the rising empire of Japan.

Yet caution was also present in the counsels of Emperor Mutsuhito in Japan. The Emperor's favourite advisor, Marquis Ito Hirobumi, who had served as Prime Minister of Japan at the beginning of the century, favoured an accommodation with Russia that would see a division of the spoils of the decrepit Chinese Empire, with Russia obtaining paramountcy in Manchuria while Japan achieved the same result in Korea. China had ceased to be Korea's nominal suzerain following the Sino-Japanese War, and Japan was increasing its influence there. The perspective of the Japanese government was a logical approach in the Age of Imperialism. But Russian imperialists demurred at what seemed to be an accommodation of the upstart Asiatic power. Ito himself, after leaving office, was rebuffed when he visited St. Petersburg in the autumn of 1901, seeking accommodation with Russia. After the failure of Ito's attempt to reach an understanding with Imperial Russia, the Japanese government proceeded to conclude the Anglo-Japanese Alliance.

A final effort to reach an arrangement or understanding with Russia was undertaken by Japan in 1903, but the portents were not auspicious. In St. Petersburg, those advisors to the Tsar who favoured Russian expansionism in Korea were in the ascendant, forcing Sergius Witte to resign his post as Minister of Finance.[4] The loss of Witte's cautious voice in the counsels of the Russian Tsar removed any sense of urgency on the part of the Russian government to reach an accommodation with Japan concerning their respective spheres of influence in the Far East. In October, 1903, Russian forces occupied the city of Mukden in Manchuria, while Japan presented itself as a promoter of the Open Door Policy that had been first articulated by the United States as a way to reduce encroachments by outside powers on the feeble Manchu Empire.[5]

In the background of Russia's disjointed policy was a hidden but important actor, the German Kaiser, Wilhelm II. Wilhelm had come to the German throne several years before Nicholas II had ascended to the throne of Imperial Russia and the Kaiser was older than Nicholas by nine years. They were cousins in an era when European royal families commonly intermarried and the familial bond, together with the assiduous cultivation of the relationship by Wilhelm, gave the German Kaiser an extraordinary degree of influence over his younger cousin. Harking back to an earlier time, they maintained personal attachés in each other's official household, which created a channel of personal communication that bypassed their chancelleries and it was one that the Kaiser used to try to influence Russian policy away from Europe, and towards the Far East.

It was a German ambition since the days of Chancellor Bismarck to reorient Russia towards Asia, and away from Europe.[6] The Kaiser wrote to his cousin the Tsar, and suggested to Nicholas that it was the duty of Russia to protect Europe from the 'yellow race.'[7] Nicholas, with his embedded prejudice towards the Japanese, was very susceptible to the Kaiser's flattery and manipulation. To reinforce his message, the Kaiser commissioned his own court painter to paint a racist portrait of Asian hordes led by the Lord Buddha being resisted by European Caucasians under the leadership of Russia and Germany, both together defending Christian principles. Wilhelm sent the painting to Nicholas who wrote back appreciatively to the Kaiser, and the Kaiser derived much satisfaction from his insight into the character of the Russian Tsar.[8]

Faced with Russian intransigence, Japan began to prepare for war.

The sense that the two empires were moving towards a collision slowly began to awaken the Tsar and his advisors to a growing danger. Japan was particularly concerned to act militarily before the completion of the Trans-Siberian Railway, because the railway, once completed, would give the Russian Empire a continuous line of communication between European Russia and the Russian Pacific coast. Nicholas informed his Pacific Viceroy, Admiral Alexieff, to avoid hostilities but by then it was too little, too late, and on February 4, 1904, the Japanese struck by launching a surprise attack on the Russian Far Eastern Fleet at Port Arthur.[9]

The surprise attack on Port Arthur was not a fatal blow to the Russian fleet, however, and of the seven Russian battleships in port only two, the *HIRMS Tsarevich*, and the *HIRMS Retvizan* were damaged, along with a cruiser the *HIRMS Pallada*. Subsequently, the Japanese laid mine fields at Port Arthur to keep the Russian fleet harbour-bound while the Japanese Army landed on the coast and worked to establish a siege of Port Arthur. The Russians countered with their own sea mining initiatives, and rather than a fleet action both sides lost capital ships to each other's minefields. An attempted sortie by the Russian Far Eastern Fleet in April resulted in the sinking of the battleship *HIRMS Petropavlovsk*, the flagship of the Russian Far Eastern Fleet, which hit a mine and went down with 700 men, including the fleet commander, Admiral Makarov.[10] When a new commander, Admiral Witgeft, led the Russian fleet on another sortie in August, 1904, he hoped for victory but faced difficult odds because his 6 battleships, 4 cruisers, and 8 destroyers faced a Japanese force of 4 battleships, 14 cruisers, 17 destroyers, and 30 torpedo boats. In the resulting Battle of the Yellow Sea, two hits on the Russian flagship killed Witgeft and caused his flagship to fall out of line. The Russian fleet retreated in disorder to Port Arthur, with some of the stragglers interning themselves in neutral ports.[11]

Now, genuinely alarmed by the possibility that Port Arthur might be lost, the Russian government decided to send the modern Russian

Baltic Fleet to the Far East, to reinforce the Far Eastern Fleet. However, such a voyage required the Baltic Fleet to sail around Africa, or through the Suez Canal, and to round the Malay Peninsula before attempting to force the Strait of Tsushima in the face of the Japanese Fleet, in order to reach Port Arthur. It was a tall order for an efficient and capable navy but the Russian navy was neither. The man chosen to lead the Baltic Fleet was Vice Admiral Zinovi Petrovich Rozhestvensky, an aggressive officer who led what became known as the Great Black Fleet in a complex navigational and logistics undertaking from its base in Latvia through the Atlantic Ocean and around Africa to Madagascar, with a port stop at Dakar, in west Africa. A few ships of doubtful seaworthiness were sent through the Mediterranean to transit the Suez Canal. More than 40 Russian ships with their black hulls and gold funnels sailed halfway around the world to their doom. Rozhestvensky made only one serious error on the outbound voyage. In the North Sea the jumpy Russians, who were nervous about the threat of a Japanese torpedo attack, mistook the British fishing fleet for Japanese torpedo boats and shot them up. The Great Black Fleet then failed to stop when the Russians realized their mistake, causing outrage in the British Empire and a major diplomatic headache for the Russian government.[12] King Edward VII minuted that it was, "A most dastardly outrage".[13] Ultimately the matter was submitted to international arbitration and Russia paid 65,000 pounds in compensation to Great Britain.[14]

The need to maximize the storage of coal led to coal being stored everywhere on the Russian ships, enveloping them in a black pall that could hardly improve the morale, or efficiency, of their crews. Many despaired. When news of revolution back home reached the fleet some of the crews became mutinous. Many Russian sailors died on the outbound voyage from physical illness, or suicide, or from one of the firing squads that were used by Rozhestvensky to put down mutiny.[15]

The core of Rozhestvensky's fleet was built around his four modern

Borodino class battleships; HIRMS *Borodino*, HIRMS *Imperator*, HIRMS *Alexander III*, HIRMS *Orel*, and HIRMS *Suvorov*, which were all armed with four 12 inch guns, as well as a six-inch secondary armament, and 3-inch guns to ward off torpedo boats. Each ship had an armour belt of 7.5 inches in thickness but the Russian ships suffered from being overweight when they were fully loaded, which impacted their effectiveness.[16]

In contrast, the Japanese fleet under the command of Admiral Togo Heihachiro possessed six modern battleships of British design, although two of them were lost to mines before the battle took place. The Japanese flagship, HIJMS *Mikasa*, was a 15,000-ton ship that could reach a maximum speed of 18 knots and was armed with four 12 inch guns, fourteen 6 inch guns in her secondary armament, as well as twenty 12 pounder weapons to ward off torpedo boats. The main armament could fire three 800 pound armour-piercing shells every three minutes. The *Mikasa* boasted a nine-inch armour belt and was equipped with modern rangefinders, telescopic sights, and a radiotelegraph, allowing Togo to control the battle effectively from his flagship.[17]

Unlike the Russians, there was a close collaboration by the Japanese Army command with the Japanese Navy command, which allowed for coordination of operations. Taking advantage of their collaboration as the Russian fleet meandered its way towards Port Arthur the Japanese Army bombarded the Russian fortress with siege artillery, destroying what remained of the Russian Far East Fleet on December 29, 1904, while Rozhestvensky was still at sea. A few days later, on January 2, 1905, the fortress of Port Arthur surrendered to the Japanese. In February the Russian Army suffered another major defeat by losing the Battle of Mukden, and the city of the same name, together with its stockpiles of supplies.[18] Compelled by the Russian government to force his way through to Vladivostok, Rozhestvensky, contemplated the probable doom of his fleet, now so far from home, but he still hoped to slip past the Japanese fleet in the Strait of Tsushima. He almost did it.

Leaving his last coaling port at Cam Ran Bay, in French Indochina, on May 13, 1905, Rozhestvensky headed north and was passing through the Strait of Tsushima between Japan and Korea on May 27, 1905, when the rearmost vessel in his fleet, a fully lit hospital ship, was detected by the Japanese.

Admiral Togo risked his ships by ordering a turn that was within the range of the Russian guns while his ships had reduced gun accuracy, owing to the loss of forward motion on his vessels. Although the Russian fleet attempted to take advantage of their good fortune they were unable to do so, and Togo got his fleet through the turn. Then he engaged the Russians from a parallel course, and although the Japanese took a few minutes to establish firing accuracy they soon rained down high explosive shells on the hapless Russians, devastating the Russian battle line. The Russian flagship, *Suvorov*, was hit hard, and Rozhestvensky was badly injured and was forced to turn over command of the fleet to his subordinate, Admiral Nebogatov. The *Alexander III* and the *Suvorov* were sunk by the Japanese, and the *Borodino* blew up, taking her entire crew to their doom with the exception of one man.

The following morning Togo renewed the battle but by that time the fate of Russia's Great Black Fleet was settled, and Admiral Nebogatov, now in command, surrendered what remained of the fleet to Admiral Togo. A few Russian warships attempted to escape but they were rounded up by the Japanese and they either surrendered or were sunk, with only two destroyers and an armed yacht succeeding in reaching Vladivostok. A few Russian ships sought sanctuary in neutral ports, including the cruiser HIRMS *Aurora*, which was interned in Manila by the Americans. Later, *Aurora* would be returned to Russia by the United States and the ship would win immortality by launching the Bolshevik Revolution in Russia in November, 1917. The Japanese released the hospital ship, the *Orel*, whose brightly burning lights, which were in accordance with international law, had led the Japanese to the Russian fleet in Tsushima Strait, and then to victory.[19] Japan lost only three small ships and 117 men killed. A total of 4830 Russian sailors lost their lives in the battle.[20] Russia also lost all eight of its battleships, seven cruisers, and nine destroyers, in the greatest naval battle fought since the Battle of Trafalgar, a century before.

The twin Japanese victories of Mukden and Tsushima sealed the fate of Russian adventurism in East Asia. The strain of war and the impact of defeats led to a revolution in Russia, and although the revolution was not sufficient to bring down the absolute monarchy of the Tsar, it shook the Russian throne to the core and forced the Tsar to institute a quasi-constitutional monarchy in which the Tsar was compelled to grant his people a parliament and to share power. Sergius Witte was recalled from retirement and sent to Portsmouth, New Hampshire, in the United States where US President Theodore Roosevelt had offered himself as a mediator to bring peace to Russia and Japan. The Japanese had been skilful in identifying their war aims and in timing their attack on the Russian Empire before the completion of the Trans-Siberian Railway. The brilliant Japanese victories on land and sea had placed Japan in a superior position for the conduct of the negotiations. Nevertheless, Witte performed brilliantly, and used his knowledge that the Japanese were constrained by a lack of the economic resources necessary to continue the war to compel the Japanese to compromise. Japan finally accepted peace without receiving a war indemnity from Russia but Russia was forced to cede the southern half of Sakhalin Island to Japan, and Russia transferred all of its interests in Manchuria (including the Manchurian Railway, and the Russian lease of Port Arthur) to Japan.

Although the gains made by Japan were solid, there were those in Japan who had expected that Japan would gain much more, and riots erupted in Tokyo, and in other centres when the terms of the settlement were made known, and the paucity of the Japanese gains became apparent. Nevertheless, there were real gains made by Japan in this war. Japan had pushed the Russian Empire farther north by obtaining southern Sakhalin Island and had gained a foothold on the Chinese mainland by obtaining both Port Arthur and the Manchurian Railway, which they subsequently used with great effect to penetrate, and eventually occupy, all of Manchuria.

Abroad, Japan was now recognized as a great power. At the outset of the war, it was inconceivable that the Japanese would defeat the greatest land empire in the western world but they had nevertheless done so. Britain's decision to enter into an alliance with Japan now looked like a wise decision for Britain, given the challenges that Britain was increasingly facing in Europe. In Asia, and Africa, the Japanese victory was stunning, and it meant that the western Caucasian nations were not invincible, thus calling into question the legitimacy of colonialism. As the twentieth century progressed the edifice of western colonialism slowly began to rot away. Japan was proof that non-western countries could succeed in the world just as the western countries had succeeded in the past.

For Russia, the loss of the Russo-Japanese War meant a retreat from the Far East and a recognition of Japan's predominant position in both Manchuria and in Korea. Convulsed by revolution, and defeat, the Russian Empire ceased to be a significant threat to Japan, or to Great Britain's control of the Indian subcontinent. Japan's defeat of Russia, and Great Britain's diplomatic support of its Japanese ally, had proved the worth of the Anglo-Japanese Alliance but the retreat of Russia now undermined one of the original purposes of that alliance. However, a new rising power in the Asia-Pacific region would soon give another focus to the alliance as the date approached to consider its renewal.

NOTES

[1] See Massie, *Nicholas and Alexandra*

[2] G P Gooch and H Temperley ed., *British Documents on the Origins of the War, 1898-1914, Vol IV*, 1929 (1951) HM Stationary Office, London, (No. 243), 260 [afterwards: BD]

[3] Storrey, 37.

[4] Massie *Nicholas and Alexandra*, 91

[5] Storrey, 61

[6] Massie, *Nicholas and Alexandra*, 88-89

[7] Massie, *Nicholas and Alexandra*, 89

[8] Cowles, 149

[9] Storrey, 63. It is ironic to note that the western press commented favourably on the brilliance of the Japanese strategy of making a surprise naval attack on the Russian fleet without a formal declaration of war – a striking contrast to western views when the Japanese followed a similar approach in the Asia-Pacific region in 1941.

[10] Massie *Nicholas and Alexandra*, 93

[11] Eric Grove, *Big Fleet Actions, Tsushima, Jutland, Philippine Sea*, Brockhampton Press, London, 1991, 10

[12] Massie, *Nicholas and Alexandra*, 94

[13] BD (No 5), 6

[14] BD (No. 29 – Ed. Note), 38

[15] Allan Villiers, *Men, Ships and the Sea*, National Geographic Society, Washington, 1963, 285.

[16] Grove, 13

[17] Grove, 17; Andrew R Wilson, *Masters of War: History's Greatest Strategic Thinkers*, The Teaching Company, Chantilly, Va., 2012, 85

[18] Storrey, 65

[19] Grove, 44-45

[20] Grove, 45

4. The Second Alliance

As the Japanese army and navy moved from one success to another in the war with Russia it became clear that Japan would prove to be the overall victor in the war. In London, there was concern that after the successful conclusion of the war, and the resulting ouster of Russia from influence in Korea, there might be a rapprochement between Japan and Russia that would prove inimical to British interests in the Far East. Such concerns prompted the Foreign Secretary, Lord Lansdowne, to invite the Japanese Minister to Great Britain, Viscount Hayashi, to discuss the Anglo-Japanese Alliance of 1902, and the prospects for a renewal of the agreement. Lansdowne found Hayashi to be enthusiastic about the prospect of an early renewal of the alliance, although the matter required careful consideration by the Japanese government in Tokyo. Hayashi was quite clear with Lansdowne that the possibility of a rapprochement with Russia after the war was not in the contemplation of the Japanese government, and it was unlikely to happen for several years.[1] Likewise, the British Minister in Tokyo, Sir Claude MacDonald, cabled Lord Lansdowne to advise him that the Japanese Prime Minister had given him assurances that there was no possibility of a rapprochement with Russia in the aftermath of the war, and that Japan remained committed to the Anglo-Japanese Alliance.[2]

With those assurances in hand, Lansdowne opened negotiations for a renewal of the alliance, and Hayashi soon received instructions from Tokyo to express the willingness of Japan to renew the agreement. Japan moved quickly, and a draft of a proposed agreement was submitted to Lord Lansdowne by Viscount Hayashi on May 10, 1905.[3] A week later Lansdowne minuted about a further meeting that he had held with Hayashi, in which he proposed the British terms for the renewal of the alliance. Rather than a straightforward renewal, the British wished to expand the agreement in two key areas, although, as with the first alliance, the focus of the alliance remained the countering of Russian expansionism in Asia.

Under the terms proposed by the British, each ally would come to the other's defence if one of the allies was attacked by any other power. This differed from the scope of the original alliance, which only called upon an ally to aid the other ally if a second power joined in an assault on Japan or Great Britain. Before, in the first alliance, the obligations of the treaty would have only required Great Britain or Japan to come to the aid of the other if both Russia and France attacked one of them. Now, under the terms proposed by Great Britain for the renewal of the alliance, the alliance partners would become obligated to come to the other's defence if any other power attacked them in Asia.

The second area of expansion proposed by the British concerned the geographical extent of the treaty. Britain now wished to expand the scope of the alliance beyond the Orient to include the Indian subcontinent, where Britain's Indian Empire lay exposed to a potential assault from the north by Russia. In the Pamirs and Himalayan mountain chains, the Great Game continued to be played out by the British and Russian Empires, as Russia sought to expand its influence southwards, and Britain sought to block Russia from obtaining access to the Indian Ocean. Although Hayashi expressed doubts about whether the Japanese government would consent to an expansion of the geographical limits of the alliance beyond the Far East that is in fact what happened, and Ambassador MacDonald advised Lord Lansdowne of the Japanese agreement in principle in a cable from Tokyo on May 25, 1905. The Japanese were careful to note that the changes in the scope of the arrangements that were being proposed by Great Britain constituted a new alliance, rather than a renewal of the existing alliance because "the basic principle [of the alliance] had been entirely altered."[4] British officials were somewhat taken aback by the alacrity with which the Japanese accepted, in principle, the British proposals to expand the scope of the alliance but the alliance was of special importance to Japan. Racial prejudice ran high and it was not only the German Kaiser who railed against the 'yellow peril'. The alliance with Britain prevented Japan from becoming internationally isolated, and it was considered to be Japan's most significant link to the international community of nations.[5]

The Japanese realized that what Great Britain was proposing was a kind of offensive-defensive alliance to replace what had been a purely defensive arrangement in the original treaty. With Japanese success in the Russo-Japanese War now largely assured by the destruction of Admiral Rozhestvensky's fleet at the Battle of the Tsushima Strait Russia was temporarily de-fanged but it still remained a formidable foe. Both Great Britain and Japan had to be concerned that Russia would recover, and then seek revenge against Japan in a new war – a war in which Great Britain itself might be drawn into and which could endanger the all-important British Indian Empire. As MacDonald reported to London in a despatch Russia was still able, thanks to the Trans-Siberian Railway, to maintain an army of 250,000 men at a distance of over 3000 miles from European Russia, a capability that made plain the potential danger to India, which lay much closer to European Russia than the far off Pacific coast of Siberia. Thus, Great Britain now proposed, through the second alliance, a policy of post-war containment in order to hold the Russian Empire in check in both the Far East, as well as on the Indian subcontinent and its adjacent territories.

Japan understood the danger that the British identified in the current geopolitical environment but the Japanese had never before accepted an obligation to potentially defend a territory so far from the Japanese homeland as British India, and therefore conceding to the British negotiating demand would only be palatable to Japanese public opinion if Japan received something concrete in return. That concrete element was Korea, where Russian intrigues had resulted in the Korean Imperial Court playing off Russia against Japan in an effort to sustain the independence of the country now that it had passed out of the orbit of Imperial China, following Japan's success in the Sino-Japanese War. For its part, Great Britain was not averse to Japan encroaching upon Korea, provided that the Open Door Principle in relation to China continued to be respected, and that the existing rights of western countries in Korea were not abrogated by the establishment of a Japanese protectorate over Korea. Ambassador MacDonald succinctly summed up the cold bargain between Great Britain and Japan by stating: "... in return for our acquiescence in the protectorate which Japan intended to establish over Korea at the conclusion of the war, she would engage to assist us should our Indian Empire be attacked by a third Power".[6] Lord Lansdowne advised Viscount Hayashi that: "... His Majesty's Government were entirely favourable to the development of Japanese influence in Corea [sic] and that, so far as [Great Britain was] concerned, the Jap[ane]se Gov[ernment]t were not likely to encounter any difficulties in giving effect to their policy".[7]

For both countries then, the new alliance would, unlike the first alliance, omit any reference to their joint desire to preserve the independence of Korea, and Japan would receive a *carte blanche* from Great Britain to pursue her interests in reducing Korea to the status of a protectorate of Japan. Perhaps any scruples that Lord Lansdowne might have had over sacrificing the interests of Korea to Japan were mollified by a second-hand report from the British representative in Korea, Sir J Jordan, who advised that "... nothing short of a protectorate will ever save the situation here. In the interests of Coreans themselves this is the only possible solution...".[8]

The main concern that Britain expressed to Japan over Korea was that Japan, in establishing its control over Korea, should not jeopardize the rights and interests of the western powers. Of particular concern to Great Britain was the possibility of a conflict, however remote, between Japan and the United States. Lansdowne made this point clear in a cable to MacDonald in Tokyo stating: "... all we desire is that we should not be compelled to go to war say with the US in the event of a violation of established Treaty rights by Japan".[9] MacDonald proceeded to press this point upon Prime Minister Katsura on July 25, 1905, noting that relations between Japan and the United States were currently on a solid footing, and "exceedingly friendly".

Japan itself had reservations about accepting an open-ended commitment to the defence of India. Although it was prepared to send troops to India to assist in its defence if Russia attacked British India, it was concerned about the British insistence that the enlarged scope of the treaty should include the border areas adjacent to India. Japan's concern was that such a broad commitment could be construed to mean that it would have to assist Great Britain in places such as Tibet, Afghanistan, and Seistan (a Persia-Afghanistan border region) where Japan had no specific interests. Ultimately, the language initially proposed ("... the regions adjacent to the Indian frontier") was tightened up to read "the security of the Indian frontier," which the Japanese found to be acceptable.

Initial efforts to specify what military forces each country would deploy, or make available to support the alliance in the future were ultimately discarded in favour of future conferencing between Japanese and British military officials. From the British perspective, military officials within the General Staff at the War Department who reviewed the proposed British obligations under the treaty had noted that Britain would be unable to send substantial forces to the Far East if Japan was attacked by Russia, although perhaps Britain could despatch some cavalry and horse artillery units in respect of which the Japanese Army was deficient. The British staff officers also felt that Japanese troops were unlikely to be a significant addition to the forces available to the Indian Army, and India could not necessarily count on them anyway if Russia launched a major attack on Japan.

The British war staff did note that Japan could be a useful ally if

Great Britain found itself at war with either Germany or France because Japan could attack the colonial possessions of those countries in the Far East and Pacific. The Japanese Navy could also be relied upon to keep the maritime lines of communication open. Somewhat surprisingly, the report also stated that:

> "In the military contingency of the United States being hostile, the Japanese troops could advantageously be employed against the Philippines, and also against the States themselves, thus indirectly assisting in the defence of Canada."

This statement perturbed Lord Lansdowne who minuted; "I do not agree with some of Gen. Grierson's arguments and there is a passage in his letter which shows I think that he somewhat misapprehends the nature of the [Japanese] obligation".[10]

Of most importance to Great Britain was the ability to significantly draw down its naval forces in the Far East. The principal military advantage of the alliance to the Royal Navy was the ability of the RN to withdraw its capital ships (i.e. battleships) from the Far East by a future reliance on the Japanese navy. The warships removed from the Far East could then be redeployed to home waters to counter the growing naval threat from Imperial Germany.

After the Japanese annihilated the Russian Navy in Far Eastern waters the Admiralty expressed the view that it was no longer necessary for the Royal Navy to maintain battleships in the Orient, a view with which the Japanese subsequently concurred while still expressing the hope that Britain would not allow its naval forces in the Orient to slip below the standard of superiority to any third-power fleet stationed there.[11] However, as Lord Lansdowne explained to Sir Claude MacDonald, it remained a particular concern of the British government to ensure that Japan understood that Great Britain would not seek to match the naval forces deployed by the United States in or near the Orient.[12]

The negotiations between Great Britain and Japan continued through the first half of 1905, while Japan remained at war with the Russian Empire. Despite the long distances between London and Tokyo, the negotiations moved swiftly considering the challenges in communications. The first draft of a new treaty was submitted to Lord Lansdowne on behalf of Japan by Viscount Hayashi on May 10, 1905. A second Japanese draft was submitted by Viscount Hayashi to Lord Lansdowne on May 26, 1905. A first British draft of a new treaty was submitted to Viscount Hayashi by Lord Lansdowne on June 10, 1905. Viscount Hayashi submitted a third Japanese draft to Lord Lansdowne on June 23, 1905. A second British draft of the treaty was submitted by Lord Lansdowne to Viscount Hayashi on July 1, 1905. Following some further representations by Viscount Hayashi, a third British draft was provided on July 19, 1905. The British final draft was provided to Viscount Hayashi on August 9, 1905, and on August 12th Viscount Hayashi called on Lord Lansdowne at his home in London and the treaty was signed by them at Lansdowne's home.

The treaty signed on August 12, 1905, was significantly different from the original alliance. Although it was still directed primarily at Russia, it was general enough to potentially address conflicts with other European powers, such as Germany. And although Great Britain had taken pains to express to Japan that Britain did not contemplate hostilities with the United States there was no language in the agreement that specifically excluded the United States from the purview of the treaty. The second alliance would now remain in force for a total of ten years, instead of the five-year term in the original alliance.

The text of the second alliance treaty was as follows:

> "AGREEMENT BETWEEN THE UNITED KINGDOM AND JAPAN
>
> Signed at London, August 12, 1905

PREAMBLE

The Governments of Japan and Great Britain, being desirous of replacing the Agreement concluded between them on the 30th January, 1902, by fresh stipulations, have agreed upon the following Articles, which have for their object;

(a.) The consolidation and maintenance of the general peace in the regions of Eastern Asia and of India;

(b.) The preservation of the common interests of all Powers in China by insuring the independence and integrity of the Chinese Empire and the principle of equal opportunities for the commerce and industry of all nations in China;

(c.) The maintenance of the territorial rights of the High Contracting Parties in the regions of Eastern Asia and of India, and the defense of their special interests in the said regions:--

ARTICLE 1.

It is agreed that whenever, in the opinion of either Japan or Great Britain, any of the rights and interests referred to in the preamble of this Agreement are in jeopardy, the two Governments will communicate with one another fully and frankly, and will consider in common the measures which should be taken to safeguard those menaced rights or interests.

ARTICLE 2.

If by reason of unprovoked attack or aggressive action, wherever arising, on the part of any Power or Powers either Contracting Party should be involved in war in defence of its territorial rights or special interests mentioned in the preamble of this Agreement, the other Contracting Party will at once come to the assistance of its ally, and will conduct the war in common, and make peace in mutual agreement with it.

ARTICLE 3.

Japan possessing paramount political, military, and economic interests in Corea, Great Britain recognizes the right of Japan to take such measures of guidance, control, and protection in Corea as she may deem proper and necessary to safeguard and advance those interests, provided always that such measures are not contrary to the principle of equal opportunities for the commerce and industry of all nations.

ARTICLE 4.

Great Britain having a special interest in all that concerns the security of the Indian frontier, Japan recognizes her right to take such measures in the proximity of that frontier as she may find necessary for safeguarding her Indian possessions.

ARTICLE 5.

The High Contracting Parties agree that neither of them will, without consulting the other, enter into separate arrangements with another Power to the prejudice of the objects described in the preamble of this Agreement.

ARTICLE 6.

As regards the present war between Japan and Russia, Great Britain will continue to maintain strict neutrality unless some other Power or Powers should join in hostilities against Japan, in which case Great Britain will come to the assistance of Japan, and will conduct the war in common, and make peace in mutual agreement with Japan.

ARTICLE 7.

The conditions under which armed assistance shall be afforded by either Power to the other in the circumstances mentioned in the present Agreement, and the means by which such assistance is to be made available, will be arranged by the Naval and Military authorities of the Contracting Parties, who will from time to time consult one another fully and freely upon all questions of mutual interest.

ARTICLE 8.

The present Agreement shall, subject to the provisions of Article 6, come into effect immediately after the date of its signature, and remain in force for ten years from that date.

In case neither of the High Contracting Parties should have notified twelve months before the expiration of the said ten years the intention of terminating it, it shall remain binding until the expirations of one year from the day on which either of the High Contracting Parties shall have denounced it. But if, when the date fixed for its expiration arrives, either ally is actually engaged in war, the alliances shall, *ipso facto*, continue until peace is concluded.

In faith whereof, the Undersigned, duly authorized by their respective Governments, have signed this Agreement and have affixed thereto their Seals.

Done in duplicate at London, the 12th day of August, 1905.

[L.S.] (Signed) TADASU HAYASHI.

Envoy Extraordinary and Minister Plenipotentiary of His Majesty the Emperor of Japan at the Court of St. James.

[L.S.] (Signed) LANSDOWNE,

His Britannic Majesty's Principal Secretary of State for Foreign Affairs."

In order to ensure that publication of the new treaty did not interfere with, or hamper, the efforts of US President Theodore Roosevelt at Portsmouth, New Hampshire, to arrange peace between Japan and Russia the publication of the treaty was delayed until after a peace treaty was negotiated.

The new alliance was greeted with relative calm by the world community. Although the original alliance in 1902 had been a surprise, given Great Britain's traditional aloofness in matters of alliances, the renewal of the Anglo-Japanese Alliance was not viewed as a significant departure in the relations between the two states. Russia clearly saw that the new alliance was stronger than the first alliance because it was no longer limited to the scenario in which a second aggressor participated in a war involving one of the two parties to the alliance.

Furthermore, the expansion of the geographical ambit of the alliance to include India, and possibly its border regions, could only be directed at Russia. However, Russia's defeat in the Russo-Japanese War (the Treaty of Portsmouth ending the war was signed a few weeks later on September 5, 1905) and the convulsions of the 1905 Revolution that followed Russia's defeat, which nearly brought down the Russian monarchy, meant that Russia would be compelled to look inwards for a number of years.

In the United States, President Roosevelt was sympathetic to Japan in its struggle with Russia and he had no objections to the second alliance seeing the Anglo-Japanese Alliance as an arrangement that was primarily directed at Russian containment after the conclusion of the Russo-Japanese War. France, though formally allied to Russia, was moving ever closer to Great Britain under the Entente Cordiale and it also expressed no objections to the new arrangement. Japan took steps to assure Germany that its commercial interests in the Far East would not be affected by the new Anglo-Japanese Alliance.

Although the second alliance was brought about to contain Russian imperialism in Asia and to guard against the possibility of a future Russian-instigated revanchist war, the aftermath of the Russo-Japanese War put aside the concerns of both nations about Russian intentions. After the convulsions of the 1905 Revolution Tsar Nicholas II issued a Manifesto granting a limited representative body, the Duma, which began to act as a limited check on the exercise of the Tsar's autocratic powers. Although Russia was by no means a completely constitutional monarchy after 1905, it had taken the first steps towards a more liberal political order and that reduced the possibility of Russian adventurism beyond its borders in Asia. Henceforth, Russia concentrated on its internal developments, and the continuing evolution of its political system. By 1907, the growing power of Germany and a suspicion of its long-run intentions served to draw Russia closer to Great Britain, a result encouraged by Russia's ally, France. A rapprochement between Great Britain and Russia was sealed by a visit to the Tsar from King Edward VII in 1907.

Japan moved swiftly after the conclusion of the Russo-Japanese War and the publication of the second alliance with Great Britain to deal with Korea. Sir Ernest Satow, the British Ambassador in Peking, cabled Lord Lansdowne on November 21, 1905, to advise that a treaty was signed by Japan and Korea on November 18, 1905, reducing Korea to the status of a protectorate of Japan and that Japan now considered it unnecessary for Britain to continue to maintain a diplomatic legation in that country.[13] Five years later Japan annexed Korea outright.

Britain and France had also developed a cooperative security arrangement through the Entente Cordiale of 1904. With Germany's Kaiser Wilhelm II bent on developing a high seas fleet that could challenge Great Britain for the trident of world-wide naval supremacy the British Admiralty under its First Sea Lord, Jackie Fisher, seized the opportunity provided by the Anglo-Japanese Alliance of 1905, to withdraw the five British battleships assigned to the China Station and based at Hong Kong, and reassigned them to the Channel Fleet in home waters to ensure that the Royal Navy could retain its supremacy in European waters. Henceforth, the Royal Navy would rely upon the Japanese Navy to control the Pacific Ocean on behalf of the two allied powers.[14]

Military talks between Japan and Great Britain pursuant to the alliance were convened in 1907 in London. The Japanese did not press the British about the withdrawal of their battleships from the China Station but they did ask the Royal Navy to agree to provide Japan with 400,000 tons of transport capacity in the event of a war with Russia in order to swiftly move the Japanese Army from Japan to Manchuria. At first, the British Admiralty demurred, but under pressure from Sir Edward Grey, the Foreign Secretary, the Admiralty relented and the Japanese received a commitment from the Royal Navy to supply the requisite transport capacity if another war with Russia came to pass.[15] On the land forces side of the talks, the Japanese were not pressed to provide troops for the defence of India. Both the General Staff and the India Office in London, together with the Government of India itself, did not want to use Japanese forces to defend the Indian Empire. The ostensible reasons given related to logistical difficulties in moving additional troops up to the Indian frontier but, significantly, there was a more underlying concern that British prestige in the East, and in India in particular, would suffer a terrible, and perhaps a fatal blow if Britain had to rely on Japan to defend its possessions in Asia.[16]

Thus, despite the intentions of both Japan and Great Britain to devise a new alliance to contain the Asian aspirations of Russia the only practical benefits of the second alliance was the ability of Great Britain to redeploy its battleships from the China Station to home waters, and a commitment to Japan by Great Britain to supply transport capacity to Japan in the event of a future war with

Russia. Nevertheless, the British did achieve much by the second alliance and the additional capacity redeployed to home waters helped the Royal Navy to maintain its numerical advantage over Germany in capital ships based in European waters. But for the first time since it had achieved worldwide maritime supremacy, the British had willingly surrendered naval control of an ocean to another power. Henceforth, the Royal Navy's writ of supremacy would not run across the Pacific Ocean where Britain would now rely on its Japanese ally to maintain naval control. All British efforts were now concentrated on meeting the growing threat of Germany's bid for naval supremacy, and those efforts would have political repercussions in Canada.

NOTES

[1] BD (No. 111), 120

[2] BD (No. 110), 120

[3] BD (No 114), 123

[4] BD (No. 117), 127

[5] Nish, *Alliance*, 373, 377

[6] BD (No. 135), 148

[7] BD (No. 103), 113

[8] BD (No. 133), 146

[9] BD (No. 143), 154

[10] BD (No. 127), 140

[11] BD (No. 122 and 123), 133

[12] BD (No. 126), 137

[13] BD (No. 108), 118

[14] Nish, *Alliance*, 353, 373

[15] Nish, *Alliance*, 358

[16] Nish, *Alliance*, 355

5. The Anglo-German Naval Race and the Birth of the Royal Canadian Navy

Throughout the nineteenth century, Canada was shielded from seaborne invasions by the strength of the Royal Navy, which was superior to every possible combination of enemies anywhere in the world following the great victory at Trafalgar in 1805. British squadrons based around the world projected the power of the empire wherever, and whenever, it was needed according to the views of policymakers in the capital of the empire at London. In the maritime colonies of British North America, the great bastion at Halifax provided the major port for the North American and West Indies Squadron, which could be reinforced relatively quickly by ships sent from the home waters of the British Isles. In the North Pacific Ocean, it was another matter. The Royal Navy maintained a Pacific Squadron in the eastern Pacific but it was based at Valparaiso, in Chile, and it was not until 1862 that the headquarters of the Royal Navy's Pacific Squadron was relocated to Esquimalt, in the Colony of Vancouver Island.

Esquimalt was an excellent choice for a naval base because it was a protected harbour that was surrounded on three sides by dense forests and it was close to the colonial capital at nearby Victoria. Although a wary eye was constantly cast southwards towards the United States the main fear in the early years of the Esquimalt base was of a possible sudden descent by a Russian fleet upon Vancouver Island. These were the years of tension in Asia as both the Russian and British empires engaged in the Great Game, seeking territories and advantages in central Asia. The tensions between the two empires gave rise to continuing concerns about the security of Britain's Pacific territories in North America, which were somewhat alleviated when the United States purchased Russian America (Alaska) from the Russian Empire in 1867, the same year that Canada came into being as an autonomous country under the British Crown. Still concerned about Russian ambitions, and their possible impacts on the west coast of Canada, the Royal Navy purchased two torpedo boats from Chile in 1885, and stationed them at Esquimalt where they served until 1903.[1]

By the turn of the century, however, the Pacific Squadron was becoming outmatched by the increasing US naval resources on the west coast of North America. In 1901, Rear Admiral Bickford, the commander of the Pacific Squadron complained to the Admiralty that his squadron of ten ships was considerably weaker than the nineteen vessels that the United States Navy maintained on the west coast of North America, calling the British squadron 'ridiculously small.' Unamused by his complaint, the Admiralty smacked down their commander on the Pacific station by thundering back: "Their Lordships do not consider it becoming in you to apply the remark 'ridiculously small' to the dimensions of the Squadron which they have thought it right to place under your orders."[2] But the truth was that by the turn of the century the British Admiralty viewed the Pacific Station at Esquimalt as of secondary importance in the overall disposition of British naval forces.

In fairness to the Admiralty, a new cause for concern was beginning to occupy the minds of British naval commanders. On March 26, 1898, the German Reichstag enacted the first of several Navy Bills that would set Imperial Germany on a course of increasing naval tension with Great Britain. The German Emperor, Kaiser Wilhelm II, was imbued with the idea of creating a great German fleet to enhance his status and the status of the German Empire abroad. Wilhelm, the eldest grandchild of Queen Victoria, was an overseas member of the extended British Royal Family, but a strident and difficult person. He had a great affection for Britain, and for its status as the leading world power, and he much desired to see the German Empire emulate it in the world. Above all else, he sought recognition and acceptance by his British relatives, and he saw the possession of a great navy as a way to reduce his feelings of inferiority in dealings with his British relatives and to force them to show greater respect to him.

What Wilhelm could never clearly see was that the possession of a great fleet by Germany, the most powerful land power in Europe, could only pose an existential threat to the security of Great Britain.[3] The world-wide possessions and responsibilities of Great Britain required the Royal Navy to maintain ships and establishments across the globe, while the lack of a large colonial empire meant that most of the German Navy's ships could be concentrated in the Baltic, and the North Sea, causing a jittery Britain to fear a sudden descent upon its coasts with an amphibious assault by the most powerful army in Europe.

In December, 1904, the Admiralty crystallised its new view of the danger in the Selbourne Memoranda, which articulated this threat from Germany, by stating: "The new German Navy has come into existence; it is a navy of the most efficient type and is so fortunately circumstanced that it is able to concentrate almost the whole of its fleet in its home waters."[4] The preceding October Admiral John (Jacky) Fisher had become the First Sea Lord, and he immediately embarked upon a wide-ranging review and restructuring of the Royal Navy to modernize it, and to ensure its continued superiority over the fleets of other nations. Among the reforms that he promoted to enhance its capabilities four measures particularly stood out. Firstly, he arranged for the scrapping of a large number of obsolete warships. Secondly, he reorganized the dockyards and created new partially-manned naval reserve squadrons that could be rapidly scaled up in an emergency. Thirdly, he created an interlocking system of fleet commands that could protect both the home islands and Britain's imperial lines of communication, especially those linking Britain to India. Finally, he embarked on rapid technological change by bringing into service a new type of capital ship, the dreadnought battleship.[5]

The German naval theory was built around the concept of the line of battle and hence Germany needed battleships if it was to contend with Britain for naval supremacy. The British innovation of the dreadnought-type ship was a game-changer since it rendered the existing pre-dreadnought line of battleships obsolete. HMS *Dreadnought* combined size, speed, and large guns of the same size in one ship, giving it enhanced gunnery, and marking a significant improvement in its offensive capability.[6] Powered by superior turbine engines in place of the older, reciprocating engines, the new battleship when fully loaded was in excess of 20,000 tons and could reach a speed of 21 knots. Its five turrets (one forward, two amidships, and two aft) were each equipped with two 12-inch guns that could simultaneously fire six shells forward, six shells aft, and eight shells in a broadside, making it equal to two, or three, of the earlier pre-dreadnought battleship designs.[7]

Germany responded by launching its own dreadnought-type warships and it sought to compete with the Royal Navy in the number of capital ships. The architect of the German Kaiser's naval ambitions, Grand Admiral Alfred von Tirpitz, believed in the risk theory, a theory that Germany only needed to threaten, or potentially injure, the Royal Navy sufficiently to compromise the British two-power standard. Under the earlier two-power standard Britain had pledged to maintain its naval superiority over the next two most powerful fleets then existing, France and Russia. Thus, by threatening the two-power standard, Germany hoped to wring concessions from Great Britain. The unintended consequence of such a policy, however, was to compel Great Britain to sort out its difficulties with France and Russia diplomatically, which it did in the 1904 Entente Cordiale with France and the 1907 rapprochement with Russia.[8] Thereafter, Germany found itself isolated in Europe in the failing Triple Alliance along with an ambivalent Italy, and a slowly disintegrating Austria-Hungary.[9]

The naval race between Great Britain and Germany produced important consequences in Canada. As part of Admiral Fisher's reforms at the Admiralty, the number of ships maintained by the Royal Navy on far distant stations was considerably reduced. Among the stations that were reduced was the Pacific Squadron based at Esquimalt, British Columbia, which was demobilized on March 1, 1905. Thereafter the Royal Navy only maintained two small guard ships at the Canadian west coast. A similar withdrawal took place in Halifax, and the two naval bases were both subsequently transferred to Canada, which now became responsible for the defence of those two naval bases, including, at Esquimalt, the graving dock at His Majesty's Dockyard (HMD).

The effective withdrawal of the Royal Navy from Canada encouraged the Canadian government to consider the need for a separate Canadian naval policy. Unquestionably, Canada would remain within the British security structure for the purposes of any new approach to naval policy but within that structure, the government contemplated the creation of a separate Canadian naval force. Prime Minister Sir Wilfrid Laurier (in office 1896-1911) made it clear, however, that a separate naval force did not mean that Canada would not rally to Great Britain if Great Britain was threatened.[10]

The need for a new naval strategy for Canada rose to the top of the policy agenda in 1909, when the debate over the naval estimates in the British Parliament made it plain that the danger of Germany's naval ambitions required Britain to authorize up to eight new dreadnought-type vessels to counter the German threat.

The policy choice that the Canadian government faced was whether to financially support the Imperial government by making a financial contribution for the expansion of the British fleet or to create a separate Canadian naval service that would be integrated with the Royal Navy. Generally, Canada did not wish to contribute towards the cost of the British naval expenses, as the Laurier Ministry was conscious of the implied protection that Canada obtained from its fortunate geographical proximity to the United States. Canada's reluctance to help pay for the costs of the Royal

Navy had caused Admiral Jacky Fisher, the First Sea Lord at the Admiralty, to characterize Canadians as "grasping" and "unpatriotic" and who only wished to use Great Britain when it was to Canada's advantage.[11] Initially, the opposition Conservatives under Robert Laird Borden agreed in principle with Laurier's Liberal Party that Canada should establish its own naval force that would be under domestic control in peacetime but would be capable of being assigned to duty with the Royal Navy in the event of a war. Parliament thereafter unanimously passed the Foster Resolution, calling for the creation of a separate Canadian naval service.

However, the question of a separate Canadian naval service created tensions in the Conservative party between those who harboured strong Imperial sentiments, and those, particularly from Quebec, who wanted a more nationalistic approach to the subject. In order to reconcile these competing viewpoints, Borden was forced to articulate a new position, by calling for financial contributions to the Royal Navy to construct battleships while proceeding to establish a separate Canadian naval service over a longer period of time.[12]

The Admiralty initially insisted on the Imperial unity of naval command, and the centralized control of the Royal Navy's forces. However, the Admiralty eventually came to recognize that local naval forces in the dominions could enhance the operational reach of the Royal Navy, and it modified its views to accommodate small local naval units under the organization and control of the separate self-governing dominions.[13]

The debate in the Canadian Parliament over the Naval Service bill was long and divisive, as it raised important questions about the place of Canada in the British Empire. The debate pitted the Liberal Party's view of a decentralized empire, with broad measures of autonomy for the individual dominions, against the opposition Conservative Party's view of a closely associated empire, with centralized control of foreign and defence issues. But the results of the debate were never really in doubt because Prime Minister Laurier commanded a majority of the seats in the House of Commons and in the Senate. In May, 1910, the naval bill was passed and shortly afterwards the Canadian Naval Service came into existence. The following year the King granted permission for the use of the Royal prefix and the service was restyled as the Royal Canadian Navy (RCN).

A Canadian officer serving in the Royal Navy, Rear Admiral Charles Kingsmill, was selected by Ottawa to command the new Canadian service, and he immediately began to plan for the acquisition of ships, and for the rehabilitation of the naval bases on the east and west coasts. At Esquimalt, Admiral Kingsmill envisaged stationing two small cruisers for training purposes and, eventually, two coastal type destroyers, and four torpedo boats, the latter to be built at the west coast in order to save costs.[14]

Despite the laser-like focus of the Admiralty on the growing threat from the German High Seas Fleet as a result of Germany's ambitious naval program, Canadian officials showed concerns about another potential threat – Japan. Although Japan was Britain's ally, and hence Canada's ally as well, there was a concern in high circles in Canada that Japan could eventually pose a threat to Canada's west coast. Those concerns were discussed in the correspondence that circulated at the highest levels of the government in the years that led up to the naval debate and the creation of the RCN. Partly the concern about Japan was fuelled by the racial prejudices that were rampant during the pre-war era, particularly in British Columbia, where the serious race riots of 1907 had been directed against immigrants from Asia. Prejudice against Asians was also a feature of the United States society in the pre-war era and, at the highest level, President Theodore Roosevelt developed a concern about the growing power and ambitions of Japan. In 1907-08 he despatched the US fleet, painted all-white for the occasion, on a round the world cruise to show the flag, the primary purpose of which was to demonstrate to Japan that too great an ambition could bring it into conflict with the United States.[15]

Canadians became fascinated with the progress of the American Great White Fleet as it journeyed around the world and none more so than the Governor General of Canada, Lord Grey, who sent cajoling missives to Prime Minister Laurier to encourage him to think about a potential Japanese threat to Canada's Pacific coast. The Governor General warned Laurier in one letter that Canada's only protection against the seizure of British Columbia by the Japanese was the strength of the Royal Navy and the existence of the Anglo-Japanese Alliance. In the absence of those two factors, the Governor General thought that Japan could take BC at its leisure.[16]

After the Vancouver race riots in 1907, Laurier had appointed William Lyon Mackenzie King, the Deputy Minister of Labour, to convene a Royal Commission to investigate those disturbances and to recommend compensation for those who had been affected by them. The riots were also the catalyst for Laurier to send the Postmaster-General and Labour Minister, Rodolphe Lemieux, to Japan to firm up agreements under which Japan would voluntarily limit Japanese emigration to Canada in order to avoid exacerbating racial tensions in British Columbia.

Observing those events, President Roosevelt invited Mackenzie King to visit him in Washington, intending to set up a back-channel between Washington, via Canada, to engage with London in the hope of persuading the British government to use their influence with Japan to obtain some restrictions on Japanese emigration to America. Prime Minister Laurier did not object to this attempt at back-channel communications as the political concerns about Japanese emigration were equally of concern to Canada. However, nothing came of this effort because Great Britain was committed to the Anglo-Japanese Alliance in order to meet her own security needs, and was averse to putting that alliance at risk over purely domestic issues in Canada, and in the United States.[17]

In any event, Japan did adhere to the agreements it made concerning Japanese emigration to Canada that were negotiated by Minister Lemieux. Part of the source for a surge in Japanese emigration to Canada (and the United States) in the early years of the twentieth century actually came from Hawaii, where a large number of Japanese immigrants had been accepted by the Kingdom of Hawaii before the kingdom was overthrown, and Hawaii was incorporated into the United States. Japanese immigrants from Hawaii, an American possession, fell outside of the scope of the Gentleman's Agreement that Canada had negotiated with Japan, and thus Japanese immigrants from Hawaii were in addition to the flow of immigrants from Japan itself.

While it may be perplexing from a great historical distance to find that some among the Canadian elite harboured concerns about the possibility of a Japanese invasion despite the British Empire's firm alliance with Japan, that was no doubt a reflection of the times. Japan proved in the Russo-Japanese War that it could militarily contend with the other major powers and that alone provoked fear of Japan. Furthermore, alliances between states were seen to be fickle among the major powers in the pre-war era. Enemies today might be allies tomorrow, and vice versa, and therefore the existence of an alliance between countries, such as the Anglo-Japanese Alliance, was not seen as a future guarantee of security to an exposed country, such as Canada. Some policy-makers considered that peace between the British Empire and Japan might not be a permanent condition. The risk of impermanence in alliances contributed to the general anxieties in pre-war society. Nevertheless, for Canada, and for the other self-governing dominions, the reality was that Pacific Ocean security in the pre-war period was securely built on the foundation of the Anglo-Japanese Alliance.[18]

In Canada, Rear Admiral Kingsmill managed to establish the new Royal Canadian Navy through the purchase of two older second-hand cruisers from the Royal Navy. Canada obtained the *Spartiate* class cruiser HMCS *Niobe*, the larger of the two cruisers, which was intended for service at Halifax. The smaller, *Apollo* class cruiser, HMCS *Rainbow* was purchased for service on the Canadian Pacific coast. Re-commissioned in England, *Rainbow* departed from Portsmouth on August 20, 1910, and arrived at Esquimalt on November 7, 1910, to the public acclaim of the residents of Victoria. Canada now had its own navy.[19]

Unfortunately for Admiral Kingsmill, his larger plans for the RCN failed to come to fruition because the fight over the naval bill had cost Prime Minister Laurier political support in Quebec, and the fight over a trade reciprocity agreement negotiated with President Taft and his administration in the United States, which subsequently became the main focus of the 1911 election campaign, lost Laurier support in much of the rest of the country. As a result, when the election returns were counted in 1911, Laurier's Liberals were ousted from office, and the Conservative Party returned to power under Robert Borden. The Conservatives fell back on their plan to provide a 35 million dollar subvention to Great Britain to build three new capital ships for the Royal Navy. The Admiralty tried to assist Prime Minister Borden by preparing a memorandum on the subject of naval supremacy in which it explained that naval supremacy was of two types, general and local. General naval superiority resulted when one navy could defeat another, or drive it from the high seas, thus ensuring complete oceanic control. Local superiority was merely the superiority that existed in one particular locale and, while important, there was no guarantee that local superiority could continue where there was an absence of general naval superiority.[20] The focus of the British Admiralty, therefore, remained determined to sustain a general superiority over the German navy, as well as a local superiority over the German Navy in Britain's home waters.

While Borden was successful in getting his naval bill through the House of Commons, where his party held a majority, it was not done without political difficulty, and Borden had to deal with a division over the issue in his Quebec caucus.[21] But despite his success in the Commons, the Liberal majority in the Senate defeated the Conservative government's subsidy proposal on May 30, 1913. The Liberal Party resisted Imperial naval centralization on a policy level. Foiled in his attempts to support the expansion of the Royal Navy with a financial contribution Prime Minister Borden made no further attempts to financially support the British navy, and he left the young Royal Canadian Navy to languish with its two second-hand cruisers.

Abroad, Germany was defeated in the naval race with Great Britain. The greater financial capacity of Britain, its greater shipbuilding capabilities, and the absence of a large standing army in Britain to drain financial resources ensured that the Royal Navy could remain the master of the waves.[22] Grand Admiral von Tirpitz would later claim that Germany's policy had forced the British to turn over control of the Mediterranean Sea to France, and the control of the Pacific Ocean to Japan, but as historians have noted that provided very little practical benefit to Germany.[23]

However, the naval race with Germany had finally forced Great Britain to abandon the two-power standard that it had formally maintained since 1889. Henceforth, according to the new First Lord of the Admiralty, Winston Churchill, Great Britain would seek to maintain a 60% level of superiority over the German High Seas Fleet in capital ships. In that endeavour Britain would prove to be successful, and when the Royal Navy entered upon the First World War in August of 1914, it possessed twenty dreadnought-type ships to Germany's fifteen.[24]

NOTES

[1] William Johnston, William G P Rawling, Richard H Gimblett, John MacFarlane, *The Seabound Coast, The Official History of the Royal Canadian Navy, 1867-1939*, Dundurn Press, Toronto, 2010, 26

[2] quoted in Gilbert Norman Tucker, *The Naval Service of Canada, Its Official History*, vol. 1, King's Printer, Ottawa, 1952, 84

[3] Robert K Massie, *Castles of Steel, Britain, Germany, and the Winning of the Great War at Sea*, Ballantine Books, New York, 2003, 10 [afterwards: Massie, *Castles*]

[4] quoted in Tucker, 89

[5] Peter Kemp, "The Naval Race" in "Germany's Bid for Sea Power," in *History of the First World War*, BPC Publishing/Imperial War Museum, Vol. 1, No. 2, BPC Publishing, London, 1969, 47 at 48.

[6] Tucker, 87

[7] Robert K Massie, *Dreadnought, Britain, Germany and the Coming of the Great War*, Ballantine Books, New York, 1991, 473 [afterwards: Massie, *Dreadnought*]

[8] Sir Llewellyn Woodward, "Germany's Bid for Sea Power", *History of the First World War*, BPC Publishing/Imperial War Museum, Vol. 1, No. 2, BPC Publishing, London, 1969, 40 at 42.

[9] Massie, *Castles*, 10

[10] Ralph Allen, *Ordeal By Fire, Canada 1910 – 1945*, Doubleday Canada Limited, Toronto, 1961, 17

[11] Margaret MacMillan, *The War That Ended Peace, The Road to 1914*, Allen Lane, Toronto, 2013, 124 [afterwards: MacMillan, *1914*]

[12] Allen, 20

[13] Johnston et al, 112-13

[14] Johnston et al, 136-37

[15] Johnston et al, 117

[16] Johnston et al, 119

[17] Johnston et al, 119

[18] Johnston et al, 143

[19] Johnston et al, 167

[20] Massie, *Dreadnought*, 828

[21] Allen, 45

[22] Woodward, 42

[23] Massie, *Dreadnought*, 827

[24] Woodward, 45-46

6. The North Pacific on the Eve of the World War

In the years from 1908 until 1914, the subject of immigration from Asia continued to require the political attention of the Canadian Government. Racial harmony was in short supply on the west coast, and it was not only in Canada that these concerns were apparent – they were shared by Canada's sister dominions in the Pacific, Australia, and New Zealand, as well as by the United States, particularly in the state of California.

Japanese immigrants to Canada did not have to pay the sordid head tax that Chinese immigrants to Canada had to pay because Japan was the formal ally of the British Empire, and hence Canada's ally, but that did not mean that Japanese immigrants were welcome in Canada. White supremacy was in its heyday in the pre-war years, and many in Canada were alarmed by Asian immigration, fearing that the cultural integrity of the country would be undermined. Matters were not helped by the practice of using recent Asian immigrants as strikebreakers in labour disputes, thus fueling the antipathy of the working class against Asian immigrants. Labour tensions, as well as outright racism, had led to the 1907 race riot against Chinese and Japanese Canadians in Vancouver. Large-scale property damage occurred when a white mob smashed windows and property in the Chinese and Japanese neighbourhoods. Although the Chinese-Canadian community was apparently cowed by the violence, the Japanese-Canadian community fought back, and it took many hours before the Vancouver Police Force was able to restore public order. This eruption of violence at the west coast led to the creation of a Royal Commission headed by Deputy Labour Minister W L Mackenzie King who eventually awarded the Japanese-Canadian community nine-thousand dollars in compensation. Those reparations at least spared the Canadian government from any embarrassment with the government of the King-Emperor's ally in Tokyo. The Chinese-Canadian community was left without compensation but subsequent public pressure resulted in reparations of twenty-six thousand dollars being paid to the Chinese-Canadian community. In the aftermath of the riots, the Laurier Ministry decided to send a Minister to Japan to attempt to negotiate an informal agreement to voluntarily restrict Japanese emigration to Canada, despite the fact that many of the immigrants of Japanese descent that came to Canada in the pre-war years came from Hawaii, and were, therefore, immigrants from the United States. Nevertheless, a 'Gentleman's Agreement' was struck by Postmaster-General and Labour Minister Rodolphe Lemieux early in 1908 with the Japanese government to govern the emigration of Japanese subjects to Canada.

In the agreement that Postmaster-General and Labour Minister Rodolphe Lemieux negotiated with Viscount Hayashi, now Foreign Minister of Japan, the admissibility of Japanese immigrants to Canada was constrained in a manner that the Laurier Ministry felt would lessen the chances of racial animosity towards Asians boiling over again at the west coast. Under the 'Gentleman's Agreement', of 1908, Japanese merchants, travellers, and students continued to be admissible to Canada but labour immigrants were excluded, subject to exceptions for Japanese immigrants employed as household servants, or as agricultural workers, and with the admissions in those categories capped at 400 persons annually. The resolution of the immigration issue was formalized by an exchange of notes in January, 1908. Canada was much more successful than other countries in negotiating immigration controls with Japan. Both Australia and New Zealand were unable to obtain equally satisfactory immigration agreements with Japan. In Washington President Theodore Roosevelt sought to learn the terms of the accord negotiated by Lemieux but Canada insisted on keeping its arrangements with Japan to itself.[1] However, President Roosevelt was also able to arrange for similar restrictions in a 'Gentleman's Agreement' between Japan and the United States.

For Japan, the immigration disputes with the British Empire dominions were a minor distraction that did not affect the strength of the Anglo-Japanese Alliance. The Japanese Government never confused its top-line policy, which was its political alliance with Britain, and its second-line policy considerations involving relations with the British dominions around migration issues. The Anglo-Japanese Alliance remained the bedrock of Japanese foreign policy in the pre-war years, as it gave Japan a recognized international status, and it avoided the international isolation of Japan.[2]

In the aftermath of the war with Russia Japan had suffered economically, partially because it was unable to obtain a war indemnity from Russia through the peace negotiations that could compensate Japan for the economic dislocations caused by the war. The country suffered through a recession between 1907 and 1910, which necessitated higher levels of taxation, and that energized opposition to the government in the Diet and required some further government belt-tightening. However, there were also new opportunities presented by the continuing consolidation of Japan's position in Korea, and in Manchuria, and the start of its systematic economic penetration of China. Japan established the South Manchurian Railway Company as an economic vehicle for the creation of a Japanese economic footprint in Manchuria and Japan quickly became commercially dominant in North-East China. A growing economic hegemony carried with it a commercial competition (and disputes) with other countries, however, and therefore an effort was made to reduce the level of friction with other countries arising from Japan's exploitation of its sphere of influence. To that end, Japan concluded an agreement with Russia on the respective spheres of influence of Japan and Russia in Manchuria in 1907, and that agreement went some way towards placating Russia and avoiding any prospect of a future war of revanchement. The Japanese-Russian Agreement was renewed in

1910, and again in 1912 and Japan also entered into a similar agreement with Russia's ally, France.[3]

The relationship between Britain and Japan was not free of economic tensions either, as Japan, in the aftermath of the Russian war, increased its economic penetration of China beyond Manchuria. Great Britain was especially sensitive to Japanese economic penetration in the Yangtze Valley, which had long been the locus of the British sphere of influence in China. However, Britain needed Japan as a counterweight to Russia so that it could concentrate the Royal Navy in European waters, and thus there was little that Britain could do about Japanese economic activity in China. In 1901, Britain had maintained 38 warships on the China Station and by 1910 it had halved that number, underscoring the naval importance of the Anglo-Japanese Alliance.[4]

The one major power that continued to look askance at Japan's rise towards strategic domination in the Asia-Pacific region was the United States. Increasingly, in the pre-war years, America took steps to reinforce its strategic posture in the Pacific. The most important step it took was the construction of the Panama Canal. In the nineteenth-century, there had been a competition between the United States and Great Britain over which of them might construct a navigable canal across Central America to link the world's two major oceans. Ultimately, the two countries had attempted to cooperate in the event such an endeavour materialized, by entering into a treaty known as the Clayton-Bulmer Treaty but, in 1901, under a new agreement, the Hay-Pauncefote Agreement, Britain released the United States from the provisions of the Clayton-Bulmer treaty so that the United States could build, control, and defend a canal on its own across the Central American isthmus. After considering the building of a canal through Nicaragua, the US decided instead to build a canal through Panama, which was then a province of Columbia because a Panamanian location permitted the construction of a canal that would be both deep and wide enough to permit the passage of dreadnought-type battleships.

Colombian sentiments over the potential American control of the canal were intended to be smoothed over by a 10 million dollar cash payment but the Colombian legislature refused to approve such a deal. The administration of President Theodore Roosevelt quickly arranged a filibuster (without the direct participation of US citizens) that led to the separation of the province of Panama from Columbia, Panama's creation as an independent state, and the grant by the new country of a sovereign US zone through the middle of Panama to accommodate the trans-isthmus canal.[5] The Panama Canal was a great undertaking that took ten years to complete. Fifty thousand men worked day and night to complete the project. Steam-shovel crews moved 765,000 cubic metres of soil, and 300 metre long locks were constructed to raise and lower ships on their passage through the canal. The Panama Canal cost 352 million dollars, and 5600 lives before it was finally completed in August, 1914.[6]

The construction of the Panama Canal meant that the United States now truly had a two-ocean navy, one that could be quickly moved from ocean to ocean to accommodate whatever circumstances might arise. The canal also meant that the United States would now be able to challenge Japan for Pacific supremacy. Although President Roosevelt worried about the prospect of a future war between the United States and Japan neither country wanted a conflict to develop, and as the construction of the canal proceeded efforts were made to put in place diplomatic mechanisms to forestall any future conflict in the Pacific between the two powers. The Taft-Katsura Memorandum of July 1904, and the subsequent Root-Takahira Agreement of 1908, acknowledged the territorial acquisitions of both the US and Japan in the Asia-Pacific Region (i.e. Hawaii, Guam, the Philippines, Korea, and the Kwantung Peninsula) and the establishment of a Japanese sphere of influence in China (in Southern Manchuria) while paying lip service to Chinese independence. Such agreements served to maintain cordial relations between the two rising Pacific powers in the pre-war era.[7]

Nevertheless, while the Japanese and American governments continually emphasized the cordiality of their relations their respective militaries began examining the possibility of an outbreak of war between them. Thus, the Japanese navy began planning for an invasion of the Philippines, and the United States military began its war planning against Japan in 1907. Roosevelt sought funding from Congress to commence the construction of significant fortifications at Pearl Harbour, Guam, and at Subic Bay in the Philippines but Congress would only authorize new fortifications at Pearl Harbour, in Hawaii.[8]

Roosevelt's decision to send the US fleet on its round the world tour in 1908 was viewed in many places as an American warning to Japan, and the appearance of the fleet in the waters of Australia and New Zealand played into the hands of those politicians, such Billy Hughes of the Australian Labour Party, who adhered to a white supremacist political philosophy. President Roosevelt asked W L Mackenzie King, the Canadian Deputy Minister of Labour, when he was in Washington for discussions with the President, whether the Canadian government would permit the Great White Fleet to call at Vancouver and Victoria. King discussed the matter with decision-makers in Ottawa, including the Governor General, Lord Grey, among others. The Canadian government decided not to invite the US fleet to Canada, ostensibly, Mackenzie King wrote later, to avoid encouraging annexationist sentiment in British Columbia, or to suggest that Canada was militarily dependent on the United States for its Pacific Ocean security.[9]

More likely, Mackenzie King was worried about the widespread presence of anti-Asian sentiments at the west coast, which he had studied during his work on the Royal Commission established in the aftermath of the 1907 race riot. Undoubtedly, King did not want to encourage another racial incident that could embarrass the Canadian government with the government of the King-Emperor's Pacific ally, Japan. Thus, the Great White Fleet came as far north as Puget Sound, in the State of Washington, before commencing its transpacific voyage. The Great White Fleet made successful visits to the antipodean dominions, and then Japan invited the American fleet to visit Japanese ports. The visit of the Great White Fleet to Japan was a success, and it contributed to the continuation of cordial relations between the US and Japan in the pre-war years.[10]

In 1910, Japan finally moved to consolidate its position on the Korean peninsula by formally annexing the Empire of Korea. In 1907, Gojong, the Emperor of Korea, had attempted to send Korean diplomats abroad to a Hague Conference in the Netherlands, notwithstanding the fact that Korea had become a Japanese protectorate at the end of the Russo-Japanese War and, as such, no longer had the right to engage in direct diplomatic relations with other states. The Emperor had hoped that he could find international support for the reestablishment of Korean independence but his Korean diplomats were unsuccessful, and they only succeeded in angering Japan. To underscore its displeasure Japan deposed the Emperor and put his heir, Sunjong, on the Korean throne. Japan also took the step of abolishing the Korean army. Subsequently, when a Korean dissident assassinated the elder statesman Marquis Ito, a former Japanese Resident-Minister in Korea, during a visit the Marquis made to China in 1909, Japan's patience with Korea finally came to an end. In 1910, Japan annexed Korea outright, deposed the recently installed Korean Emperor, and confined the Emperor and the royal family to their palace.

In 1911 the two allies, Britain and Japan, began to contemplate the future of the Anglo-Japanese Alliance. Although the 1905 treaty would not run out until 1915, both countries had reasons to consider the advantages of an early renewal. For Japan, the pending completion of the Panama Canal in 1914, would provide the United States with the flexibility to reinforce its fleet in the Pacific Ocean, and the growing military footprint of the United States in the North Pacific Ocean was a long-term cause for Japanese concern. The Imperial Japanese Navy was particularly aware of the potential for the US Navy to challenge Japan for naval supremacy in the Pacific. Early renewal of the alliance would at least confirm Britain's continuing diplomatic support for Japan, and thus avoid the prospect of Japan becoming isolated among the great powers.

Great Britain also had good reasons to consider an early renewal of the alliance. The naval race with Germany was in full force, as each country sought to out-build the other in battleships and battlecruisers. Increasingly, there was a belief in both countries that a political collision between them was possible. The naval threat that Germany was posing to Great Britain had forced the British Empire to resolve its outstanding issues with both France and Russia. With France, Britain had entered into the Entente Cordiale in 1904, resolving many colonial disputes between the British and French Empires in Africa and in North America. Although the Entente Cordiale was not a formal military alliance, unlike Britain's alliance with Japan, a subsequent naval agreement between the two powers allowed the French fleet to concentrate its ships in the Mediterranean, while the British concentrated their fleet in the North Sea, and the English Channel. That agreement meant that, in wartime, the French navy would protect British possessions in the Mediterranean from Germany's Triple Alliance partners, Austria-Hungary, and Italy, while the British would protect the French Atlantic coast from the possibility of an attack by German naval forces. The strategic situation facing Britain compelled the continuation of the British policy of concentrating the Royal Navy in home waters to face the potential German threat, and it underscored the need for both the naval agreement with France and the Anglo-Japanese Alliance, in order to ensure that the threat of the Imperial German Navy across the North Sea could be met by the Royal Navy.

A subsidiary factor for Great Britain concerned the political development of the Empire. While the 1902 and 1905 alliance treaties with Japan had been negotiated by the Imperial government without much regard for the far-flung components of the empire, such an approach could no longer be countenanced by the constitutional developments that had occurred within the Empire in the interim. In the nineteenth century the only self-governing dominion in the Empire was Canada, but in the first ten years of the twentieth century several more were added; Australia (1901), New Zealand (1907), Newfoundland (1907), and South Africa (1910). The dominion governments were autonomous to varying degrees although they lacked an internationally-recognized status as separate states. Within the British Empire, however, their status created an expectation that they would be consulted about major foreign policy initiatives that might affect them, and the continuation of the Anglo-Japanese Alliance was one of those initiatives.

The Imperial government in London was concerned that the racial prejudice against Asian immigration was so apparent in each of Australia, New Zealand, and Canada, that it might affect Britain's ability to obtain a consensus within the Empire on the renewal of the Anglo-Japanese Alliance. The Imperial government did not wish to wait until the alliance treaty was close to expiration before considering renewal because obstructionism from the dominions could seriously impact the length and course of the diplomatic negotiations. Thus, an early renewal that left plenty of time to bring the recalcitrant dominions on board with the strategic policy being pursued by London was seen as beneficial.

In early 1911 the Japanese made an initial overture to Great Britain concerning the possibility of early renewal of the treaty, and the British Foreign Minister, Sir Edward Grey, was immediately amenable to its consideration. However, Britain had noted the growing US strategic presence in the Pacific Ocean, a presence that would only increase with the pending completion of the Panama Canal, and Britain was increasingly concerned about the possibility that its alliance with Japan could embroil the Empire in a conflict with the United States – something that British foreign policy now adamantly wished to avoid. The two Atlantic countries had continued to grow closer together both politically, and culturally, as a result of the modern improvements in transportation and communications.

In order to prevent any possibility of war between the British Empire and the United States, Britain advised Japan that it wanted a clause inserted into the treaty for the renewal of the alliance that would exempt Great Britain from having to come to the aid of Japan if a war between Japan and another power involved a power with which Britain had entered into a general arbitration treaty for the resolution of disputes. At the time that the early renewal of the Anglo-Japanese Alliance was being considered in 1911, Great Britain was actively pursuing a general arbitration treaty with the United States and all indications were that those negotiations would soon come to fruition. Thus the proposed clause containing an exemption for general arbitration treaties was intended to let Great Britain escape any military obligations to Japan if the latter found itself at war with America.

Japan was obviously reluctant to grant an exemption for so-called general arbitration treaties, the more so as the potential for an American threat to Japan could only grow as American power in the Pacific Ocean increased over time. However, Japan also understood that the British would not give way on this subject, and, reluctantly, they agreed with the British proposal but only if the exemption clause was structured around general arbitration treaties with third powers. The Japanese would not agree to explicitly exempt Britain from the obligations of the Anglo-Japanese Alliance if a conflict were to occur between Japan and the United States.

In all other respects, the renewal treaty of 1911 retained its scope of application in the Far East and India, although the British no longer insisted on a commitment by Japan to assist with the defense of the frontiers of India.[11] The British proposed, and Japan agreed, that the term of the renewed alliance would be ten years from the date that it entered into force. Negotiations were completed relatively quickly, and the renewal of the Anglo-Japanese Alliance was signed in London on July 13, 1911. The text of the renewed treaty was as follows:

"AGREEMENT BETWEEN THE UNITED KINGDOM AND JAPAN

Signed at London, July 13, 1911,

Preamble

THE Government of Great Britain and the Government of Japan, having in view the important changes which have taken place in the situation since the conclusion of the Anglo-Japanese Agreement of the 12th August, 1905, and believing that a revision of that Agreement responding to such changes would contribute to general stability and repose, have agreed upon the following stipulations to replace the Agreement above mentioned, such stipulations having the same object as the said Agreement, namely;

(a.) The consolidation and maintenance of the general peace in the regions of Eastern Asia and of India;

(b.) The preservation of the common interests of all Powers in China by insuring the independence and integrity of the Chinese Empire and the principle of equal opportunities for the commerce and industry of all nations in China;

(c.) The maintenance of the territorial rights of the High Contracting Parties in the regions of Eastern Asia and of India, and the defence of their special interests in the said regions:-

ARTICLE I

It is agreed that whenever, in the opinion of either Great Britain or Japan, any of the rights and interests referred to in the preamble of this Agreement are in jeopardy, the two Governments will communicate with one another fully and frankly, and will consider in common the measures which should be taken to safeguard those menaced rights or interests.

ARTICLE II

If by reason of unprovoked attack or aggressive action, wherever arising, on the part of any Power or Powers, either High Contracting Party should be involved in war in defence of its territorial rights or special interests mentioned in the preamble of this Agreement, the other High Contracting Party will at once come to the assistance of its ally, and will conduct the war in common, and make peace in mutual agreement with it.

ARTICLE III

The High Contracting Parties agree that neither of them will, without consulting the other, enter into separate arrangements with another Power to the prejudice of the objects described in the preamble of this Agreement.

ARTICLE IV

Should either High Contracting Party conclude a treaty of general arbitration with a third Power, it is agreed that nothing in this Agreement shall entail upon such Contracting Party an obligation to go to war with the Power with whom such treaty of arbitration is in force.

ARTICLE V

The conditions under which armed assistance shall be afforded by either Power to the other in the circumstances mentioned in the present Agreement, and the means by which such assistance is to be made available, will be arranged by the Naval and Military authorities of the High Contracting Parties, who will from time to time consult one another fully and freely upon all questions of mutual interest.

ARTICLE VI

The present Agreement shall come into effect immediately after the date of its signature, and remain in force for ten years from that date. In case neither of the High Contracting Parties should have notified twelve months before the expiration of the said ten years the intention of terminating it, it shall remain binding until the expiration of one year from the day on which either of the High Contracting Parties shall have denounced it. But if, when the date fixed for its expiration arrives, either ally is actually engaged in war, the alliance shall, *ipso facto*, continue until peace is concluded.

In faith whereof the Undersigned, duly authorised by their respective Governments, have signed this Agreement, and have affixed thereto their Seals.

Done in duplicate at London, the 13th day of July, 1911.

E. GREY,

His Britannic Majesty's Principal Secretary of State for Foreign Affairs.

TAKAAKI KATO,

Ambassador Extraordinary and Plenipotentiary of His Majesty the Emperor of Japan at the Court of St. James."

In Japan, there was some public dissent about the renewal treaty because a comparison of the respective obligations of Great Britain and Japan under its terms suggested that the scope of the British obligations were reduced in comparison to those obligations accepted by Japan. However, the Japanese Government held firm on both the utility and the importance of the treaty for Japan. Both Prime Minister Katsura, and Foreign Minister Komura, who, remarkably, were both in office when the first alliance treaty was signed in 1902, and also when the second alliance was signed in 1905, remained firm backers of the British alliance. They saw, as did other Japanese statesmen, that the alliance with Britain was crucial to Japanese foreign policy because it confirmed Japan's status as a great power, and of Japan's acceptance as a geopolitical equal by one of the major European world powers.[12]

In Britain, Sir Edward Grey, the Foreign Minister, was left with the delicate task of selling the renewal of the alliance to the dominion governments which, coincidentally, were meeting in London in 1911 at an Imperial Conference being held in conjunction with the coronation of the new King-Emperor, George V, who had succeeded to the British throne in 1910, upon the death of his father, King Edward VII. The Imperial Conference took place during the last stages of the negotiation of the renewal of the alliance and therefore it became an important topic at the conference. For Sir Edward Grey it was important to assuage the particular concerns of Australia, and New Zealand, which continued to be concerned about the level of Japanese immigration into their countries. Due to the sensitivity of the alliance in the dominions, Grey arranged for the discussions about it to take place in a meeting of the Committee for Imperial Defence, which had restricted attendance, and secrecy rules that insulated the colonial politicians from any temptation toward political grandstanding by prohibiting them from releasing details of the revised arrangements to the public. In that Committee, Grey emphasized how important it was for the British Empire to sustain the alliance, arguing that the existence of the alliance precluded aggression by Japan and that the combined forces of Japan and Great Britain in the Pacific would be sufficient to protect the dominions from any military threats that they might face.

On the question of Japanese immigration, Grey stated that Japan had affirmed to the British government that Japan would not promote Japanese emigration to countries that did not want Japanese immigrants, although that did not mean that the Japanese government could wholly stop Japanese emigration. Grey made the novel argument that if there was no alliance between the British Empire and Japan the immigration issue faced by the dominions could be worse because then Japan would not have any incentive to try to restrain Japanese emigration.[13] Grey pointed to the 1908 'Gentleman's Agreement' that Canada had negotiated with Japan as proof that Japan did not want large numbers of her people to emigrate to western countries, even if Japan could not wholly prohibit Japanese emigration. For his part, Sir Edward Grey continued to encourage Japan to promote the emigration of Japanese to Korea and Manchuria, in order to avoid upsetting the three British Pacific Ocean dominions.[14]

In the end, the dominion Prime Ministers, including the Canadian Prime Minister Sir Wilfrid Laurier, agreed with the Imperial Government that the Anglo-Japanese Alliance should be renewed and that it should also be extended for a further period of ten years. Prime Minister Laurier was very much in favour of the continuation of the alliance with Japan because it removed all threats of conflict between Canada and Japan. In Laurier's view, it was actually desirable to extend the treaty of alliance beyond the proposed ten-year period.[15]

Advance notice of the renewal of the Anglo-Japanese Alliance was given by the signatories to the United States, France, and Russia but not to Germany. British relations with Germany were increasingly strained owing to the naval race, and the Kaiser's rants about the 'Yellow Peril' and other racist statements had upset Japanese officials and had created a negative impact on German-Japanese relations.[16] As for the United States, the arbitration treaty that Britain had looked to as a means of legally exempting Great Britain from any potential obligation to assist its Japanese ally if Japan entered into a conflict with the United States had failed to gain the sanction of the US Senate, and the Anglo-Japanese Alliance was therefore left without any legal reservation to preclude a British obligation to Japan in a Japanese-American war. Although the Japanese relied on the strict text of the treaty, Japanese officials were realistic about the support that Japan could expect to receive from the British Empire if Japan and the United States ever came to blows.[17]

In 1911, Great Britain also entered into a new commercial treaty with Japan on behalf of the British Empire. The new treaty of commerce and navigation was signed on April 3, 1911, and it contained provisions relating to travel and immigration that immediately caused concern to the Laurier Ministry in Canada. The new treaty provided for travel by the subjects of each empire between their respective territories, with the right of entry into those territories, and the right to settle within those territories. However, the Imperial government in London added a stipulation that the commercial treaty would not apply to any of the British dominions unless the dominion concerned provided formal notice of adherence to the treaty within two years of its signing date. Fearful of Japanese immigration, and of the political effects of that in British Columbia, Prime Minister Laurier declined to adhere to the treaty but he proposed that Canada would continue to follow the previous commercial treaty between the British Empire and Japan for an additional two years, which Japan considered to be an acceptable compromise.[18] For Laurier, the 'Gentleman's Agreement' that had been negotiated by Rodolphe Lemieux reflected the Federal Government's policy on Japanese immigration to Canada, and Laurier knew that any departure from its terms would cause significant political difficulty in British Columbia in the forthcoming 1911 general election.

As the world moved inexorably towards a collision in Europe between the great powers other changes were occurring in the North Pacific, and in the Far East. In 1912, Mutsuhito, the Meiji

Emperor of Japan, died. He had seen his country emerge from obscurity to claim an important place in the world and Japan's great achievement was at least partially due to the Emperor himself, who was no mere cipher. However, his successor, Yoshihito, the Taisho Emperor, was mentally enfeebled, and he could not effectively assume the Meiji Emperor's place in the Japanese political structure, leaving the Crown with a more symbolic, and less active role, in the forthcoming events.

In China, the long decline of the Manchu Empire led to the outbreak of revolution in October, 1911. The spark for the revolution was an actual explosion that was accidentally set off by military conspirators in the city of Wuhan, which led to a local mutiny in the Imperial Army that soon spread across the country. The Imperial Court was paralyzed but Dowager Empress Longyu had the presence of mind to summon the indefatigable Yüan Shih-k'ai to put down the rebellion. However, Yuan, after accepting the imperial assignment, decided to double-cross the Dowager Empress and he arranged a political deal with the head of the revolutionary insurgency, Sun Yat-sen, in which Sun would step aside as Provisional President and allow Yuan to become the President of China if Yuan would support the revolution against the Manchu, and the creation of a republic. The deal was struck, and the Imperial Army went wholly over to the revolution. Manchu rule collapsed. On February 12, 1912, the regents for Pu Yi, the boy Emperor of China, signed an abdication on his behalf and the Chinese monarchy, the oldest and greatest of the world's monarchies, fell into ruin.

In Canada, a general election was held in the autumn of 1911, and it was remarkable for being one of only two general elections in the twentieth century in which foreign policy was a major focus of the election (the other being the 1988 general election). In both cases trade reciprocity with the United States was the major foreign policy issue and, in 1911, it was the Liberals under Laurier that were seeking a mandate for a free trade agreement with the United

States. The country was not yet ready to fully embrace the United States in trade, however, and the election resulted in the defeat of the Liberal Ministry that had held office since 1896. Sir Wilfrid Laurier accepted defeat and stayed on as Leader of the Opposition in the House of Commons. Robert Borden had at last reached the highest elective position in Canada, and he now promoted a new naval policy, offering subsidies to support the Royal Navy in the Anglo-German naval race, rather than expending Canadian funds to create a purely local naval force in Canada. Consequently, the Royal Canadian Navy languished, while Borden's measure to offer Great Britain 35 million dollars for the construction of battleships struggled through the House of Commons only to suffer an ignominious defeat in the Senate.

During Borden's naval fight the RCN was placed in limbo, and its two cruisers, HMCS *Niobe* in Halifax, and HMCS *Rainbow* in Esquimalt were essentially tied up at dockside. Training was stopped, and only reduced crews were maintained on board, although HMCS *Rainbow* at the Pacific coast was at least able to conduct short cruises in 1913, to support fisheries enforcement, and *Rainbow* arrested an errant American schooner that was caught fishing illegally in Canadian waters.[19] Nevertheless, the Royal Canadian Navy remained largely moribund in the run-up to the outbreak of the war, and by 1914 its manpower strength had fallen from 800 to 350. It was a sad contrast to the newly formed Royal Australian Navy, Canada's dominion counterpart in the southern hemisphere which, in 1914, could boast of having in deployment one battlecruiser, four cruisers, and three destroyers.[20]

Across the Pacific, on the Royal Navy's China Station, at Hong Kong, a new commander in chief in the Far East arrived in 1913, in the person of Vice Admiral Sir Thomas M Jerram. The British squadron now consisted of a battleship, HMS *Triumph*, a pre-dreadnought type battleship that was armed with ten-inch guns, and two armoured cruisers, HMS *Minotaur*, and HMS *Hampshire*, as well as two light cruisers, HMS *Yarmouth*, and HMS *Newcastle*. The deployment of HMS *Triumph* to the Far East had been intended to give the British squadron the capability of successfully engaging with the German East Asiatic Squadron based at the German concession port at Tsingtao, China.

Jerram could also potentially look for support from Britain's Entente Cordiale partner France, which maintained two cruisers in the Pacific Ocean, the FS *Montcalm*, and the FS *Dupleix*. But it was to Japan, the preeminent naval power in the Pacific, that Great Britain relied upon for the control of the Pacific Ocean, and Jerram took the initiative to meet with the senior Japanese civil and military officials. Those meetings helped to improve operational preparedness between the two allies.[21]

Since the 1890's the Canadian Pacific Steamship line had provided fast, comfortable service across the North Pacific between the Far East and Canada, being true to its popular advertising slogan "Canadian Pacific Spans the World," which first appeared in the pre-war years, and was emblazoned on the CPR Pavilion at the 1913 Panama-Pacific Exposition held in San Francisco.[22] An increase in demand in the transpacific trade persuaded the company to order new passenger ships for its transpacific service and in 1910 it ordered two large passenger liners for Pacific service, the RMS *Empress of Asia* (16,908 gross tons), and the RMS *Empress of Russia* (16,810 gross tons), both of which entered service in 1913.[23] The new CP steamers continued the company's passenger and royal mail service between Vancouver, Victoria, Yokohama, Kobe, Nagasaki, Shanghai, and Hong Kong, providing communications between Canada, Japan, and China (and Manila, in the Philippines, was subsequently added) giving Canada a significant presence in the Far East. Canadian Pacific was also present in the Atlantic Ocean, having bought two smaller shipping lines engaged in transatlantic service. By 1914, Canadian Pacific Steamships was one of the largest ship-owners in the world.[24] In conjunction with its passenger railway services, Canadian Pacific could provide marine passengers with a through service from the Far East to Europe, using the Canadian Pacific Railway network across Canada.

In the North Pacific, as well as in the Atlantic, the pre-war Edwardian Age had been an era of growing prosperity built upon increasing linkages between countries, as exemplified by the growing reach of the Canadian Pacific rail and steamship transportation empire. By 1914 increasing globalization had contributed to a common sense of civilizational progress among both the great and lesser powers of the world, and many people across the globe looked forward to better lives for themselves, and their families. As midsummer 1914 approached, however, no one could foresee the great storm that now lay just beyond the political horizon, a storm that would sweep away the optimism of the age.

NOTES

[1] Ian H Nish, *Alliance in Decline: A Study In Anglo-Japanese Relations 1908 – 1923*, University of London/The Athlone Press, London, 1972, 23 [afterwards: Nish, *Decline*]

[2] Ian Nish, "Japan Declares War" in *History of the First World War*, BPC/Purnell, London, 1969, 316 [afterwards: Nish, *War*]

[3] Nish, *War*, 315

[4] Hew Strachan, *The First World War, Vol. 1 To Arms*, Oxford University Press, Oxford (UK), 2001, 443

[5] McDougall, 434-35

[6] McDougall, 505

[7] McDougall, 453, 485; Nish, *Decline*, 25

[8] McDougall, 480

[9] Johnston et al, 120

[10] Nish, *Decline*, 24

[11] Nish, *Decline*, 58

[12] Nish, *War*, 316

[13] Nish, *Decline*, 63

[14] Nish, *Decline*, 7, 69

[15] Roger Sarty, "There will be trouble in the North Pacific: The Defence of British Columbia in the Early Twentieth Century," in BC *Studies, The British Columbian Quarterly*, Vol. 61, *Spring*, 1984, University of British Columbia, Vancouver, 1984, 3 at 13

[16] Nish, *Decline*, 26

[17] Subsequently, during the administration of US President Woodrow Wilson, Great Britain managed to successfully negotiate a Conciliation Treaty with the United States in September, 1914, and Sir Edward Grey claimed that the Conciliation Treaty met the intent of the arbitration exemption in the 1911 renewal of the Anglo-Japanese Alliance Treaty. Thus, Grey held that Britain was exempt from coming to Japan's aid if Japan engaged in a war with the United States. From a strictly legal perspective, Grey was wrong about the effect of the Conciliation Treaty because conciliation is a consensual dispute resolution process while arbitration is a binding determination process. Nevertheless, Japan did not take exception to Grey's declaration and merely stated that a legal analysis was not required, as Japan understood Britain's position in the event of a war between Japan and the United States.

[18] Pringsheim, 19

[19] Johnston et al, 203

[20] Strachan, 440

[21] Nish, *Decline*, 95

[22] Leighann C. Neilson, *John Murray Gibbon (1875-1952): The Branding of a Northern Nation*, Sprott School of Business, Carleton University, Ottawa, [ojs.library.carleton.ca E pcharm. [accessed April 27, 2020]

[23] Pigott, 40

[24] Johnston et al, 283

7. The Outbreak of World War One and a West Coast Panic

On a bright summer day at the end of June, 1914, the heir to the throne of one of Europe's great empires, the Austro-Hungarian Empire, came to the city of Sarajevo in the southern province of Bosnia and Herzegovina for a ceremonial visit. Archduke Franz Ferdinand was accompanied by his morganatic wife, Sophie, Duchess of Hohenberg, who ordinarily could not accompany him on official visits because the rigid protocol of the Austrian Court prevented the august Imperial heir from being accompanied by a person of her lesser social rank on state occasions. However, she was present on this occasion because the Archduke's primary purpose in visiting Sarajevo was to witness military manoeuvres as an officer of the Imperial Army, and therefore it was not viewed as a state occasion. There was a great deal of political unrest in the southern reaches of the Austro-Hungarian Empire, a polyglot multi-ethnic state held together by the forces of historical inertia, and respect for its old Emperor, Franz-Josef I, who had ruled the empire since 1848.

Archduke Franz Ferdinand knew that there was an element of danger in his visit to Sarajevo because the population was ethnically Slavic, and was influenced by the Slavic irredentism of the neighbouring Kingdom of Serbia. Political unrest due to separatist sympathies in the southern provinces increased the risk of political assassination. Nevertheless, Franz Ferdinand decided to make the visit because he believed that the Slavic population of the empire could eventually be successfully integrated into the complicated political structure of the empire, perhaps by converting what was described as the Dual Monarchy (the separate but joined realms of Austria and Hungary) into a supranational federation that recognized the Slavic and other national populations of the empire. Such a development was opposed by radicals in Serbia, who wished to create a greater Slavic nation in the Balkan region of Europe. Unbeknownst to Franz Ferdinand, secret societies formed, or manipulated, by officers in the Serbian government's military intelligence service were plotting an attempt on Franz Ferdinand's life when he visited Bosnia and Herzegovina in order to forestall the Archduke's future plans and to promote unrest in the province. During the visit of Archduke Franz Ferdinand and Duchess Sophie on June 28, 1914, a bomb was thrown at their motorcade, which missed the couple but injured some of the officials accompanying them. The royal couple afterward decided to visit the injured in the hospital and they re-entered their motorcade to make the hospital visit. However, due to a mix-up in the instructions concerning the route, the driver of the car in which the Archduke and his consort were riding made a wrong turn, and the car was directed to stop and turn back by an official accompanying the party. At that moment one of the group of plotters against the Archduke happened to be at the location where the motorcade had stopped, and he stepped forward and fired two shots with a revolver, killing the Archduke and the Duchess.

The assassination of the heir to the Austro-Hungarian throne, and his wife, sent shock waves across Europe and precipitated the European Crisis of July, 1914. Suspicion in Vienna fell immediately upon the Serbian government, and a group of senior Austro-Hungarian officials promoted retribution through a punitive military confrontation with Serbia, which they hoped would lead to the eclipse of Serbia as a political actor in the Balkans. The conflict between Austria-Hungary and Serbia however, would inevitably draw Russia into the confrontation, since Russia considered itself to be the protector of the Slavic states in south-eastern Europe. Austria-Hungary, as a member with Germany and Italy in the Triple Alliance, needed to know that it would receive strong backing from

Germany, the most important power in the Triple Alliance if a confrontation between Austria-Hungary and Serbia broadened to include Russia. To that end, Austro-Hungarian diplomats engaged with their German counterparts, which led to an important meeting between the Austro-Hungarian ambassador in Berlin and Kaiser Wilhelm II. German foreign policy favoured a military confrontation between Austria-Hungary and Serbia because it was thought in Berlin that the Austro-Hungarian Empire was slowly disintegrating and that a successful military expedition against Serbia could help to fortify the empire against the disintegration caused by the increasing nationalism among the empire's constituent peoples. Although Russia was a factor in Berlin's considerations, there was a considered view in Berlin that the Russian Empire was in no shape to come to Serbia's aid. The Russian Empire had escaped from an unsuccessful revolution less than ten years previously but in the summer of 1914 it was once again convulsed by strikes and labour disruptions, and so it was thought in Berlin that Russia would not be able to undertake aggressive military actions in 1914.

There was also a personal factor that animated the German response to the assassination. Kaiser Wilhelm II and Archduke Franz Ferdinand were friends, and the Kaiser and his wife had visited the Archduke and his wife shortly before the assassination. The Kaiser was therefore personally affected by the death of people who were in his personal circle, and no doubt there was also sympathy for the three young children of the Archduke and his Duchess, who were now orphaned. Those factors led the Kaiser into a fateful error. During a luncheon with the Austro-Hungarian Ambassador to Germany, Count Ladislaus von Szögyény on July 5, 1914, the Kaiser gave an assurance to the ambassador that Germany would support Austria-Hungary no matter what action it decided to take in regards to Serbia, in response to the assassination. Taking his cue from the Kaiser, the German Chancellor, Theobald von Bethmann Hollweg, formally advised Vienna of Berlin's support, and German foreign policy swung away from containing the crisis, and towards promoting it as a means of shoring up the failing Austro-Hungarian Empire. The Kaiser then left Germany for his annual cruise to Scandinavia on board his yacht, the SMY *Hohenzollern*.

Prodded by Germany, Austria-Hungary prepared an ultimatum to Serbia that was designed to be rejected so that military action could be taken by Austria-Hungary against its smaller neighbour. Those preparations were undertaken in great secrecy so that other European nations would not get wind of the Austro-Hungarian ultimatum before it was sprung upon Serbia, and thus preclude any attempts by other powers to promote a diplomatic solution to avoid a war. In fact, the delivery of the Austro-Hungarian ultimatum to Serbia on July 23, 1914, was deliberately delayed until Raymond Poincaré, the President, and René Viviani, the Premier, of France, who were visiting their Russian ally in St. Petersburg, were actually at sea on their return journey to France and were therefore unable to coordinate a diplomatic response with France's ally, Russia.

Although there was a great concern in European capitals when the terms of the Austro-Hungarian ultimatum became known, the Serbian government surprised the other European countries by accepting almost every demand posed to it by Vienna. Only Austro-Hungarian demands that would have constituted a real infringement on the sovereignty of Serbia were not accepted by that country. Even Kaiser Wilhelm II rejoiced at what appeared to be the makings of a diplomatic triumph by Austria-Hungary. However, the war party in Vienna would not be dissuaded by an abject attempt of Serbia to avoid a military confrontation, and the Serbian response to the ultimatum was rejected. Events now rapidly escalated as the pre-war system of interlocking alliances began to activate in the face of the broad European crisis that emerged out of the Balkans. Austria-Hungary broke diplomatic relations with Serbia after delivering its ultimatum, and upon rejecting the Serbian response Austria-Hungary declared war on Serbia on July 28, 1914.

Russia had perceived the danger to the European peace as soon as the terms of the Austro-Hungarian ultimatum to Serbia were revealed, and despite the internal problems it was facing, and the fact that the process of rebuilding and modernizing its military following the disastrous Russo-Japanese War was still a work in progress, it felt that it must offer support to its fellow Slavic state, Serbia. Russia perceived that if it failed to support Serbia in the face of the Austro-Hungarian ultimatum it would lose international respect as a great power, and henceforth be restricted to a marginal political role in the Balkans. Yet Tsar Nicholas II hesitated to commit his military to a course of action that he knew would, in all probability, lead to a general European war. When his Foreign and War Ministers sought his authority to mobilize the Imperial Russian Army the Tsar refused to grant a general mobilization order, although he did authorize the mobilization of Russia's southern armies facing Austria-Hungary.

Now alarmed by the course of events, Kaiser Wilhelm II and Chancellor Bethmann-Hollweg sought some means by which war between Austria-Hungary and Russia could be avoided, and they tried to persuade the Tsar not to mobilize. In that attempt, they were unsuccessful because the Tsar's own military officials had by then persuaded the Tsar that he must authorize a general mobilization in order to avoid anarchy in the mobilization process, as the Russian mobilization plans were built around a general mobilization in Europe, and did not contemplate a partial mobilization. Reluctantly, Tsar Nicholas agreed, and he authorized a general mobilization of Russian forces on July 31, 1914.

The Russian mobilization triggered Germany to act immediately because Germany's war plan called for an immediate advance in the west against France with almost all of its military might, while taking advantage of the slower Russian mobilization to maintain a mere holding, or screening function, in the east against Russia. With Russian mobilization, Germany was compelled to move to a general mobilization so as not to lose its advantage against France. Germany, therefore, declared war on Russia on August 1, 1914.

Germany issued an ultimatum to Russia's Dual Alliance partner, France, which France rejected, resulting in a German declaration of war on France on August 3, 1914.

Germany had also issued an ultimatum to Brussels on August 2, 1914, demanding that Belgium grant permission to German forces to pass through, and occupy Belgium while disclaiming any intention on Germany's part to permanently annex Belgium. Belgium refused the German request, and it was invaded by Germany on August 3rd. Meanwhile, on August 3rd the remaining member of the Triple Alliance, Italy, declared itself neutral and its defection effectively sundered the Triple Alliance. Italy declared that Austria-Hungary's actions towards Serbia amounted to a war of aggression, and therefore it did not meet the test of the Triple Alliance, which was only intended to be a defensive alliance.[1]

During this period Great Britain, in the person of its Foreign Minister, Sir Edward Grey, had been in constant contact with the Foreign Ministers of the great powers, and Grey had assiduously sought to obtain their consent for an international conference, or an international mediation, to attempt to settle the matters that were leading Europe to war. However, intransigence in Vienna, and an unwillingness in Berlin to cooperate with British efforts, led to the failure of Sir Edward Grey's attempts to formulate a diplomatic solution to the crisis. Britain was part of the Triple Entente with France and Russia but unlike the Triple Alliance, the Triple Entente was not a formal three-party military alliance. Yet Great Britain had made important naval commitments to France, whereby France could concentrate its major warships in the Mediterranean against Italy, which was a member of the Triple Alliance, leaving Great Britain to defend France's Atlantic shores. In return, Great Britain had been enabled by its arrangements with France to redeploy British battleships from the Mediterranean to home waters to counter the German naval build-up in the North Sea. Those naval commitments meant that Great Britain, at the very least, would have to take steps to defend France from a seaborne assault by Germany along France's Atlantic coast.

The invasion of Belgium on August 3rd however, put a new element before the British Cabinet, which was in grave danger of splitting over the question of British involvement in a general European war. Great Britain was one of three signatories (along with France and Germany) of Belgium's neutrality and inviolability, which Germany had now tossed aside by the German invasion of Belgium. The British commitment to Belgium was a responsibility that most of the British Cabinet could accept as a *casus belli*, leading to British participation in the war. Accordingly, Great Britain now delivered an ultimatum to Germany requiring it to agree to withdraw its troops from Belgium, failing which a state of war would exist between Great Britain and Germany. When Germany failed to respond by the British deadline, a state of war automatically ensued between the two empires as of August 4, 1914. On August 6, 1914, Austria-Hungary declared war on Russia, and on August 12th both Great Britain and France declared war on Austria-Hungary.

In Canada, the crisis was slow to capture the complete attention of the government. After an unpleasantly cold winter the glory of summer was looked upon as a reward for Ottawa's endurance and after Parliament had risen for the summer official Ottawa decamped for the well-earned pleasures of the lakeside or the mountains. As the crisis slowly mounted, and the days of July slipped by, the Prime Minister, Sir Robert Borden, was to be found enjoying the beach and golf links in Muskoka, in the Lake Huron country north of Toronto. The Governor General, Prince Arthur, the Duke of Connaught, was taking in the mountain airs of Banff, Alberta.[2] As a European diplomatic crisis began giving way to a general European war, however, ministers and officials scurried back to the capital. On July 29, 1914, the Warning Telegram arrived in Ottawa from the Admiralty at almost the precise moment that the Deputy Minister of the Department of the Naval Service, J. G. Desbarats, was signing the newly drafted Canadian War Book, detailing naval operations in the event of a war.

A Cabinet meeting of available ministers in Ottawa was held on July 30, 1914, to discuss the European situation, and on the following day, the Prime Minister arrived back in the capital.[3] At a subsequent Cabinet meeting on August 1, 1914, the government undertook the preliminary steps necessary to put the country on a war footing, including the recall of naval personnel, authorization to recruit more sailors, and orders to prepare HMCS *Rainbow* and HMCS *Niobe* for active service under the direction of the British Admiralty. The two cruisers were formally placed under Admiralty control by the Canadian government on August 4th.[4] On that same momentous day, the Governor General arrived back in the capital from his holiday in Alberta, as did the former Prime Minister and current Leader of the Opposition, Sir Wilfrid Laurier.[5] The Cabinet met twice on that day and then in the evening, as Prime Minister Borden subsequently recounted:

> "We were in Council on August 4th at eleven and again at four. During the evening, while again in Council, at 8:55 p.m. the momentous telegram arrived announcing that war had been declared. Immediately an Order-in-Council was passed summoning Parliament to meet on August 18th."[6]

The almost moribund Royal Canadian Navy had existed in a sort of suspended animation while Prime Minister Borden had attempted to put his failed Royal Navy subvention scheme through Parliament but now with war declared the naval service became a necessary component of Canada's national defense. In July the cruiser HMCS *Rainbow* had been placed into operations at the west coast for the purpose of frustrating the immigration into Canada of a party of Sikhs from India, who had crossed the Pacific in the steamship SS *Komagata Maru* from Hong Kong in order to resettle in Canada. Although Canada took in large numbers of immigrants in the years before World War One, the population of Canada generally, and in

British Columbia in particular, exhibited a strong racial prejudice against immigrants from Asia. Just as immigrants from China and Japan found it difficult to immigrate to Canada so too did those who originated in India. A difficulty for the Federal government was the fact that Indians were British Subjects, as were Canadians, and therefore they could not be considered as foreigners, unlike prospective Chinese and Japanese immigrants. The SS *Komagata Maru* was a Japanese-owned steamship that had been chartered to bring 376 mostly Sikh passengers to Canada. At that time, Canada maintained in force an immigration regulation known as the Continuous Journey Regulation which mandated that ships bringing immigrants to Canada must have made a direct voyage from the country of origin to Canada without stopping along the way for rest and replenishment. As a practical matter, that regulation was intended to stop Indian immigration to Canada, since the great distance between India and Canada generally precluded a single passage from India to Canada.

When the *Komagata Maru* arrived in Vancouver immigration officers took immediate steps to stop the landing of a majority of the prospective immigrants, although a few of them did manage to secure entry. Perceiving that they would be denied entry to Canada the prospective immigrants seized the ship at anchor in Vancouver harbour. When police and immigration officials tried to intervene on July 18, 1914, they were pelted with rocks of coal from the ship's coal supplies. A court case was launched on behalf of the passengers of the *Komagata Maru* but their attempt to secure a positive judicial intervention from the British Columbia courts was unsuccessful. Meanwhile, Vancouver officials had called upon the military to assist the civil power, and HMCS *Rainbow* was sent to Vancouver where it slowly circled the *Komagata Maru*, whose passengers declared to the Rainbow that their only weapons consisted of pieces of coal. Eventually, the disconsolate immigrants agreed to return to India provided that the Federal government supplied them with food for the journey. An initial reluctance on the part of the government to resupply the vessel was overcome, and on July 23rd the SS *Komagata Maru* departed from Vancouver for the return voyage to India.[7] Its mission accomplished without having to fire a shot, the HMCS *Rainbow* returned to Esquimalt, arriving back in port on August 1st.[8]

At Esquimalt, HMCS *Rainbow* was alone at the base because the two small Royal Navy station vessels at Esquimalt, the outdated sloops HMS *Algerine*, and HMS *Shearwater*, were both employed as part of an international naval squadron formed under US command to operate off the west coast of Mexico, which was then embroiled in a civil war. The purpose of the international squadron was to facilitate the evacuation of foreign citizens from western Mexico as Carranzanist forces took control of western port cities. The international squadron based at Mazatlán included the cruiser SMS *Nurnberg* from the German East Asiatic Squadron at Tsingtao, China, which was relieved on July 7th by the cruiser SMS *Leipzig*. The antiquated British sloops HMS *Algerine* and HMS *Shearwater* were at, respectively, Mazatlán and Ensenada, Mexico. The Japanese armoured cruiser HIJMS *Idzumo* was also at Mazatlán. By the end of July, the foreigners had been safely evacuated, and Carranza's forces had entered Mazatlán.[9]

As the international situation in Europe continued to deteriorate, the residents of south-western British Columbia became increasingly alarmed, knowing that Germany possessed a powerful naval force in the North Pacific, and that Canada's navy, and the small British ships based at Esquimalt, were ill-prepared to defend the west coast. A type of panic ensued at the west coast, and several actions were taken out of a fear that Vice Admiral Count von Spee and his German East Asiatic Squadron would suddenly appear off of Canada's west coast and bombard its cities. The local banks began transferring cash and securities to eastern bank branches, and millions of dollars were spent by British Columbians purchasing bombardment insurance for their properties after the *Victoria Daily Colonist* published a story about the rules of bombardment under international law. Some residents made plans to leave the coast for the relative safety of an inland location, and families were removed from the family quarters that were maintained at the Esquimalt naval base. The City of Victoria, which was constructing a sewer network, had to stop its blasting activities because the noise unduly alarmed its residents.[10]

Part of the worry that consumed British Columbians and their Premier, Sir Richard McBride, was the fear that Japan might now switch sides, despite the existence of the Anglo-Japanese Alliance, and join Germany in a war against Britain (and Canada). Half a world away from the Premier's office in Victoria, BC, someone else who was contemplating the imminent outbreak of war was also thinking along the same lines as British Columbia's Premier. The Chief of the German General staff, General Helmuth von Moltke, wrote to the German Foreign Minister Gottlieb von Jagow, pressing him to search for potential allies on the eve of the World War. His memorandum, dated August 2, 1914, reviewed a number of potential possibilities in Europe and countries further abroad, including Japan. In relation to Japan, Moltke emphasized that Japan should be encouraged to satisfy her aspirations in the Far East by going to war with Russia. If, according to von Moltke, Japan was willing to side with Germany, and attack Russia, Germany should promise Japan anything.[11]

General von Moltke was reaching for straws, however, in pleading with the German Foreign Minister to find additional allies for Germany. Japan never considered resiling from the Anglo-Japanese Alliance, which was crucial to Japan's aspirations to be treated as one of the great powers. In any event, there would be plenty of spoils for Japan if it engaged in a war with Germany, as Germany had extensive colonial possessions in the Pacific Ocean, an ocean in which Japan now possessed the dominant navy. And Japan had not forgotten the role that Germany had played almost twenty years before in Triple Intervention, which had forced Japan to disgorge the gains it had made from the Sino-Japanese War. A reckoning of the accounts between the two countries now beckoned.

Back in Victoria, an unusual meeting was held at the offices of the Union Club on July 29, 1914, as the international situation deteriorated. The President of the Seattle Construction and Drydock Company, James Paterson, declared to a half-dozen men present at the meeting that his company had available for sale at Seattle, Washington, two submarines that had recently been constructed under licence from the Electric Boat Company of Connecticut for the Chilean government Paterson explained that the Chilean authorities were refusing to complete the original transaction with the Seattle company because they deemed the submarines to be overweight, and therefore not able to meet the sea endurance standards stipulated by Chile. Accordingly, Paterson was prepared to make the submarines available to Canada instead. The matter was complicated, however, because Chile had paid a substantial sum towards the contract price of USD $818,000, and Chilean officials were in Seattle, still hoping to work out some arrangement with Paterson's company to take possession of the submarines. In addition, the prospect that war would soon be declared in Europe meant that President Wilson would soon issue a Neutrality Proclamation, and once done that would preclude any possibility of a future transaction with Canada involving military goods as Canada would become a belligerent when the British Empire entered the war. Premier McBride was informed of this situation, and he immediately began to convene a series of urgent meetings to discuss the structure of a transaction with Paterson for the purchase of the submarines.

Smelling the panic in British Columbia, Paterson demanded USD $575,000 for each boat, a considerable advance over the contract price that the government of Chile had agreed to earlier, and Paterson refused to negotiate over that price. His Majesty's Dockyard at Esquimalt informed Naval Service Headquarters (NSHQ) in Ottawa that the submarines were available, and NSHQ cabled the Admiralty seeking its advice as to the utility of the two submarines. Obviously engaged by many other responsibilities with the outbreak of war now fast approaching, the Admiralty did not immediately respond. Paterson increased the pressure on Premier McBride by warning that the transaction must be completed, and the submarines must leave US waters no later then the night of August 4/5 to avoid the consequences of President Wilson's expected Neutrality Proclamation. Premier McBride, worried that British Columbia would lose the ability to obtain the submarines, now took it upon himself to authorize the purchase transaction on behalf of the government of British Columbia by agreeing to pay Paterson out of provincial funds the sum of USD $1,150,000 for the two submarines, an advance of USD $332,000 over the price Chile had agreed to pay. Included in the negotiated purchase price was a USD $40,000 personal commission payable to Paterson.

It was dark, and visibility was obscured by mist, as the two submarines cast off from the Seattle Construction and Drydock Company's docks in Seattle, Washington, around ten PM on the night of August 4th, moving almost silently on their electric motors, and under the control of company crews. Once out of the harbour at Seattle, the diesel engines were started and the two submarines headed north, without first obtaining clearance to leave port from the US harbour authorities. In the early morning of August 5th, near Canadian waters, the two submarines were met and inspected by a retired Royal Navy submariner, who pronounced them fit, and a Provincial government cheque was produced for the total purchase price that had been agreed upon and delivered to Paterson.[12] Royal Canadian Navy crews took over the two boats and they proceeded to Esquimalt, where they arrived in daylight on August 5th. On that same day in Washington, DC, President Wilson signed the US Neutrality Proclamation, which banned the export of military goods, and all US ports were advised. The next day, August 6, 1914, the cruiser USS *Milwaukee* was despatched from the Bremerton Naval Yard in Puget Sound, Washington, to look for the two missing submarines, both of which were now safely ensconced at HMD in the Esquimalt RCN base, and flying Canadian colours.

Sir Richard McBride had spent a considerable sum out of provincial coffers for the submarines without the prior authorization of the British Columbia Legislature, which was technically an unconstitutional action. Furthermore, under the British North America Act, 1867, which served as Canada's Constitution, the military and naval forces of Canada were the responsibility of the Federal government and not the Provincial governments. The government of British Columbia lacked constitutional authority to purchase and maintain naval vessels. Accordingly, Premier McBride was anxious for the Federal government to give its *ex post facto* approval of the unusual transaction. Fortunately, the Admiralty had finally gotten around to answering the questions posed to it by NSHQ at Ottawa, and the Admiralty advised the Federal government that the two submarines would be a useful purchase towards the defense of British Columbia. With the Admiralty's endorsement in hand, the Federal government was more than happy to take over responsibility for the two submarines and to reimburse McBride's government for their purchase cost. Prime Minister Borden wired to Premier McBride: ". . . we appreciate most warmly your action which will greatly tend to increase security on the Pacific coast, and send hearty thanks."[13] On August 7th the two submarines were transferred to the Federal government, thus bringing to an end to the two-day lifespan of the British Columbia navy.

Meanwhile, on the other side of the Pacific Ocean Japan was contemplating whether it would, or should, be drawn into the war that now touched every continent. On August 1, 1914, Sir Edward Grey advised the Japanese ambassador that it appeared that Great Britain would enter the war to support France and Russia but that it was unlikely that Great Britain would need to call upon Japan for assistance under the Anglo-Japanese Alliance Treaty. The current thinking in London was that there would be no precipitate challenge to British interests in the Far East and Indian theatre of operations.[14] On that basis, the Japanese Foreign Ministry advised the British ambassador to Tokyo, Sir Conyngham Greene, that it would render assistance under the alliance only if Britain requested its assistance.[15] The Foreign Ministry also issued a public statement suggesting that Japan would remain neutral in the conflict unless Great Britain asked for assistance pursuant to the alliance.[16] Grey responded to the public position that Japan expressed by privately recalling to the Japanese government that Japan had shown restraint in asking for help from Britain during the Russo-Japanese War, and Great Britain intended to show a similar reticence in its demands of Japan during the current conflict.

However, that British attitude began to change on August 5th when it became obvious to the Admiralty that the Royal Navy could not meet all of its commitments in the Pacific without Japan's assistance. The Admiralty's responsibilities in the Pacific, in addition to the defence of the Canadian Pacific coast, included the following operational demands:

- The New Zealand troop convoy to Australia
- The Combined ANZAC troop convoy to Europe
- The British Far East garrisons convoy to Europe
- The Indian Army troop convoys to replace the British Far Eastern garrisons
- The New Zealand attack convoy to German Samoa
- The Australian attack convoy to German North East New Guinea.[17]

In light of the existing Admiralty commitments in the Pacific theatre, Grey despatched a request to Japan on August 5th, in which he said that the British government would "gladly avail themselves" of Japanese assistance in protecting British shipping in the Far East from the depredations of German raiders while realizing that in offering such assistance to Great Britain Japan would have to declare war against Germany.[18]

The British Empire was asking for military assistance in the light of the treaty relationship between the two powers. Upon receipt of the British request for aid Foreign Minister Baron Kato Takaaki met with Prime Minister Okuma Shigenobu to discuss the Japanese position. They both decided that Japan should provide assistance to their alliance partner by commencing hostilities against Germany but that Japan should not restrict its war activities to chasing down German warships, or auxiliary cruisers. On August 7th Japan decided at a Cabinet meeting to declare war on Germany and to discuss the explanations for Japan's decision to go to war with Great Britain. Japan wanted to be able to state to the world that its entry into the war resulted from its alliance relationship with Great Britain and it did not want to let itself be portrayed as taking advantage of the world crisis to advance its own position in the Far East. Additionally, the invocation of the alliance relationship by Great Britain would be a further confirmation of Japan's status among the great powers.

On August 9th Japan replied to the British request stating that it would enter the war pursuant to the Anglo-Japanese Alliance but upon joining the war its joint objective with Great Britain would be the destruction of German power in East Asia.[19] However, the fact that Germany had not commenced any open hostilities against the British possessions in the Far East, or the Pacific, was perceived to be an impediment to invoking the precise terms of the alliance and, in any event, Foreign Minister Grey began having second thoughts about what the entry of Japan into the war would mean to great power rivalries in the Orient. Therefore, on August 11th Grey advised Japanese Ambassador Inouye Katsunosuke that in light of the absence of any present danger to British possessions, Great Britain would not formally invoke the alliance treaty but the British were amenable to the issuance of a joint statement stating that Great Britain and Japan would take action to protect their interests pursuant to the Anglo-Japanese Alliance. However, Grey tried to limit the scope of Japanese operations in the Far East by proposing that Japan would only carry out active operations against Germany in the China Seas and Asiatic waters adjacent thereto, and would not operate eastwards into the North Pacific Ocean, nor invade any territories on the Asian continent other than the territories that were under German occupation. Grey told the Japanese that such a statement was desirable in order to avoid any misapprehension on the part of other countries.[20]

Sir Edward Grey was trying to find some diplomatic formula that would allow Great Britain to obtain Japanese assistance but at the same time restrict the participation of Japan in the war. After requesting a limited but nevertheless hostile intervention from Japan, Grey spent much of his time trying to stop a Japanese attack on Kiaochow, and when that did not seem possible he sought to restrict Japan from undertaking general operations in the Pacific Ocean. Grey's attitude towards Japan's participation in the war was disturbing to the First Lord of the Admiralty, Winston Churchill, who knew that Britain needed the help of the Japanese navy in the Pacific and he warned Grey against offending the Japanese.[21]

In Canada, rumours of Japanese mobilization caused anxiety in British Columbia, where the Premier of British Columbia, Sir Richard McBride, became so worried about the possibility of Japanese perfidy that he telegraphed Prime Minister Borden to relate his fears that a British naval defeat in the Pacific, presumably at the hands of the German East Asiatic Squadron, could well be the catalyst for Japan to defect from the Anglo-Japanese Alliance and to side with Germany in the war. He stated in his telegram to Borden that a naval defeat in the Pacific by the British Empire would lead to Japan unhesitatingly cooperating with Germany in the war, and that the existing treaty with Canada and Britain would be irrelevant in those circumstances.[22] Seeking to find a way to assure McBride of Japan's loyalty Borden sent McBride's concerns on to the First Lord of the Admiralty, Winston Churchill in London, stating:

> "Following telegram just received from Premier McBride and

submitted for your consideration. Begins. Press reports indicate Japan mobilization. It would be well get in touch with Admiralty personally. Do not hesitate to say that in event British loss Japan would not hesitate co-operate with Germany. I know of treaties with Canada and England but in this time these of little or no consequence. Without intending any serious alarm would like to have you consider as I have outlined. Ends. Borden."[23]

Churchill, however, facing an unprecedented situation, and knowing that Great Britain did not have the strength to dominate the remote Pacific and Indian Oceans, while facing the German High Seas Fleet across the North Sea, without Japan's assistance, was having none of these alarmist colonialist sentiments. He responded to Prime Minister Borden the next day, wiring:

"Secret. Japan has had grievance against Germany since 1895 and her alliance with us involved her very closely in the war. In these circumstances a menacing communication from the German Ambassador to the Japanese Foreign Minister has been decisive. Japan enters the war of her own free choice. She must be welcomed as a comrade and an ally. The naval situation is very secure everywhere but entry of Japan will of course make Pacific absolutely safe very soon. Tell McBride we are sending two powerful British cruisers to Pacific coast. Please reassure him privately. Any declaration against entry of Japan into war would do harm. We are full of admiration here for all your doings. Churchill"[24]

The Japanese government was naturally unwilling to accept any restrictions on its participation in the war, once war had been declared against Germany by Japan, and having now made the decision to enter the war in response to Sir Edward Grey's request on behalf of Great Britain for naval assistance in the Far East, Japan issued an ultimatum to Germany on August 15, 1914, in the following terms:

> "We consider it highly important and necessary in the present situation to take measures to remove the causes of all disturbance of peace in the Far East, and to safeguard general interest as contemplated in the Agreement of Alliance between Japan and Great Britain.
>
> In order to secure firm and enduring peace in Eastern Asia, the establishment of which is the aim of the said Agreement, the Imperial Japanese Government sincerely believes it to be its duty to give advice to the Imperial German Government to carry out the following two propositions:
>
> (1) Withdraw immediately from Japanese and Chinese waters the German men-o'-war and armed vessels of all kinds, and to disarm at once those which cannot be withdrawn.
>
> (2) To deliver on a date not later than September 15th, to the Imperial Japanese authorities, without condition or compensation, the entire leased territory of Kiaochau, with a view to the eventual restoration of the same to China.
>
> The Imperial Japanese Government announces at the same time that in the event of its not receiving, by noon on August 23rd, an answer from the Imperial German Government signifying unconditional acceptance of the above advice offered by the Imperial Japanese Government, Japan will be compelled to take such action as it may deem necessary to meet the situation."[25]

Japan gave Germany a full week to respond to the ultimatum because direct communications between the two countries had been interrupted by the outbreak of the war. Berlin did not actually receive the ultimatum until August 17th.

After requesting Japan's help on August 5th, Sir Edward Grey continued to spend much of the remainder of the month in a futile effort to restrain Japan from doing more than Great Britain wanted it to do. Grey was unhappy that the Japanese ultimatum to Germany did not contain the geographical limitations on Japan's freedom of action that he had sought. He advised that such limitations were necessary in order to reassure the dominion governments, and other governments, of Japan's friendly intentions and pointedly sought confirmation that Japan would:

- return conquered German territory in China to the Chinese government at the war's end
- not occupy German-owned islands in the Pacific Ocean
- not intervene in the Pacific coastal regions of North America
- not seize the Netherlands East Indies.[26]

But Japan had its own national interests in mind, and like the European powers, it was motivated to acquire both influence and territory from the German Empire in China and the Pacific Ocean. Obviously, Japan had no interests in North America, and as for the Dutch colonies, the Netherlands was a neutral country, and Japan's entry into the war was clearly stated in the ultimatum to be within the general parameters of its alliance with Great Britain, and thus Japan posed no threat to the Netherlands.

Grey's attitude towards Japan was paternalistic, and it was offensive to Japanese sensibilities, as Churchill tried to warn. Probably, Grey was mainly motivated by concerns over the attitude of the United States, which expressed its concerns over the possibility of a Japanese expansion in the Asia-Pacific region, despite assurances by Foreign Minister Kato to US ambassador George Guthrie that Japan did not intend to engage in territorial aggrandizement.[27]

On August 17th Prime Minister Okuma issued a formal statement of Japan's war intentions, stating that Japan sought the elimination of German influence in China, which menaced the peace of Asia, and was an objective that was in conformity with the country's alliance with the British Empire. Japan forswore any "selfish end," and Prime Minister Okuma stated that Japan had no designs for a "territorial aggrandizement" but would only undertake actions that were necessary, and that were aligned with Japan's own interests.[28]

Sir Edward Grey remained unhappy with Japan's refusal to accept the limitations that Great Britain sought to impose on Japan's war operations in the Pacific theatre, and on the same day as the issuance of the Japanese declaration, the British government released its own public statement which said that the British government understood that Japan would not undertake actions in the Pacific Ocean outside of the China Seas unless it was necessary to protect Japanese shipping, nor would it extend military operations east into the Pacific Ocean or upon any territory that was not then under the occupation of Germany on the Asian continent.[29]

Needless to say, Japan did not accept the British government's formulation of its own war intentions, which was frankly insulting to its ally, and Foreign Minister Kato made it clear to the British ambassador that Japan would not accept Sir Edward Grey's formulation. To underscore the strong feelings that Grey's pronouncement created in the minds of the Japanese, Kato also ceased working with Grey on the issuance of a joint note to China which had been intended by Sir Edward Grey to allay any Chinese concerns over Japan's belligerency. Subsequently, Grey lamely attempted to smooth over the dispute by pointing to the prefatory words in the British statement, which said that "It is understood," as an acknowledgement that the British statement was only a British supposition about Japan's war objects.[30]

The question that remains is why did Sir Edward Grey press the Japanese to restrict their war operations after initially asking for assistance from Japan, and even suggesting that Japan would of necessity have to declare war on Germany to assist Great Britain? It seems that Grey was concerned about the Japanese taking advantage of the European war to enhance its position in China vis-a-vis the other great powers, and perhaps leaving Japan in a paramount position in China at the end of the war. Great Britain had extensive commercial interests in China, and naturally, Britain wanted to maintain its commercial position in China on the other side of the war.

The other British consideration involved the extensive German Pacific island colonies. The World War was a war to contest political domination in Europe, and colonies were to be the spoils of that war. Germany's Pacific islands were part of that play and the British Empire wanted its share – a share that could be (and later was) denied to the British Empire by the naval operations of Japan in the Pacific. Churchill, in his book *The World Crisis*, paints a picture of British Cabinet Ministers carving up the German Empire as early as August, 1914, with Australia and New Zealand anxious to take over the German Pacific possessions.[31] If Japan had not entered the war Britain and its dominions might have taken German Micronesia at their leisure, and much later in the war when they had time to set aside sufficient resources to mount an occupation. Japan's entry into the war upset that timetable because Japan's powerful navy could act immediately to conquer the German islands, thus foiling the intentions of the British Empire concerning those islands.

In the end, Japan decided to overlook the British ingratitude towards Japan's entry into the war. Japan also chose to overlook the offensiveness of some of the language in the heavy-handed British attempts to restrict Japan because it was in Japan's national interest to participate in the war, and in the division of the German Empire that would follow the war. Although the British request for assistance was the catalyst for the Japanese ultimatum to Germany, it was actually Japan's own interests in expanding its control over new territories, and the extension of Japan's economic footprint in China, that motivated Japan to act as it did. Japan's approach to the war was also reflected in the fact that Japan initially refused to sign the Declaration of London, which was signed by Great Britain, France, and Russia on September 4, 1914, and which committed its parties to refrain from making a separate peace with Germany and Austria-Hungary. Although the Japanese Ambassador to France, Viscount Ishii, recommended that Japan sign the Declaration of London, Foreign Minister Kato refused to permit Japan to sign it on the grounds that the Anglo-Japanese Alliance already committed Japan and Great Britain to refrain from separate peace negotiations, and the signature of Japan on the Declaration of London would detract from the Anglo-Japanese Alliance, which remained the foundation of Japanese foreign policy.[32] The firm reliance of Japan on the Anglo-Japanese Alliance as the basis for its war effort limited the geographical commitment that Japan made to the allied cause, and gave it a plausible diplomatic reason for refusing to commit its troops to the European or African battlefields.

Realizing their vulnerability in the Far East, the Germans made some half-hearted efforts to divest themselves of Kiaochow before the active war erupted but those efforts did not avail them. Germany made no formal response to the Japanese ultimatum and, after its expiration, Japan declared war on Germany on August 23, 1914. At Tsingtao, in addition to the German naval forces that were present there, Austria-Hungary maintained a protected cruiser, SMS *Kaiserin Elisabeth*, at the German naval port. To maintain the diplomatic niceties prior to laying siege to Tsingtao Japan presented an ultimatum to Austria-Hungary, requiring it to remove its warship from Tsingtao. When Austria-Hungary refused to do so, Japan declared war on Austria-Hungary on August 25, 1914. War in the Pacific against the Central Powers was now fully underway.

NOTES

[1] In 1915 Italy would join the war on the side of Entente powers by declaring war on Austria-Hungary on May 23, 1915, after formally withdrawing from the Triple Alliance on May 3rd. Declarations of War against the Ottoman Empire and Bulgaria followed but, curiously, Italy did not declare war on Germany until late in the summer of 1916.

[2] Allen, 63

[3] Colonel G W L Nicholson, *Canadian Expeditionary Force 1914-1919*, Queen's Printer, Ottawa, 1962, 6

[4] Johnston et al., 217

[5] Tucker, 215

[6] Quoted in Tucker, 215

[7] When the SS *Komagata Maru* arrived back in Calcutta on September 27th the colonial officials in India considered the passengers to be political agitators and attempted to arrest some of them, leading to a dockside riot in which 19 people lost their lives and considerably more were arrested, some of whom then remained under restricted movement orders for the duration of World War One. The *Komagata Maru* incident is now seen as a shameful example of the racial prejudice inherent in Canadian immigration policy in the early twentieth century, and political efforts have been undertaken in the twenty-first century to publicly acknowledge the harm caused by those policies. Formal public apologies for the *Komagata Maru* incident have been made by both Prime Minister Stephen Harper and Prime Minister Justin Trudeau.

[8] Johnston et al, 230

[9] Tucker, 263

[10] Tucker, 290; Bryan Elson, *Canada's Bastions of Empire, Halifax, Victoria and the Royal Navy 1749-1918*, Formac Publishing, Halifax, 2014, 176

[11] Von Moltke to Jagow, in Imanuel Geiss (ed.) *July 1914, The Outbreak of the First World War, Selected Documents*, Charles Scribner Sons, New York, 1967, p. 353-54.

[12] Johnston et al, 241

[13] Quoted in Tucker, 289

[14] Nish, *Decline*, 116

[15] Charles Stephenson, *The Siege of Tsingtao, The German – Japanese War 1914*, Pen & Sword Books (e-book), Great Britain, 2017, 155

[16] Nish, *Decline*, 116

[17] Winston S Churchill, *The World Crisis*, Charles Scribner's Sons and Maxwell Macmillan Canada, New York/Toronto 1931 (1992), 185 [afterwards: Churchill: *Crisis*]

[18] Stephenson, 163

[19] Nish, *Decline*, 120

[20] Stephenson, 166

[21] Stephenson, 168

[22] Johnston et al, 245

[23] Department of External Affairs, *Documents on Canadian External Relations Vol. 1, 1909-1918*, Ottawa, Queen's Printer for Canada, 1967, 43, no. 59 [afterwards: DCER Vol. 1]

[24] DCER Vol. 1, 44, no. 62

[25] https://wwi.lib.byu.edu/index.php/Japanese_Ultimatum_to_Germany

[26] Nish, *Decline*, 123

[27] Stephenson, 176

[28] Nish, *Decline*, 124

[29] Nish, *Decline*, 124

[30] Nish, *Decline*, 125

[31] Churchill, *Crisis*, 179

[32] R P Dua, *Anglo-Japanese Relations During the First World War*, S Chand & Co. (Pvt.) Ltd., Ram Nagar, New Delhi (India), 1972, 175

8. The German Raider Threat

War in the Pacific in 1914 found Canada ill-equipped to ward off any seaborne assaults by the enemy, owing to the fact that the Royal Canadian Navy had fallen largely into desuetude following the ouster of the Laurier Ministry, and the ill-fated attempt of the Borden Ministry to financially support the Royal Navy by subsidizing the cost of two dreadnought battleships. With Canadian naval policy all at sea, so to speak, the state of naval defences on the west coast was far below what it should have been. The public in British Columbia was quite aware of the poor condition of the west coast naval defences, and that fact contributed to public alarm, and a sense of panic, at the thought of a sudden descent on Victoria, or Vancouver, by the Imperial German Navy. Regardless of the insufficiency under which it laboured, however, the RCN stepped up with what it had available in order to address the immediate threats to the Pacific coast.

The first threat that the naval authorities at Esquimalt faced was the prospect of an attack by detached German cruisers operating along the west coast of the Americas. In the summer of 1914, the continuing political instability in Mexico had drawn the warships of several nations to Mexico's west coast in order to protect their national citizens residing in Mexico. Among the ships sent to Mexico were the two remaining British station ships at Esquimalt, the sloops HMS *Algerine*, and HMS *Shearwater*. Both were fitted with steam engines but they retained their sailing rigs and *Algerine*, at least, was still capable of sail propulsion, although it appears that the sails may have been removed from HMS *Shearwater* by 1914, despite the continuing presence of her masts.[1] United States naval vessels were also present in Mexican waters, as was a German cruiser, initially the SMS *Nurnberg*, subsequently relieved by the SMS *Leipzig*, and a Japanese armoured cruiser, HIJMS *Idzumo*.

On August 1st NSHQ in Ottawa ordered HMCS *Rainbow* at Esquimalt to prepare for sea. *Rainbow* had been brought up to strength with local drafts supplemented by other RCN personnel, and by crew from the Royal Navy. NSHQ advised the *Rainbow*'s captain, Commander Walter Hose, that both SMS *Nurnberg* and SMS *Leipzig* were reported to be off the western coast of North America.

HMCS *Rainbow* had entered service with the Royal Navy in 1892, as an *Apollo* class protected cruiser, and had served in the RN until the ship's transfer to the fledgeling RCN in 1910. HMCS *Rainbow* was a 3700-ton vessel with a range of 8000 nautical miles at ten knots, and a maximum speed of 19.75 knots. Lightly armoured, she carried an armament of two 6-inch guns, six 4.7-inch guns, eight six-pounder guns, and four torpedo tubes, and was served by a crew of 273 men. Aged 22 years by 1914, HMCS *Rainbow* was considered to be obsolete but still sufficient for duties on the Canadian Pacific coast, which largely consisted of showing the flag, naval training, and supporting the civil authorities in fisheries and immigration enforcement. Now, however, the ship was being asked to undertake the defence of the west coast against more modern and more powerful German cruisers. HMCS *Rainbow* also suffered from a lack of high explosive shells in its armoury, which placed it at a serious disadvantage if it found itself in a battle with modern German cruisers. In addition, the ship's wireless only had a range of 200 miles, and there were no pre-arranged coaling facilities for the ship south of its base at Esquimalt.

Nevertheless, on August 2nd, HMCS *Rainbow* received an order from the Admiralty in London to proceed to sea and search for SMS *Leipzig*, which had been reported at Mazatlán, Mexico, on July 30th. Commander Hose, asked NSHQ for confirmation of the order because operational control of *Rainbow* had not yet been transferred from Canada to Great Britain, and Ottawa confirmed the order on August 3rd stating:

"You are to proceed to sea forthwith to guard trade routes

North of Equator, keeping in touch with Pachena [wireless station] until war has been declared [-] obtain information from North Bound Steamers . . . No further news of Leipzig."[2]

August 3rd found HMCS *Rainbow* cruising off the coast of the State of Washington, awaiting word of developments in Europe. Shortly after 8 PM on August 4th, the *Rainbow* was informed that war had been declared, and the ship was recalled to Esquimalt to coal, after which it was ordered to proceed south to find and escort the British warships HMS *Algerine*, and HMS *Shearwater* returning to Esquimalt, which were now in potential danger from SMS *Leipzig*, or SMS *Nurnberg*. Lloyds of London was warning all British shipping that both the *Leipzig* and the *Nurnberg* were believed to be in North American waters.

By the end of July, the crisis on the Mexican coast was ending as Carranza's forces entered Mazatlán, and the prospect of a world war began the dispersal of the naval units that had been present at Mazatlán. On July 31st the Canadian collier SS *Cetriana* had arrived at Mazatlán under charter to coal the SMS *Leipzig*, and on August 1st the *Leipzig* began preparing for sea, its commander prudently taking the precaution of assuming control of the *Cetriana*'s wireless until the coaling of *Leipzig* from the collier was completed. Meanwhile, HMS *Shearwater* was at Ensenada, and HMS *Algerine* had left Mazatlán.[3]

HMCS *Rainbow* sailed south looking for the two wayward British sloops. HMS *Shearwater* was a 980-ton *Condor*-class sloop originally constructed in 1899, and had a range of 3000 nautical miles at ten knots, although she could reach a maximum of 13 knots. Originally possessed of a sail plan with a barque, and then later a barquentine rig, her sails were apparently removed before the war. *Shearwater* was armed with six 4-inch 25 pounder guns, and four 3-pounder guns, but only had light armour protection over her boilers and machinery. The *Shearwater* carried a crew of around 125.

The slightly larger HMS *Algerine* was a twin-screw 1050 ton steam sloop, also fitted with a sail plan rigged as a barquentine but the ship normally relied on steam propulsion. Like the *Shearwater*, HMS *Algerine* was capable of steaming at 13 knots and had a similar range. Her armament consisted of six 4-inch 25 pounder guns, four 3-pounder guns, and three maxim guns. She was lightly armoured over her boiler and machinery areas.

In 1914 both the *Algerine* and the *Shearwater* were obsolete vessels that contributed little to the defence of Canada's west coast. They had been left behind as station vessels when the Royal Navy withdrew from Esquimalt largely because the RCN had not yet been formed when the British withdrew, and at the time there was no adequate Canadian naval protection for the naval base at Esquimalt. Their main duty had been to enforce the Bering Sea Sealing Convention with the United States. Now, with the German cruisers at large, there was great concern about the whereabouts of the two ill-equipped British warships.

HMCS *Rainbow* sailed south and reached San Francisco, California, on August 7th. The United States had now declared its neutrality in the war, and therefore the *Rainbow* was denied full coaling privileges while in port but she nevertheless managed to acquire a small amount of coal. The presence of HMCS *Rainbow* at San Francisco was widely reported to the German merchant marine however, and German freighters operating off of North America immediately sought the safety of American harbours as a consequence. Once in port, some of the cargoes from the German merchantmen were transferred to American-flagged vessels.[4] Commander Hose discovered that the SMS *Nurnberg* had also been at San Francisco but the *Nurnberg* had left San Francisco on July 21st heading west to return to Tsingtao.

Intelligence reports on August 8th suggested that a German schooner had departed San Francisco with supplies for SMS *Leipzig*, and so Commander Hose took HMCS *Rainbow* to sea and patrolled slowly to the south on August 9th but the Rainbow did not encounter any ships. By August 10th HMCS *Rainbow* was beginning to run short of coal supplies, and the refusal of US officials at San Francisco to bend the neutrality rules for Canada's benefit meant that Commander Hose had to return to Esquimalt. Hose also surmised that both HMS *Algerine* and HMS *Shearwater* must have passed on to the north if they had not already fallen to the German cruiser. Thus, Hose calculated that his best chance of making contact with the wayward British steam sloops at this point was to head north towards home. Accordingly, on August 10th, HMCS *Rainbow* headed north from San Francisco.

In the meantime, Captain Johannes Haun of SMS *Leipzig* was cruising north from Mexico and looking for HMCS *Rainbow*, having been warned of the Canadian cruiser's approach to San Francisco. The *Leipzig* actually arrived in the waters off San Francisco on August 11th, missing a rendezvous with HMCS *Rainbow* by only one day. SMS *Leipzig* was a modern light cruiser commissioned in 1906. The cruiser displaced 3756 tons and had a maximum speed of 22 knots. The *Leipzig*'s range was 4690 nautical miles at 12 knots, and she carried a crew of around 290 men. Her armament consisted of ten 4.1-inch guns, ten maxim guns, and two torpedo tubes. Although HMCS *Rainbow* possessed two guns of greater calibre than SMS *Leipzig*, the *Rainbow* was outmatched by the *Leipzig* in speed, crew training, and crew efficiency, and there is considerable doubt about whether HMCS *Rainbow* could have prevailed in a contest between the two vessels. While naval battles are unpredictable and much happens that cannot be foreseen, most writers have come to the conclusion that HMCS *Rainbow* was outmatched by SMS *Leipzig*, and a contest between them would have been unlikely to result in a Canadian victory.[5]

After patrolling off San Francisco for a few days in hopes of encountering HMCS *Rainbow*, and going as far north as Cape Mendocino,[6] the *Leipzig* entered San Francisco on the night of August 16-17 in order to obtain coal. The presence of this powerful warship in American waters caused all British and Canadian shipping along the west coast of North America to remain harbour-bound until the danger presented by the *Leipzig* had passed.[7] Captain Haun made the most of his stop in San Francisco, meeting with the American press and letting it slip that he was searching for HMCS *Rainbow*. The public relations impact of *Leipzig's* appearance at San Francisco reinforced the caution of allied ship masters all along the west coast of the Americas.

On August 18th, the *Leipzig* departed San Francisco and on September 3rd, Captain Haun was advised by the Kaiserliche Marine (KM) in Berlin to "transfer cruiser warfare to southwest America and the Atlantic."[8] After subsequently operating unsuccessfully between South America and the Galapagos Islands, Captain Haun received instructions on October 1st to attempt a rendezvous with SMS *Dresden*, which had by then entered the South Pacific Ocean.

After proceeding north back to Esquimalt, HMCS *Rainbow* found HMS *Shearwater* approaching the Strait of Juan de Fuca and escorted her back into Esquimalt. The Rainbow then went back out and found HMS *Algerine* along the Washington coast where she had run short of coal and been found by HMCHS *Prince George*, a hastily fitted out hospital ship that was also searching for the *Algerine*. The Rainbow escorted both ships back to Esquimalt. Meanwhile, SMS *Leipzig* departed San Francisco harbour on August 18th, heading south. Rumours continued to circulate about the presence of German cruisers off the Pacific coast. HMCS *Rainbow* sailed north to investigate reports of a sighting of German cruisers off Prince Rupert but nothing was discovered, nor was there any real basis in fact for the purported sighting.[9]

After leaving San Francisco on July 21st, SMS *Nurnberg* proceeded west across the Pacific, and arrived at Honolulu, Hawaii, on July

27th, where Vice Admiral Count von Spee ordered her to rendezvous with the German East Asiatic Squadron at Ponape in the Caroline Islands. The KM in Berlin had advised von Spee of the existence of strained relations between the Triple Alliance partners of Germany and Austria-Hungary with the Dual Alliance partners of France and Russia.[10] Although the *Nurnberg* was well out of North American waters by the time the war broke out the uncertainty about her whereabouts was a major cause for concern at both the Admiralty in London and at NSHQ in Ottawa. The possibility of more than one German cruiser operating off the west coast of North America would clearly mean that Canada's naval forces in the area were inadequate to contain the threat. Thus, Germany actually had effective local control of the seas off of the west coast of North America because the RCN lacked the strength to hunt down and destroy any of von Spee's cruisers operating in North American waters, notwithstanding the valiant efforts of HMCS *Rainbow*. To buttress Canada's defences the Admiralty, On August 18th, ordered the Commander-in-Chief in the Far East, Admiral Sir Thomas Martyn Jerram, to despatch the light cruiser HMS *Newcastle* from Yokohama, Japan, to Esquimalt.[11]

After Japan entered the war on August 23, 1914, an immediate request was made by Great Britain to Japan for Japanese naval assistance to protect western Canada. As a result, Imperial Japanese Naval Headquarters ordered the Captain of HIJMS *Idzumo*, which was then still in Mexican waters, to immediately head to Canada to protect commerce and defend Japan's North American ally.[12] The *Idzumo* sailed immediately for Canada and arrived at Esquimalt on August 25th. Only from that date did allied forces reacquire local control of the seas off of North America by virtue of superior forces.

HIJMS *Idzumo* was an armoured cruiser of 9353 tons and had the capability of making 21.75 knots, with a range of 7000 nautical miles at 10 knots. She had an armour belt of between three and one-half and seven inches, and two and one-half inches of deck armour.

The ship was armed with four 8-inch guns in a fore and aft twin turret layout, fourteen 6-inch guns, of which ten were casemated, twelve 12-pounder guns, and eight 2.5 pounder guns, as well as four torpedo tubes. The *Idzumo* was a major naval unit that outclassed any of the German East Asiatic Squadron's light cruisers, such as the *Leipzig*. *Idzumo*'s arrival at Esquimalt went far to alleviate the public alarm that had existed in the west coast cities of British Columbia since the outbreak of the war. Even before Japan entered the war the *Victoria Times* had taunted the German cruiser by underlining the threat that SMS *Leipzig* faced if she was forced to fight HIJMS *Idzumo* after the Japanese ultimatum to Germany expired: "Unhappy cruiser Leipzig! For the next six days she is going to be stalked wherever she may go by a warship big enough to swallow her with one bite."[13]

On August 30th HMS *Newcastle*, a British light cruiser arrived from the Far East, and with the addition of the *Newcastle*, the allied naval forces at Esquimalt were now overwhelmingly superior to any German light cruisers that might be operating off the west coast of North America. The commander of HMS *Newcastle*, Captain F A Powlett, in his capacity as the senior Royal Navy officer, assumed command of the allied flotilla at Esquimalt and extended his authority to His Majesty's Dockyard at Esquimalt. There had been a loss of administrative efficiency in the management of the port facilities, and so Captain Powlett considered his assumption of authority to be justified by the circumstances but he had taken control of HMD without being authorized to do so by NSHQ in Ottawa. With the active encouragement of the Premier McBride of British Columbia, Captain Powlett also arranged for mining of the northern reaches of Vancouver Island, the removal of guns from the obsolete British sloops *Algerine* and *Shearwater*, and their subsequent installation in the Strait of Georgia adjacent to Seymour Narrows.[14]

On September 3rd, HMS *Newcastle* and HIJMS *Idzumo* left Esquimalt and sailed south to look for SMS *Leipzig*. The *Idzumo* patrolled off

San Francisco while the *Newcastle* went as far south as the Gulf of California. HMCS *Rainbow* and the two submarines purchased by Premier McBride, HMCS C1 and HMCS C2 were left behind at Esquimalt to defend the naval base, and the sea approaches to Vancouver.[15]

Meanwhile on the far side of the North Pacific Ocean war preparations had been underway at Tsingtao since news of the assassination of the Archduke Franz Ferdinand on June 28th first reached the Far East. That news had electrified the officers of the Austro-Hungarian protected cruiser SMS *Kaiserin Elisabeth*, stationed at Tsingtao as the Austro-Hungarian guard ship in the Far East. Captain Richárd Makovicz of *Kaiserin Elisabeth* warned Captain Karl Friedrich Max von Müller of SMS *Emden*, who was temporarily in command of the naval forces at Tsingtao in the absence of Vice Admiral Count von Spee, that the assassination of the Austro-Hungarian Archduke would precipitate a war. Von Muller immediately sent news of the assassination to von Spee, who was cruising through the German-held Caroline Islands with the bulk of his squadron.

Von Muller also issued orders to German agencies in Tokyo and Shanghai to arrange for coal and other supplies to be sent to two secret rendezvous points in the North Pacific, to support the future war cruises of the German East Asiatic Squadron.[16] Then he took the SMS *Emden* to sea to search for prizes before heading for a rendezvous with Vice Admiral von Spee. At that point, the Royal Navy almost caught the *Emden*, and on the night of August 2/3 the *Emden* and the British China Station Squadron passed by each other 50 miles apart at sea. On August 4th the Emden captured the new Russian passenger liner SS *Ryazan* as a prize, and sent her into Tsingtao to be converted to naval use as an auxiliary cruiser. But the real prize that von Muller sought was the Canadian Pacific liner RMS *Empress of Japan*, which was completing a trans-Pacific voyage to Hong Kong, after completing an intermediate stop at the port of Yokohama, Japan. Von Muller hoped to take the *Empress of*

Japan as a prize. He returned to Tsingtao on the morning of August 5th, coaled, and then departed in the evening with the SS *Prinz Eitel Friedrich*, which he planned to use to take the passengers off of the *Empress of Japan* if he was able to find and capture her.

On the night of August 7th the *Emden's* wireless picked up signals from what appeared to be a passenger liner heading for Hong Kong, and the *Emden* stealthily followed, overtaking the ship on the morning of August 8th. After forcing the passenger vessel to heave-to the German boarding crew discovered that it was not the CP liner that they had hoped to take as a prize but rather a (still) neutral Japanese passenger liner, which the *Emden* had to release. The Japanese vessel promptly began transmitting a warning about the presence of the *Emden* to all ships within its wireless range, foiling von Muller's plan to capture the RMS *Empress of Japan*. Von Muller was left with no choice but to proceed on to his scheduled rendezvous with his Admiral in the Mariana Islands.[17] The Canadian Pacific liner *Empress of Japan*, which had found herself two days out from Yokohama when the war erupted on August 4th, avoided capture by the SMS *Emden* and reached Hong Kong safely, where it disembarked its passengers, and was then immediately taken over by the Admiralty to be converted into an armed merchant cruiser under a tripartite agreement between the Canadian Pacific Steamship Line, and the Canadian and British governments.[18]

A final addition to the German cruiser fleet operating in the Pacific Ocean came in the form of the light cruiser SMS *Dresden*. The *Dresden* had been operating off the east coast of Mexico before the outbreak of the war to protect German citizens swept up by the political instability in Mexico at the time. Just before the outbreak of war the *Dresden* was relieved by SMS *Karlsruhe* but the commencement of hostilities prevented *Dresden's* return to Germany. The *Dresden* began commerce raiding operations off the east coast of South America but with limited success. Searching for happier hunting grounds her commanding officer, Captain Fritz

Ludecke, decided to try the South Pacific Ocean, and the *Dresden* headed for Cape Horn, which the ship rounded on September 5, 1914. The *Dresden* then proceeded up the western coast of Chile, having been instructed by the KM in Berlin to operate in conjunction with SMS *Leipzig*, which was then heading south from North American waters.

After von Spee's defeat at the Battle of the Falkland Islands later in the year, the remnants of the German East Asiatic Squadron continued to bedevil the allies into 1915. SMS *Geier*, an antiquated gunboat which had a large coal capacity as well as auxiliary sails, had been despatched from German East Africa prior to the outbreak of the war to join Vice Admiral Count von Spee, and she passed through the Bismarck Archipelago before reaching the Marshall Islands in September,[19] taking one British prize en route. The *Geier* missed her rendezvous with the German East Asiatic Squadron however, so she continued on to Honolulu, where she was effectively blockaded in port by HIJMS *Hizen*, and HIJMS *Asama*, as a result of which the *Geier* was interned by the United States on November 8th, and then subsequently seized by the US in 1917, when America entered the war.

In the western Pacific the auxiliary merchant cruiser SMS *Komoran II*, the ex Russian *Ryazan*, which had originally been taken as a prize by Captain von Muller of SMS *Emden* at the outset of the war, had taken shelter at Lamotrek Atoll in the Caroline Islands, following the Japanese declaration of war against Germany. The *Komoran II* lacked sufficient coal to continue cruiser warfare, and an attempt to secure additional supplies by sending a small boat to the neutral island of Guam, a US territory, was unsuccessful. Warned by native Caroline Islanders that the Japanese Navy was at nearby Truk lagoon, the *Komoran II*'s commander, Captain Zuckschwerdt, resolved to make a dash to Guam with the *Komoran II*. On December 12th the ship left Lamotrek atoll and on December 14th the *Komoran II* reached Guam.[20] Unable to procure sufficient coal from the limited supplies available at Guam the *Komoran II* accepted internment at Apra harbour in Guam, where the ship remained until the US declaration of war against Germany in April, 1917. When war was declared between the United States and Germany, Captain Zuckschwerdt blew up his ship to prevent it from falling into American hands as a prize.[21]

A more successful merchant cruiser was SMS *Prinz Eitel Friedrich*, which the energetic Captain von Muller also converted from a passenger liner upon the outbreak of the war, using crews and armaments from the outdated Tsingtao gunboats SMS *Luchs*, and SMS *Tiger*. Commissioned at Tsingtao on August 5th and placed under the command of Captain Max Therichens, the *Prinz Eitel Friederich* sailed with the convoy escorted by SMS *Emden* to the German East Asiatic Squadron rendezvous at Pagan Island in the Mariana Islands in early August. On August 13th von Spee despatched the SMS *Prinz Eitel Friederich* to engage in cruiser warfare in Australasian waters. During a career that spanned seven months in the South Pacific, and South Atlantic, the raider sank 11 Allied ships amounting to 33,423 tons. Then, running short of coal, and with no possibility of obtaining more, the *Prinz Eitel Friederich* sought port at Newport News, Virginia, in the United States, where she was interned.

After escaping the German disaster at the Battle of the Falklands, SMS *Dresden* hid among the bays and inlets, many of them unexplored, in Chilean waters at Tierra del Fuego well into 1915. The British under Rear Admiral Stoddart sent warships to seek out and destroy *Dresden*, and a game of naval hide and seek ensued for several months. *Dresden's* presence, and the possibility that she could move north, kept the Japanese North American Squadron active off the west coast of North America and kept the cruisers assigned to Admiral Stoddart's South American station active on the west coast of South America. Captain Ludecke eventually decided to head north from Chile after he had been threatened with internment and he sailed to the Juan Fernandez Islands, escaping a possible capture by the cruiser HMS *Kent* along the way. Short of coal, the *Dresden* made port at the Chilean island of Mas á Tierra, where Captain Ludecke decided to permit internment by Chilean authorities. In the interim, however, the Royal Navy closed in with HMS *Kent*, HMS *Glasgow*, and HMS *Otranto* converging on the island. Captain Luce of HMS *Glasgow* refused to accept the protestations of the German captain that he was protected by Chilean neutrality because *Dresden* had earlier flouted Chilean neutrality by hiding in Tierra del Fuego. He attacked the *Dresden* in Chilean waters and the *Dresden*, being unable to escape, was scuttled by her crew on March 14, 1915, thus ending the threat of German naval attacks in the Pacific.

On the other side of the ocean, the cruiser SMS *Emden* had a very successful career as a commerce raider in the Indian Ocean. The *Emden* attacked the British port at Penang, in Malaya, and sank a Russian cruiser and a French destroyer, which caused the Admiralty to assign powerful escorts to the forthcoming ANZAC troop convoy. Captain von Muller was praised for his chivalry as a combatant, even by the allied press.[22] The *Emden* took 19 prizes and sank over 70,000 gross tons of allied shipping, causing great alarm amongst the allied merchant fleets. At one point von Muller told his officers that the *Emden* was being pursued by 16 allied warships.[23] The end of the *Emden* came when von Muller, like Count von Spee, decided to attack a British settlement, in von Muller's case, the wireless station at Cocos Islands. On November 9, 1914, the *Emden* launched an attack on Cocos Island but before the wireless station could be destroyed it broadcast a message alerting the passing ANZAC troop convoy, which was then close by, and being escorted by HMAS *Sydney*, HMAS *Melbourne*, and HIJMS *Ibuki*, of the *Emden*'s presence. HMAS *Sydney* was despatched to Cocos Islands, much to the chagrin of the commander of HIJMS *Ibuki*, who was very anxious to win battle honours for the IJN. HMAS *Sydney* arrived and engaged the *Emden* in a single ship action in which the heavier 6-inch guns of the *Sydney* prevailed over the 4.1-inch guns of the *Emden*. The *Emden* was turned into a flaming wreck, suffering heavy casualties, and Captain von Muller chose to beach the ship and raised the white flag in surrender. After HMAS *Sydney* removed the wounded they were transferred to the former Canadian Pacific liner HMS *Empress of Russia* for transport to a hospital, and then on to a prisoner of war camp.[24]

NOTES

[1] HMS *Algerine* had retained her sails. Her logbook for August 3, 1914, shows that in preparing for war the *Algerine* unbent her square sails, struck her topgallant, topsail, and lower yards, and housed her top masts in preparation for a possible battle with SMS *Leipzig*.

[2] Quoted in Tucker, 265

[3] Tucker, 263

[4] Johnston et al, 233

[5] Johnston et al, 237

[6] There have been suggestions in the historical literature that SMS *Leipzig* perhaps went as far north as the Strait of Juan de Fuca (see in particular, Massie, *Castles* at 193 fn, and Bryan Elson, *Canada's Bastions of Empire* at 195)) and those suggestions may have found support in a report by the master of an American flagged vessel that he was stopped by the *Leipzig* north of California. However, *Leipzig*'s presence north of Cape Mendocino has never been confirmed, and the *Leipzig*'s logbook was lost when the ship was sunk at the Battle of the Falkland Islands. Cape Mendocino is the farthest north confirmed location of *Leipzig*. (Tucker, 274)

[7] Johnston et al, 239

[8] Quoted in Massie, *Castles*, 193 fn

[9] Johnston et al, 249

[10] Massie, *Castles*, 184

[11] Tucker, 270

[12] Rear Admiral Yoichi Hirana, "From Pupils to Partners" in Ian Gow, Yoichi Hirama and John Chapman (ed.), *The History of Anglo-Japanese Relations, 1600-2000, vol.* 3, Palgrave Macmillan, Houndmills, Basingstoke, Hampshire (Eng.), 2003, 53

[13] Quoted in Tucker, 270

[14] Tucker, 233

[15] Tucker, 272; Elson, 225

[16] Fred Clement, *Guns in Paradise*, McClelland and Stewart Limited, Toronto, 1968, 33

[17] Clement, 45

[18] Kirsten Weisenburger and Marc Dinsdale "First Class Warrior Empress, Memories of the luxury liner that once linked Vancouver to Asia", in *Pacific Rim Magazine*, http://langaraprm.com/1998/travel/first-class-warrior-empress/ [accessed May 24, 2020]

[19] Stephenson, 509

[20] Robert F. Rogers, *Destiny's Landfall: A History of Guam*, University of Hawaii Press, Honolulu, 1995, 135

[21] Rogers, 139

[22] A A Hoehling, *Lonely Command*, Modern Literary Editions, New York, 1957, 143

[23] Hoehling, 63. The pursuing allied warships, according to von Muller, were the Royal Navy's cruisers *Hampshire*, *Minotaur*, *Weymouth*, *Gloucester* and *Yarmouth*, auxiliary cruisers (ex. Canadian Pacific liners) *Empress of Russia* and *Empress of Asia*, the Royal Australian Navy's *Sydney* and *Melbourne*, the French Navy's cruiser *Montcalm*, the Japanese cruisers *Ibuki*, *Yahagi*, and *Chikuma*, and the Russian Navy's *Askold*.

[24] Hoehling, 145

9. The Japanese North American Squadron

The outbreak of the war in the Pacific brought home to the British Admiralty how limited was the reach of the Royal Navy in the Pacific, and the absolute necessity of relying on Britain's Japanese ally for naval control of the Pacific Ocean.[1] To command the Pacific the Royal Navy only had the limited resources of the China Station Squadron at Hong Kong, under Vice Admiral Sir Thomas Jerram which consisted of the old pre-dreadnought battleship HMS *Triumph*, the armoured cruisers HMS *Minotaur*, and HMS *Hampshire*, and the light cruisers HMS *Newcastle*, and HMS *Yarmouth*. Worse yet, the *Triumph* was undergoing repairs when the war started and she was not immediately available.

In the South Pacific Ocean the Royal Australian Navy, commanded by Rear Admiral Sir George Patey, presented a more powerful force in the form of the 19,200-ton battlecruiser HMAS *Australia*, which was armed with eight 12-inch guns. In addition, Admiral Patey had two 5400 ton light cruisers, HMAS *Sydney*, and HMAS *Melbourne*, each armed with eight 6-inch guns, and three destroyers, and two submarines. The powerful Australian naval force was superior to the German East Asiatic Squadron but it was based far from the centre of German naval activity in the North Pacific Ocean. There were also two antiquated French cruisers, FS *Montcalm*, and FS *Dupleix*, both serving as colonial guard ships, which were placed under the operational control of the British Admiralty by France upon the outbreak of the war. Neither of the French cruisers was a match for the cruisers of the German East Asiatic Squadron.

The commitments of the British Empire in the Pacific made it imperative to obtain support from the Imperial Japanese Navy, especially in the absence of concrete information concerning the whereabouts of the German East Asiatic Squadron. As a result of its weakness in the Pacific, the British Admiralty turned over to Japan the responsibility for exercising full allied naval control over the North Pacific Ocean, except for Canadian coastal waters. It was a responsibility that Japan assumed and would continue to exercise, until the end of the war.[2] The IJN quickly despatched the new battlecruiser HIJMS *Kongo* on August 23rd, to patrol in the mid-North Pacific as far east as US-owned Midway Island.

A particular concern remained the west coast of North America, where Japan was already playing an important role with the deployment of HIJMS *Idzumo* to Esquimalt. To reinforce the *Idzumo*, the IJN despatched an armoured cruiser, HIJMS *Asama*, and later HIJMS *Hizen*, a former Russian battleship captured in the Russo-Japanese War, to the eastern North Pacific to form the nucleus of a Japanese North American Squadron together with HIJMS *Idzumo*, the whole squadron coming under the command of Rear Admiral Moriyama Keizaburo. Subsequently, the allies became aware that SMS *Geier*, a rather antiquated German gunboat from German East Africa, had crossed the Indian Ocean and entered the Pacific reaching Honolulu on October 15, 1914. Her commander was able to ward off internment by the United States for some time owing to the condition of her engines, which necessitated extensive repairs and to weather circumstances. To prevent SMS *Geier* from undertaking commerce raiding after her repairs, the *Hizen* and the *Asama* were diverted to Hawaii to maintain a watch on the German ship. However, the *Geier* could not indefinitely delay its departure from the neutral port of Honolulu, and when the Japanese showed no signs of terminating their watch on Honolulu the *Geier* reluctantly had to accept internment in the United States. Relieved of the responsibility for watching SMS *Geier*, the *Hizen* and the *Asama* sailed for their North American station.

By the middle of autumn in 1914, the allied navies still did not know where Count von Spee was in the Pacific Ocean, and the possibility still existed that an attack on Canada might be undertaken by the

German squadron. Consequently, it was decided to maintain a powerful covering force off the North American coast in case von Spee appeared with his warships. That became a particularly critical matter after the defeat of the Royal Navy at the Battle of Coronel on November 1, 1914. As a result, the Australian battlecruiser HMAS *Australia* was despatched to North American waters, and a multi-national allied naval squadron was put together in November, 1914, around HMAS *Australia*, flying the flag of the RAN navy commander, Rear Admiral Patey, and including the old battleship, HIJMS *Hizen* (ex-Russian *Retvizan*), the armoured cruisers HIJMS *Idzumo*, flying the flag of Rear Admiral Moriyama, and HIJMS *Asama*, and the light cruiser HMS *Newcastle*. HMCS *Rainbow* was too slow to keep up with the squadron itself and too obsolete to risk in a fleet action against the German East Asiatic Squadron, but it was attached to the allied squadron as a wireless relay vessel, in order to maintain communications between the squadron and Esquimalt.[3] This multi-national allied squadron provided a crucial covering force for the Canadian Pacific coast at a time when it was potentially vulnerable to an attack by the German East Asiatic Squadron. Around November, 1914, the allied naval forces began to use Barkley Sound on Vancouver Island as a basing area in lieu of Esquimalt because of concerns that German spies were keeping a watch on the Straits of Juan de Fuca.[4]

That a descent by the German East Asiatic Squadron on the coast of North America was at least a possibility at this time is revealed by the war diary of Count von Spee who wrote on August 13, 1914:

> "If we were to proceed toward the coast of America, we should have both [coaling ports and agents] at our disposal, and the Japanese fleet could not follow us thither without causing great concern in the United States and so influencing that country in our favour."[5]

The participation of the Imperial Japanese Navy in the west coast covering force provided an important addition to the forces available for the naval defence of Canada. After the subsequent defeat of the German East Asiatic Squadron at the Battle of the Falkland Islands the multi-national squadron continued to remain off the coast of North America because of the still-present danger of the escaped German cruiser SMS *Dresden* but Admiral Patey was ordered to take HMAS *Australia* into the Atlantic, and Rear Admiral Moriyama thereafter assumed tactical operational command of the remaining vessels, marking one of the first times that British and Canadian warships came under the command of an officer of the Imperial Japanese Navy.[6]

However, Vice Admiral Count von Spee had been perceptive in surmising that American public opinion would be aroused by the presence of Japanese fleet units in North American waters. His prediction was borne out by the saga of HIJMS *Asama*, which was part of the multi-national allied naval squadron that was responsible for allied naval defence on the west coast of North America. After assuming tactical command of the multi-national squadron, Rear Admiral Moriyama reconnoitered the waters off Central America before concluding that the remaining German threats along the west coast of the Americas, the cruiser SMS *Dresden*, and the auxiliary cruiser SMS *Prinz Eitel Friedrich*, may have sailed north and therefore Moriyama headed north towards the Mexican coast.

Admiral Moriyama arrived at Magdalena Bay on January 23, 1915, and from there he despatched HIJMS *Asama*, commanded by Captain Yoshioka Hansaku further north to Puerto San Bartolome by way of Mazatlán. He then took HIJMS *Idzumo* to patrol between Hawaii and San Francisco, because he was worried about the safety of a Japanese diplomatic representative, Baron Dewa Shigoto, who was travelling to San Francisco, on his way to the formal ceremonies marking the opening of the new Panama Canal.[7]

On the afternoon of January 31, 1915, the *Asama* entered Puerto San Bartolome and she promptly struck hard on an uncharted rock, leaving a hole in the hull bottom that was estimated to be at least

15 metres in length. The rupture left the ship's boiler and engine rooms flooded, and the ship was without power and stranded on the rock. Captain Yoshioka had to put out kedge anchors and moved the ship's ammunition out of *Asama's* magazine before it flooded. All of the crew who were not required for emergency operations, together with the ship's provisions, were transferred to a British-flagged collier that was accompanying the *Asama*. With her power out the *Asama* could not signal Admiral Moriyama about the *Asama's* distress, and *Asama's* collier did not have wireless capabilities, so it was not until a second collier arrived that word could be sent via San Diego, California, to notify Admiral Moriyama of the difficulties that the *Asama* had encountered.

At the same time, the US government became aware of the accident through its consulate at Mazatlán, and Rear Admiral Howard, the commander of the US Navy's Pacific fleet, based at San Diego, California, immediately sailed south to investigate, and to offer assistance if required. The US State Department authorized the port of San Francisco to release a chartered vessel that had been contracted by the Japanese consulate in San Francisco to assist the *Asama*, the State Department having first determined that it would not violate US neutrality law for a chartered vessel to assist a stricken warship provided that no naval stores were carried on board the chartered vessel.[8]

Admiral Howard arrived with the USS *Raleigh*, and the USS *San Diego*, on February 5th, and he assessed the damage to HIJMS *Asama* as substantial. Relations between the American fleet commander and Captain Yoshioka were cordial but the Japanese declined any assistance from the Americans. The US ships soon departed because they were neutrals, and they were displaying lights and smoke, thus potentially giving away the *Asama's* position if SMS *Dresden*, or SMS *Prinz Eitel Friedrich*, were anywhere near the Mexican coast.

Rear Admiral Moriyama arrived aboard HIJMS *Idzumo* on February

12th, and he immediately sent a message to the Japanese Admiralty in Tokyo requesting that substantial assistance be sent to rescue the *Asama*. The cruiser HIJMS *Chitose*, the supply vessel SS *Konan Maru*, the repair ship SS *Kamakura Maru*, and the armoured cruiser HIJMS *Tokiwa*, which was *Asama*'s sister ship, were despatched from Japan and arrived by March 19th to assist the *Asama*. The *Tokiwa* also carried Admiral Moriyama's relief, Vice Admiral Tochinai Sojiro, who assumed command of the North American Squadron of the IJN. Rear Admiral Moriyama returned to Japan on a rotational reassignment. An additional repair ship, the SS *Kanto*, also arrived on March 24th, carrying 250 shipwrights from Japan.[9]

As a result of a protest by the German Ambassador in Washington, who had learned of the American efforts to assist the stricken *Asama*, the US Neutrality Board placed new restrictions on any potential American aid to the Japanese at Puerto San Bartolome. The arrival of substantial assistance from Japan, however, dispensed with any further need for US assistance to refloat the *Asama*.

There matters quietly rested until the *Los Angeles Times* published a lurid page one article in its Wednesday, April 14, 1915, edition charging that the Japanese were establishing a naval base at Puerto San Bartolome and that the *Asama* was not impaled on a rock but had been deliberately beached in soft mud as a pretext to allow Japan to establish a naval base in close proximity to the state of California.

The *Los Angeles Times* article played to the prejudices of the American public towards Japan, and the fears of Japanese aggrandizement in the Americas. There had been earlier stories, in 1912, about the Japanese potentially establishing a base at Magdalena Bay, Mexico, which had sharpened Californian suspicions of Japan. The *Asama* story was taken up by the American wire services, and it also appeared in the *New York Times*. The *Asama*'s predicament was used by the American yellow press to heighten American sensitivity to the role of Japan in the Pacific during the war by giving rise to unfounded fears of Japanese aggression. The Japanese embassy in Washington refuted the story that ran in the *Los Angeles Times* as preposterous, and the US Navy at San Diego denied that Japan had mined the harbour. Meanwhile, a San Diego newspaper, which had earlier reported on the incident responsibly, took pains to disabuse the American public of any fears of Japanese imperialism in the Americas by emphasizing a factual account of the *Asama's* distress.

The salvage work continued at Puerto San Bartolome, and the *San Diego Union* newspaper was able to report in August that the *Asama* had been refloated. On August 23, 1915, Captain Yohioka took his cruiser back to sea with twelve steel patches lining the bottom, one patch being as much as 24 square feet in size. The *Asama* also carried an additional 250 tons of cement liner to ensure the ship's watertight integrity. Accompanied by the SS *Kanto* and HIJMS *Chitose*, the *Asama* began a long, slow voyage north to Esquimalt, arriving at Royal Roads, the entrance to the Esquimalt naval base, on September 4th.[10]

Canadian and Japanese work crews at His Majesty's Dockyard in Esquimalt put another 43 plates on Asama before she could begin her long return voyage to Japan in company with the SS *Kanto*. Still pumping up to 100 tons of water out of the ship each hour, Captain Yoshioka sailed from Esquimalt for Yokosuka Naval Station on October 23, 1915, arriving home safely on December 18th.

The departure of the HIJMS *Asama* and SS *Kanto* marked the final end of the role of the IJN's North American Squadron. The purpose of the squadron as a cover force had been fulfilled earlier, in May, 1915, with the elimination in the North Pacific of the German cruiser threat, and by October the Japanese ships other than the *Asama* and *Kanto* had been redeployed. Nevertheless, the presence of the Japanese squadron throughout the period of danger in 1914-15 had been a welcome addition to Canadian defenses, owing to the poor condition of the Canadian naval defences at the outset of the war.

The presence of the Japanese naval forces in North American and Canadian waters also contributed to a lessening of overt displays of racial disharmony in the Canadian west coast population, although it did not eliminate the existing prejudices against the Japanese-Canadian population. Japanese immigration remained unpopular in British Columbia, and the *Vancouver Sun* editorialized that although the help that the *HIJMS Idzumo* had brought to Canadian west coast naval defence was certainly appreciated it would not soften the opposition of British Columbians to Japanese immigration into Canada.[11]

Racial discrimination could be seen even in west coast Canadian army recruitment centres. Some Japanese-Canadian men who were resident in British Columbia, and who sought to volunteer for service in the Canadian Army, found it difficult, or impossible, to enlist in British Columbia, and they were compelled to travel to Alberta, where racial discrimination was less of a factor in army recruitment in order to enlist.

NOTES

[1] Churchill, *Crisis*, 185

[2] Churchill, *Crisis*, 183; Tucker, 280

[3] Johnston et al, 254; Tucker, 278

[4] Tucker, 233

[5] Quoted in Tucker, 263

[6] Ian T M Gow, "The Royal Navy and Japan 1900 – 1920: Strategic Re-evaluation of the IJN" in, *The History of Anglo-Japanese Relations, 1600 – 2000, vol. 3*, 44.

[7] Donald H Estes, "Asama Gunkan: The Reappraisal of a War Scare" in, *The Journal of San Diego History*, San Diego Historical Society Quarterly, San Diego (CA), Summer 1978, Volume 24, Number 3.

[8] Estes, 11

[9] Estes, 15

[10] Estes, 19

[11] Elson, 200

10. The Cruise of the German East Asiatic Squadron

The summer of 1914 began delightfully for the commander of the German East Asiatic Squadron in Tsingtao, China, Vice Admiral Count Maximilian von Spee, a Catholic aristocrat and amateur naturalist, who had held the command of Germany's only major foreign naval detachment since December, 1912. In June, he received a visit from his British counterpart, Vice Admiral Sir Thomas Martyn Jerram and his flagship, HMS *Minotaur*, which provided an opportunity for von Spee's German officers to socialize with their brother officers from the Royal Navy. The British visit included parties, dances, and sporting competitions. Afterwards, von Spee planned to take the bulk of the German East Asiatic Squadron on a long summer cruise, leaving behind only the light cruiser SMS *Emden*, and SMS *Kaiserin Elisabeth*, the station ship of Germany's Triple Alliance ally, Austria-Hungary, in Tsingtao as guard ships. Von Spee planned to cruise first through Germany's Pacific islands in Micronesia, the Mariana, Caroline, and Marshall Islands, before heading south-east to the harbour at Apia, in German Samoa. After stopping at Samoa he intended to take the squadron west, visiting British-held Fiji, before heading to Bougainville, in the German Solomon Islands, and then on to the German-held Bismarck Archipelago, and mainland German New Guinea. Finally, he would sail north back to his base at Tsingtao, in the German-leased Kiaochow Bay Concession, where he expected to arrive at his home port in the Far East on September 20, 1914.[1]

The armoured cruiser SMS *Gneisenau* sailed first on June 20th, taking a meandering route through the Mariana Islands to Truk Atoll (now Chuuk Atoll) in the Caroline Islands where she eventually rendezvoused with her sister ship SMS *Scharnhorst*, and the rest of the squadron, which had departed Tsingtao at a later date. In late

June came word of the assassination of Archduke Franz Ferdinand of Austria-Hungary but as yet there was no immediate cause for alarm in the Pacific. But in early July, von Spee received word that the political situation in Europe was not to Germany's satisfaction, and von Spee decided to continue to the island of Ponape (now Pohnpei island) where he ordered SMS *Nurnberg*, which was returning from North America, to rendezvous with him. Now the news came thick and fast from Europe. On July 27th Berlin advised him of strained relations between Germany, Russia, and France. Back in Tsingtao, von Muller, the Captain of the SMS *Emden*, had acted energetically to prepare a supply convoy for the squadron and to issue orders for colliers and supply vessels to meet the German East Asiatic Squadron at prearranged secret locations in the North Pacific Ocean. On July 31, 1914, the *Emden* sailed from Tsingtao with the auxiliary merchant cruiser SMS *Prinz Eitel Friedrich*, and eight colliers to rendezvous with von Spee. On August 1, 1914, von Spee received the war warning message from Berlin, and the very next day, August 2, 1914, he learned that Germany was at war with Russia. On August 3rd, Germany declared war on France, and on August 5th word arrived that a state of war now existed between Great Britain and Germany from August 4, 1914.

SMS *Nurnberg* arrived at Ponape on August 5th, and on August 6th von Spee went to sea with his squadron, now comprised of SMS *Scharnhorst*, his flagship, and SMS *Gneisenau*, both armoured cruisers of about 13,000 tons and armed with eight 8-inch guns, six 6-inch guns, and eighteen 3.5-inch anti-torpedo boat guns. Both cruisers also mounted four torpedo tubes. They were a very formidable pair, crack ships with highly trained and experienced crews and together they constituted the major German naval threat in the Pacific Ocean. In addition, von Spee had with him the light cruiser *Nurnberg*, with the light cruisers *Emden* and *Leipzig* temporarily detached. All of the light cruisers were about 3500 tons displacement, and they were armed with ten 4-inch guns. The light cruisers were the greyhounds of von Spee's squadron, capable of steaming at 25 knots.

Von Spee headed for Pagan Island in the northern Mariana chain, where he expected to meet with Captain von Muller of SMS *Emden* and the supply convoy that he was shepherding. Von Spee arrived first at the fine natural harbour at Pagan on August 11th, and later on the same day von Muller arrived with *Emden*, *Prinz Eitel Friedrich*, and the convoy of colliers and coastal freighters hauling supplies for the fleet. Von Spee convened a council of captains to discuss the course that should be followed by the German East Asiatic Squadron now that a world war had erupted. Von Spee did not know whether Japan would join its alliance partner Great Britain in the conflict but he thought that Japan probably would join the war on the side of the Entente powers. The German war plan for the East Asiatic Squadron had envisaged that in a war with France and Russia alone an attack on Cochinchina, with German marines from Tsingtao and supported by the German East Asiatic Squadron, would be contemplated.[2]

Now, however, the entry of Great Britain into the conflict mandated that different plans be formulated. One possibility was to engage in cruiser warfare in the Pacific. But the prospective entry of Japan into the war forced those plans to be cast aside because the overwhelming superiority of the IJN in the Pacific would make it very likely that any individual German cruisers operating as raiders would soon be caught and sunk. A return to Tsingtao however, was now out of the question because it was obvious that Kiaochow would soon be invested by a Japanese invasion force. Nor could von Spee hope to successfully play hide and seek among Germany's Micronesian islands for any great length of time, owing to the large fleet that Japan would be able to deploy against him. Reflecting, after the war, on the predicament that was faced by Vice Admiral Count von Spee, the wartime German naval commander, Grand Admiral Tirpitz, rendered this opinion:

> "The entry of Japan into the war wrecked the plan of a war by our cruiser squadron against enemy trade and against British war vessels in those seas, leaving our ships with nothing to do but to attempt to break through and reach home."[3]

Thus, it was the command of the seas by the two allies, Japan and Great Britain that foreclosed all other options to Vice Admiral Count von Spee, and led Churchill to compare von Spee to a cut flower in a vase, soon to fade.[4]

The bleak future of a force such as the German East Asiatic Squadron had also been prophesied by Kaiser Wilhelm II's favourite naval strategist, Captain Alfred Thayer Mahan, of the United States Navy, who had said a quarter-century before that:

> "The renewal of coal is a want more frequent, more urgent, more peremptory, than any known to the sailing ship. It is vain to look for energetic naval operations distant from coal stations. It is equally vain to acquire distant coaling stations without maintaining a powerful navy; they will but fall into the hands of the enemy. But the vainest of all delusions is the expectation of bringing down an enemy by commerce-destroying alone, with no coaling stations outside the national boundaries."[5]

Although many different opinions were expressed by his captains when he convened them in the war council, von Spee ultimately decided that his only realistic course of action was to attempt to take the German East Asiatic Squadron home by crossing the Pacific, rounding Cape Horn, and then running up the Atlantic Ocean and trying to break through the British naval blockade in Europe to reach the German naval base at Wilhelmshaven. The chances of success in such a venture appeared quite slim but nevertheless, von Spee considered that it was more palatable than his other options. The die was cast. The German East Asiatic

Squadron would leave the Pacific Ocean and make a dash for home through the Atlantic. Von Spee believed that he would stand a much better chance of keeping his hungry ships supplied with coal off the coast of South America, where all of the independent countries were neutral and were quite often friendly towards Germany.

On August 13th the German East Asiatic Squadron sortied from the harbour at Pagan and began its long trans-Pacific journey. The next day, August 14th, von Spee, by prearrangement with von Muller, detached SMS *Emden* and sent her on her way alone to conduct independent cruiser warfare. Von Spee had full confidence in von Muller, who was anxious to try his luck as a German raider, and his confidence in the abilities of *Emden's* captain would not be misplaced. On August 19th, von Spee arrived at Eniwetok atoll in the German Marshall Islands where he stayed for three days amid the sounds of the surf and the swaying of the palm trees. The German squadron departed Eniwetok atoll on the 22nd and then moved on to Majuro atoll, arriving on August 26th. At Majuro, on August 28th, von Spee was met by the auxiliary merchant cruiser SMS *Komoran II* (ex. Russian *Ryazan*) which von Muller in the *Emden* had taken as a prize in the Far East immediately after the outbreak of war with Russia. SMS *Comoran II* was escorting four much-needed supply vessels for von Spee.[6]

On August 29th the squadron departed Majuro atoll and headed for British-owned Christmas Island. On the way, von Spee, on September 6th, detached SMS *Nurnberg*, and the tender SMS *Titania*, which had cable-cutting equipment, to attack the British territory of Fanning Island, where the Cable and Wireless Company operated the British Empire's Trans-Pacific Cable, part of the All-Red Route of the Imperial Cable System[7].

The *Nurnberg* and the *Titania* arrived at Fanning Island on September 7th, and the *Nurnberg* flew false French colours upon arrival to lull the civilian staff at the cable relay station into believing they were in the presence of allied ships. A German landing party destroyed the station and the cable was cut, causing $150,000.00 in damages, and leaving the Pacific cable between Bamfield, British Columbia, and Suva, Fiji, out of service for two weeks. The Trans-Pacific Cable could only be restored after a local diver went down and located the severed ends, allowing the cable to be reattached. Following *Nurnberg*'s return to his fleet on September 8th, von Spee sent the ship into Honolulu to acquire news, and to communicate over the American international cables with KM naval headquarters in Berlin, in order to advise the naval high command of his decisions, and of his future plans.

September 7th found the East Asiatic Squadron at British-owned Christmas Island, one of the Line Islands, where von Spee learned that German Samoa had now been occupied by New Zealand forces. Von Spee decided to go on to Samoa regardless, to see if any allied warships were present in the harbour at Apia, and could be taken by surprise. Von Spee actually hoped that he might find the battlecruiser HMAS *Australia* serenely anchored at Apia, and in a vulnerable position, but when the German East Asiatic Squadron arrived at Apia on September 14th the roadstead was deserted, and the New Zealand forces were firmly in control of the German colony. The German Squadron cruised past the islands but made no attempt to reconquer them because von Spee knew that if he retook the islands he would not be able to hold them against a return of allied forces.

To confuse the British, and the New Zealanders, about his future intentions von Spee set his squadron on a north-west course after departing from Samoa, and then he turned south-east and doubled back towards South America after his squadron was out of sight. This sleight of hand manoeuvre was successful in confusing the allied commands in the Pacific as to the whereabouts of von Spee and his squadron, and it contributed to the squadron's subsequent success off the west coast of South America. Continuing on with his voyage von Spee passed by British-owned Suvorov Atoll and made landfall on September 21st at Bora Bora in French Polynesia. There, the squadron pretended to be British, as a ruse, and the Germans were successful in acquiring many necessary provisions from the locals, for which the squadron's officers paid in gold.[8] As the squadron departed Bora Bora, however, the islanders hoisted the French tricolour and the German East Asiatic Squadron obligingly (and rather foolishly) responded with the German naval ensign, no doubt much to the chagrin of the islanders.[9]

After putting the luscious island of Bora Bora behind him, von Spee headed for exotic Tahiti, the main island of the French-owned Society Islands, but when he arrived there on the morning of September 22nd it was impossible to engage in any further subterfuges because the Tahitians had been forewarned by the islanders on Bora Bora that the ships had displayed the German naval ensign upon their departure from Bora Bora. The German squadron found that the French had removed the navigational aids from the harbour as a precaution, and the local coal stocks were on fire. Frustrated, von Spee did not attempt to land but he commenced a bombardment against the French shore batteries, and against the French gunboat FS *Zélée* in Papeete harbour, which the Germans sunk before departing. Two local civilians were killed in the bombardment, while the Germans suffered no casualties.

Von Spee was not yet done with French Polynesia however. He took his squadron to the Marquesas, where they arrived at Nuka Hiva on September 26th. Here the squadron stayed seven days to re-provision, and to allow the crews' shore leave. After leaving Nuka Hiva on October 2nd von Spee headed south-east and on October 4th, having become aware of the presence in South American waters of SMS *Dresden*, he ordered the *Dresden* to meet him at Easter Island. Von Spee's signal to the *Dresden* was intercepted by a British station in Fiji however, and it provided the British with much-needed intelligence as to von Spee's whereabouts, and of his likely movements. SMS *Dresden* arrived at Easter Island on October 11th, and von Spee and his squadron arrived at the rendezvous on the 12th. Finally, SMS *Leipzig* arrived with three colliers on the 14th, having heard about the rendezvous at Easter Island from SMS *Dresden*. The German East Asiatic Squadron was now once again at full strength.

Easter Island was Chilean, and therefore neutral territory but the inhabitants had not yet been informed of the outbreak of the war. Von Spee did not wish to inform them of the existence of hostilities because the administrator of the local island ranch was English. Maintaining cordiality throughout the visit, von Spee remained six days on Easter Island and left the community no wiser about the war when the squadron put back to sea again on October 18th, now headed for the Juan Fernandez Islands.

After a stop at the Juan Fernandez Islands, von Spee took the German East Asiatic Squadron back to sea again on October 28th, departing from Más Afuera Island (modern Alejandro Selkirk Island). On October 30th, the coast of South America came into view at last, and von Spee could take pride in having completed a prolonged cruise under difficult wartime conditions. Von Spee's squadron had steamed 12,000 across the Pacific without running short of fuel, or essential supplies, and without encountering any significant mechanical breakdowns, while still ensuring the health and morale of the ship's crews.[10] The movement of a powerful squadron of warships with significant demand for coal, and other supplies, through a vast ocean where there were no friendly ports after leaving German waters in Micronesia, was a notable logistical achievement. The secrecy by which von Spee's movements were conducted also required the allied navies in the Pacific to keep large numbers of warships on stations where a sudden descent upon a coast could prove disastrous, and thus kept many allied vessels away from other important duties. The allies lack of knowledge about von Spee's whereabouts actually delayed the departure of Australian and New Zealand troop convoys in the South Pacific Ocean.

When Admiral von Spee left Pagan Island in the Mariana Islands he had faced a choice and made an important decision. Given the likelihood that Japan would honour its alliance with Great Britain, and enter the war, he could have dispersed his squadron and sent each vessel on its own way to engage in commerce raiding across the Pacific, or he could have concentrated his force to maintain a fleet in being with which to engage, and perhaps destroy less-powerful enemy ships, or evenly matched allied naval squadrons. Von Spee chose to concentrate his ships and embark on a perilous voyage home to Germany by way of Cape Horn. Along the way though, he had hoped to take advantage of the strengths of his German East Asiatic Squadron's overall efficiency, prowess at gunnery, and high morale to attack and destroy enemy vessels. Hence, his descent upon German Samoa, so recently conquered by New Zealand forces, in hopes of catching a major allied naval target, perhaps even HMAS *Australia*, riding at anchor in Apia harbour. When that proved fruitless von Spee moved on through French Polynesia, and then on to Chile's Easter Island on his way to the South American coast, where he hoped to find the supplies he needed to round Cape Horn, and then commence a dash through the Atlantic back to Germany.

The British, Australian, Japanese, and Canadian navies had been patrolling in the Pacific Ocean looking for von Spee's ships without success. However, after von Spee stopped at Easter Island the Admiralty was convinced that the German East Asiatic Squadron was headed for South America, and probably for Chile, where there was some pro-German sentiment. The Admiralty had few ships to spare for South America, as the overwhelming naval might of Great Britain had to remain in home waters lest the German High Seas Fleet mount a sortie, and successfully attack the British Grand Fleet. As an island nation, Britain's political and military leaders knew that everything depended upon the ability of the Royal Navy to successfully defend the kingdom from the German navy poised across the North Sea. With so few ships available for more remote service some older, and even obsolete, ships had to be pressed back into service and assigned to overseas British trade routes, to protect

British merchantmen in foreign seas bringing needed supplies to Britain. In the result, the Royal Navy was very thin in places other than the North Sea, and that, in turn, jeopardized the prospects of any British squadron that had to face the powerful German East Asiatic Squadron. As the noted American theorist Mahan had once said; ". . . it is not possible to win a great victory while trying to maintain a show of force everywhere."[11]

Among the obsolete vessels that were restored to service in the Royal Navy were two old armoured cruisers that had seen much better days, HMS *Good Hope*, and HMS *Monmouth*. Built in 1902, HMS *Good Hope* was a 14,100-ton vessel that could make 23 knots. She was armed with two 9.2-inch guns and sixteen 6-inch guns. However, her 6-inch guns were in broadside casements, and only her two 9.2-inch guns were arrayed on the centre line of the ship, and thus were able to fire to each side of the vessel.[12]

The 9800 ton HMS *Monmouth* was armoured as well but only had seven 6-inch guns, which left her severely under-gunned as a cruiser. Both ships were brought up to strength with reservists at the outbreak of the war but they had no real opportunities for intensive training.[13] Four RCN Midshipmen who had been assigned to HMS *Suffolk* at Halifax at the outbreak of the war were subsequently transferred to HMS *Good Hope* when it became the flagship of Rear Admiral Sir Christopher Cradock, the commander in chief on the North America and West Indies Station.

In September, Admiral Cradock was also appointed the RN commander on the South American Station, and he was warned that von Spee and his German East Asiatic Squadron might be headed there. To ensure that Cradock would have sufficient firepower in the South Atlantic, and South Pacific, to engage von Spee, the Admiralty assigned to him the light cruiser HMS *Glasgow*, an efficient cruiser with a permanent RN crew, and the pre-dreadnought battleship HMS *Canopus*, which was obsolete but was armed with four 12-inch guns, and twelve 6-inch guns. Rounding out Cradock's South American force was the armed merchant cruiser HMS *Otranto*, a converted passenger liner armed with eight 4.7-inch guns.[14]

When it became clear that von Spee was making for the South American coast Admiral Cradock brought his small squadron around Cape Horn and sailed up the Chilean coast looking for the German cruisers. A concern arose (mistakenly, as it turned out) that the engines on HMS *Canopus* were worn out, and that the ship could not maintain speed with the other vessels of the squadron, so Cradock instructed HMS *Canopus* to follow north with the squadron's colliers at a slower pace. In the meantime, Cradock proceeded north flying his flag in HMS *Good Hope* and keeping in company with HMS *Monmouth*, HMS *Glasgow*, and HMS *Otranto*. Without the *Canopus*, Cradock's squadron was seriously outmatched by the German East Asiatic Squadron, but Cradock probably hoped to catch individual German units and finish them off before they could be supported by the major units of the German squadron.

On October 31st off Coronel, Chile, the British squadron picked up signals from SMS *Leipzig*, seemingly alone, and Admiral Cradock decided to hunt down the *Leipzig* before she could rendezvous with the main units of Admiral von Spee's squadron. However, the *Leipzig* was not alone, and when HMS *Glasgow* went to identify suspicious smoke on the horizon she found SMS *Leipzig* in company with SMS *Scharnhorst*, and SMS *Gneisenau*, the major units of the German East Asiatic Squadron.

Von Spee held off from attacking the British squadron until SMS *Dresden*, and SMS *Nurnberg* could be brought up into the German line of battle. Admiral Cradock's only hope was to close quickly with the German warships, and hope that the lighter armament of his squadron could find their mark and disable one or more of the major German ships before the British squadron was overwhelmed.

Initially, the two squadrons were formed in two lines separated by 18,000 yards of sea, with *Good Hope, Monmouth, Glasgow,* and *Otranto* facing *Scharnhorst, Gneisenau, Leipzig* and *Dresden*. As the sun crept into the sea, and the fading light outlined the British warships in relief, the German squadron opened fire with the 8.2-inch guns of the German armoured cruisers at a range of 12,000 yards. The German East Asiatic Squadron had highly trained crews, and excellent gunnery – the *Gneisenau* had won the Kaiser's Gold Cup, the preeminent prize in the German Navy for gunnery. Von Spee's ships soon found the range of the British squadron and both HMS *Good Hope*, and HMS *Monmouth* were hit repeatedly. One of the 9.2-inch guns on the Good Hope was put out of action early in the engagement, which cut the British squadron's heavy armament in half. The 6-inch guns of the British squadron were ineffective against the Germans, and the heavier weight of the German firing soon began to tell against the British. The completely vulnerable *Otranto* was straddled by shot from the *Gneisenau* and she pulled out of the British line to save herself. HMS *Monmouth* caught on fire, and sagged out of the line of battle, listing to port. Meanwhile, concentrated fire from SMS *Scharnhorst* had turned HMS *Good Hope* into a charnel ship, the 6-inch gun crews fighting until the flames or steel shards stopped them. At 7:42 PM, with the ship having been turned into a floating wreck, HMS *Good Hope* turned and sped towards the German line, disrupting their fire, and forcing the German warships to turn away. After that brief respite SMS *Scharnhorst* and SMS *Gneisenau* returned and raked the *Good Hope* with broadside after broadside, forcing her engines to stop, and her guns to fall silent as she burned in the early night. At 7:53 PM the fires found the *Good Hope*'s magazine and a huge explosion rent the ship, sending her to the bottom of the ocean.[15] The four RCN midshipmen serving aboard HMS *Good Hope* were lost, and they became the first Canadian casualties of World War One.

HMS *Monmouth*, disabled by German fire, had drifted out of the battle and that left only HMS *Glasgow* in the British line of battle.

Incredibly, the *Glasgow* had suffered only minimal damage, and although she was hit five times by enemy shells none of those hits had disabled the ship. Although *Glasgow* had primarily exchanged fire with the German light cruisers *Dresden* and *Leipzig* the *Glasgow* did manage one hit on the *Gneisenau*, but it did not cause any serious damage.

At 8:30 PM *Glasgow* broke off the action and searched for the *Monmouth*. When *Monmouth* was discovered the *Glasgow* saw that the *Monmouth* was badly damaged but that her damage control parties were getting a handle on the ship's damage, and there was a chance that in the night HMS *Monmouth* might evade the German cruisers who were still hunting for her. The *Glasgow* however, could not face the superior German threat alone, and she left the *Monmouth* to her fate and went off to find the *Otranto*. HMS *Monmouth* might have escaped but for the late arrival into the battle zone of SMS *Nurnberg*, which had missed the main action due to the state of the *Nurnberg*'s propulsion system, which had prevented the *Nurnberg* from closing with the rest of the squadron before the battle. But now, the *Nurnberg* arrived at the battle zone, and suddenly found itself near the badly wounded HMS *Monmouth*, which was underway, and had her repair parties working feverishly to effect emergency repairs.

Nurnberg waited to see if the British ship would surrender and kept its searchlight focussed on the white ensign flying from the ship as if beseeching the surviving British officers to strike their colours. But the *Monmouth* would not strike her colours, and therefore she remained legitimate prey. With HMS *Monmouth* refusing to surrender and, indeed, preparing to turn about to utilize her remaining starboard battery against the *Nurnberg*, Captain von Schonberg decided he had no choice and he opened fire on *Monmouth*, ripping into her hull and sending her to the bottom at 10 PM.[16] By 10:15 PM von Spee had decided that the remaining British warships had probably escaped and he broke off the action. Von Spee remained concerned about the old battleship HMS *Canopus*, which he knew was in the vicinity, and he decided not to proceed further south in order to avoid running into her, and her potentially superior armament. Far to the south, much farther away than von Spee had assumed, Captain Grant of HMS *Canopus* decided that his primary duty following Admiral Cradock's defeat was to shepherd the withdrawal of HMS *Glasgow* and HMS *Otranto*, and together with his accompanying colliers to beat a retreat to Port Stanley in the Falkland Islands, on the other side of Cape Horn. That is where the surviving vessels of Admiral Cradock's squadron now sought refuge.[17]

After the battle, von Spee stopped briefly at Coronel, Chile, before returning to Más Afuera Island in the Juan Fernandez group in early November. While stopped at Más Afuera Island, von Spee had SMS *Titania* fitted out as a raider and under her commander, Captain Friedrich Vogt, *Titania* cruised the Chilean coast, taking one sailing vessel with a cargo of coal as a prize. However, *Titania* was too slow to make the anticipated dash home to Germany through the Atlantic Ocean, and so Admiral von Spee ordered her to be scuttled at Más Afuera on November 19th.[18]

Cradock's defeat vindicated von Spee's decision to keep his fleet in being, and to attempt to use it to defeat an equivalent or lesser British naval force. The German victory at the Battle of Coronel was the most significant naval victory of the Imperial German Navy in World War One, and it confirmed German local naval superiority in the waters off of South America. Von Spee could now threaten British mercantile operations of the coasts of South America, and particularly the trade from Argentina, which was the source of much of Britain's foodstuffs.

The defeat at Coronel was also a great psychological blow to the prestige of the Royal Navy. In the Admiralty, professional opinion blamed Cradock, who died in the battle, for the defeat because he engaged a superior force without waiting for the old battleship *Canopus* to come up and join his line. Regardless, however, it remained a stunning setback for the Royal Navy, and immediate action was required by the Admiralty to retrieve the situation.

The solution that the First Lord of the Admiralty, Winston Churchill, and the First Sea Lord, Admiral Jacky Fisher, decided upon was to detach two powerful battlecruisers from Admiral John Jellicoe's Grand Fleet, and to send them south with escorts to find and destroy von Spee's squadron. Accordingly, orders were issued to HMS *Inflexible*, and HMS *Invincible*, to sail from home waters to the South Atlantic Ocean, and to search for the German East Asiatic Squadron. The two battlecruisers were powerful vessels, and between them mounted eight 12-inch guns, more than enough to defeat the *Scharnhorst* and the *Gneisenau*. The two battlecruisers were placed under the command of Vice Admiral Sir Frederick Doveton Sturdee, flying his flag aboard HMS *Invincible*.

After an uneventful voyage, Sturdee arrived at Port Stanley in the Falkland Islands on December 7th with his two battlecruisers, and the cruisers HMS *Carnarvon*, HMS *Bristol*, and HMS *Glasgow*. The squadron began coaling immediately and continued coaling on the following morning, December 8, 1914.

Meanwhile, the German East Asiatic Squadron had entered the South Atlantic Ocean after rounding Cape Horn and had begun its long journey north to Germany. However, von Spee decided to attack the Falkland Islands on the way, hoping to add to his coal supplies. When von Spee told his captains about his plan some of them demurred because they felt that intelligence on British dispositions at the Falklands was insufficient. Nevertheless, von Spee decided to forge ahead with an attack on the British colony. The operation was scheduled for the morning of December 8, 1914. That morning von Spee detached the *Gneisenau* and the *Nurnberg* to carry out the attack on Port Stanley. When the warships approached the island, however, they spied the tall radio masts that could mean only one thing – powerful British capital ships were at anchor in Port Stanley![19]

The *Gneisenau* and the *Nurnberg* had found the British squadron in a vulnerable condition, as the ships were coaling in preparation for an extended ocean search. Now, here were the Germans on their doorstep. The British squadron quickly reacted by preparing for sea and at 8:30 AM the order was given to proceed to sea. At 9:20 AM HMS *Canopus*, which had been beached at Port Stanley as a stationary battery, opened fire, and a ricochet shot struck the funnel of *Gneisenau*, causing only minor damage.[20]

SMS *Gneisenau*, and SMS *Nurnberg*, returned to the German East Asiatic Squadron, and the Germans attempted to flee but the British squadron was soon in hot pursuit. The British cruisers HMS *Kent*, and HMS *Glasgow* left the harbour first and then shortly before 10 AM the battlecruisers HMS *Inflexible*, and HMS *Invincible*, sailed with the cruisers HMS *Carnarvon* and HMS *Cornwall*, leaving behind the armed merchant cruiser HMS *Macedonia* and the beached HMS *Canopus* to defend the port. From the halyards of HMS *Invincible* Admiral Sturdee raised the signal 'General Chase'.

SMS *Leipzig* was slowing the progress of the German East Asiatic Squadron's escape but even if she had been left behind the speed of the remaining ships under von Spee's command could not outrun the British battlecruisers. Von Spee had gambled on easy prey at Port Stanley but now he was trapped by a superior force and the intact German squadron had no means of escape. His choices now were to keep the squadron together and hope (a forlorn hope) that he could bring the squadron within the range of the German guns and then one or two lucky shots might disable the British battlecruisers. Alternatively, he could scatter the squadron and allow each individual ship to attempt an independent escape. If he kept his force concentrated the likelihood was that the British battlecruisers would make short work of his entire force, and if he scattered his squadron the British had enough ships to pursue each one individually with an equal or superior force. Neither choice was palatable, but the German Admiral decided to keep his force together for the battle.

The Germans were able to keep ahead of the British through the morning because Admiral Sturdee was forced to reduce the speed of his battlecruisers in order to allow his cruisers to close with his flagship. However, seeing that he could not both gain on his German quarry and reduce speed sufficiently to allow his cruisers to catch up he decided to accelerate and catch the Germans, and he ordered speed increased to 26 knots on the two battlecruisers, and on the swift cruiser *HMS Glasgow*. Von Spee set his course so that smoke would obscure the ability of the British battlecruisers to determine the fall of their shot. Finally, at 12:50 PM Admiral Sturdee ordered his battlecruisers to open fire and the artillery duel commenced.[21]

At first, the British naval artillery was ineffective but the British pursuit was dogged, and relentless, and von Spee saw that his light cruisers were beginning to fall behind. He determined that his light cruisers had the best chance of escaping and so at 1:20 PM he released the light cruisers and ordered them to try to escape. The light cruisers heeled to starboard while von Spee took the two armoured cruisers to port. The battle now began in earnest with the British battlecruisers and the German armoured cruisers in range of each other. German gunnery was superior to British gunnery and von Spee scored first, hitting *HMS Invincible* with a shell from the *Scharnhorst*. Sturdee then moved his battlecruisers out of German range but still within British range and hit both the *Scharnhorst* and the *Gneisenau*.[22]

By 3 PM the two German armoured cruisers and the two British battlecruisers were engaged in a slugging match, blasting each other with high-explosive shells. Then a fine square-rigged ship flying neutral colours intruded upon the scene, blissfully unaware that a naval battle was underway! It soon fled. The battle continued and the British lyddite high-explosive shells began to tell on the German ships, which were wrecked and on fire by the time von Spee ordered *Gneisenau* to attempt to escape at around 6 PM, while he turned the *Scharnhorst* towards the British battlecruisers. Von

Spee hoped that the sacrifice of the *Scharnhorst* would give the *Gneisenau* a chance to escape. The *Scharnhorst* was too far gone, however, to reach the British line of battle and she rolled over and sank. The *Gneisenau*, alone now, did not last much longer. Incapable of maintaining speed, she was caught by both the *Inflexible* and the *Invincible*, who were joined now by HMS *Carnarvon*, and together the three British ships pounded *Gneisenau* until finally Captain Maerker ordered the ship scuttled. The charges were fired and she sank at 6 PM, the crew cheering their Kaiser as their ship succumbed to the deep.[23]

Meanwhile, the three German light cruisers had attempted to make their escape but they were hotly pursued by the British cruisers *Glasgow*, *Kent*, and *Cornwall*. HMS *Glasgow* concentrated fire on SMS *Leipzig*, and by alternately closing and increasing the range the *Glasgow* forced the *Leipzig* to manoeuver, thus slowing the *Leipzig* enough to allow HMS *Cornwall* to come into action, with the result that the two British warships soon pounded the German cruiser into a wreck. She succumbed to the sea after Captain Haun ordered her scuttling at around 9:50 PM.[24]

SMS *Nurnberg* was chased by HMS *Kent*, an old cruiser that strained to overtake the much more modern German cruiser. It seemed that thickening mists would allow *Nurnberg* to escape the fate of the *Leipzig* but suddenly two of *Nurnberg*'s boilers exploded, sealing her fate. HMS *Kent* caught her and pounded her into submission with its 6-inch guns. Captain von Schonberg struck his colours in order to give his crew a chance to escape a watery fate but none of the *Nurnberg*'s lifeboats were serviceable, and at 7:30 PM the *Nurnberg* sank.[25]

Of the German light cruisers, only SMS *Dresden* was able to escape destruction, owing to the better condition of her engines, and she disappeared to the south.

Count von Spee's decision to attack Port Stanley was a serious miscalculation that cost him his command, and his own life, as well as the lives of many of the men who served with him including his own two sons who served with him in the German East Asiatic Squadron. Poor intelligence concerning British warship movements deprived him of any warning that superior British units were on the way to intercept him. Nor was he helped by the German High Seas Fleet, which did not put any pressure on the Royal Navy in British home waters during von Spee's passage across the Pacific and into the Atlantic. Had the German Navy been more aggressive in the North Sea, the Admiralty might have been more reluctant to despatch two capital ships to the South Atlantic.

As it was, the victory of Admiral Sturdee at the Battle of the Falklands was the most significant British naval victory since Trafalgar, and it left the Royal Navy and its allies in strategic control of the oceans. Germany would threaten Great Britain later in the war with its U-boat campaign until new strategies were employed to mitigate that threat, but the German surface fleet would never again pose a threat commensurate with the threat that the German East Asiatic Squadron had provided in the early days of the war. The sole general fleet sortie of the German High Seas Fleet that resulted in a general fleet engagement occurred at Jutland in 1916, and it ended in a strategic defeat for the German fleet because the High Seas Fleet never again ventured out from its safe harbours to do battle with the Royal Navy.

NOTES

[1] Massie, *Castles*, 183

[2] Clement, 20

[3] Quoted in Tucker, 275

[4] Churchill, *Crisis*, 185

[5] Mahan, 329, fn

[6] Massie, *Castles*, 191

[7] Clement, 73. The Imperial Cable System was jointly owned by Great Britain, Canada, Australia, and New Zealand.

[8] The Germans spoke only French or English to the local inhabitants to maintain their ruse.

[9] Massie, *Castles*, 192

[10] Massie, *Castles*, 195

[11] Mahan, 414

[12] Geoffrey Bennett, *Coronel and the Falklands*, Pan Books, London, 1967, 16

[13] Bennett, 18

[14] Bennett, 18

[15] Barrie Pitt, "The Battle of Coronel" in *History of the First World War*, Vol. 2 No. 3, BPC/Purnell, Bristol (UK), 1970, 517

[16] Pitt, 518

[17] Stephenson, 40

[18] Ohrdruf, "SMS Titania – Unlisted German Raider, 1914," *Axis History Forum*, https://forum.axishistory.com/[accessed February 8, 2021]

[19] David Mason, "Converging of the Fleets" in *History of the First World War* Vol. 2, No. 3, BPC/Purnell, Bristol (UK), 1970, 525

[20] David Mason, "Battle of the Falklands" in *History of the First World War*, Vol. 2, No. 3, BPC/Purnell, Bristol (UK), 1970, 528 [afterwards Mason: *Falklands*]

[21] Mason, *Falklands*, 528

[22] Mason, *Falklands*, 529

[23] Mason, *Falklands*, 535

[24] Mason, *Falklands*, 535

[25] Mason, *Falklands*, 536

11. The South Pacific 1914-15

The South Pacific was also an important theatre of allied naval operations in the 1914-15 Pacific naval campaign and, as in the North Pacific, the British Admiralty was forced to rely upon Japan to provide some of the necessary naval resources to protect the imperial troop convoys, and to search for the German raiders. On August 26, 1914, the IJN despatched the battlecruiser HIJMS *Ibuki*, and the light cruiser HIJMS *Chikuma* to Singapore, to help support the Royal Navy in the search for enemy raiders. Shortly afterwards, the *Ibuki* was assigned to provide cover for the ANZAC[1] troop convoy, and for the allied troop convoys from French Indochina, while the *Chikuma* was ordered to patrol into the Indian Ocean as far west as Ceylon in a search for German raiders.[2] Subsequently, the very real concerns about the presence of German raiders prompted the Japanese Admiralty to despatch the battleship HIJMS *Satsuma*, and the light cruisers HIJMS *Yahagi*, and HIJMS *Hirado*, to patrol off Australia in the search for enemy warships and auxiliaries.

In November, the British Admiralty still found that its resources were stretched far too thin, and the IJN was asked to assume the temporary theatre command in the Indian Ocean, east of 90 degrees east longitude. Vice Admiral Tochinai Sojiro assumed command of a Japanese naval squadron consisting of the battlecruisers HIJMS *Ibuki* and HIJMS *Ikoma*, three armoured cruisers, HIJMS *Tokiwa*, HIJMS *Yakuma*, and HIJMS *Nisshin*, and three light cruisers, HIJMS *Hirado*, HIJMS *Yahagi*, and HIJMS *Chikuma*. This powerful group remained in the Indian Ocean theatre until the threat to allied shipping vanished with the destruction of the German cruisers SMS *Emden*, and SMS *Konigsberg*.[3]

However, the naval operation in the South Pacific and Indian Oceans that was of the most critical importance to the war effort in 1914, was the transportation of the ANZAC troop convoy to the war fronts in Europe, and the Near East. The Admiralty had suggested to New Zealand that its troop convoy should get underway on September 20, 1914, under naval escort to Western Australia, where it would meet up with the Australian troop convoy. However, the only escorts that the British Admiralty could provide for New Zealand were three obsolete cruisers currently stationed in New Zealand and Australia, HMS *Philomel*, HMS *Pioneer*, and HMS *Psyche*, all built in 1889 or 1890, and each of them obsolete by the beginning of World War One. With von Spee's German East Asiatic Squadron unleashed and prowling somewhere in the Pacific Ocean there was considerable anxiety in New Zealand about the adequacy of the proposed escort for the New Zealand troop convoy should it meet with the German cruiser squadron at sea. When von Spee took the German East Asiatic Squadron past New Zealand-occupied German Samoa he exacerbated the anxiety over the protection available for the New Zealand troop convoy.

The British Admiralty did arrange for the armoured cruiser HMS *Minotaur*, and the battlecruiser HIJMS *Ibuki*, to rendezvous at Freemantle, in Western Australia, with the Australian and New Zealand troop convoys and to protect them on their voyage across the Indian Ocean, waters where the cruisers SMS *Emden*, and SMS *Konigsberg*, were known to be active. However, there was no equivalent protection for the troop convoys on their journey to Freemantle and that was a matter of concern to both Australia and New Zealand, and especially for the latter.

The Admiralty had directed HMS *Philomel*, and HMS *Psyche* to convoy the New Zealand troops from Wellington to Australia.[4] However, the Australian government began to question even the safety of its own troop transports that were carrying Australian soldiers in Australian coastal waters. On September 24th, shortly after the departure of the New Zealand troop convoy to Australia, the Governor General of Australia cabled his counterpart across the Tasman Sea, the Governor General of New Zealand, to advise him that the Australian government now considered that the Tasman

Sea was unsafe. Upon receipt of this advice, the New Zealand government immediately recalled the New Zealand troopships that were already underway and prohibited those waiting to leave from departing until a secure escort could be arranged. As a consequence, the British Admiralty was forced to despatch HMS *Minotaur*, and HIJMS *Ibuki* to New Zealand to assist HMS *Philomel* and HMS *Psyche* in escorting the ten New Zealand troop transports to Western Australia.[5]

The New Zealand troop convoy sailed from Wellington on October 16th with *Minotaur*, *Ibuki*, and the two light cruisers as an escort. The New Zealand ships arrived at King George Sound in Western Australia on October 28th, and on November 1st the entire ANZAC troop convoy got underway with HMS *Minotaur*, HIJMS *Ibuki*, HMAS *Sydney*, and HMAS *Melbourne* as escorts.[6] Von Spee's unknown whereabouts had certainly delayed the sailing of ANZAC troop convoy, and it had particularly delayed the New Zealand component of the convoy, but poor German intelligence prevented von Spee from attempting to physically interfere with the passage of the troop convoys.

The IJN was also called upon for assistance in another matter in the South Pacific Ocean during the early months of World War One. The emergency concerned a violent mutiny of the Indian Army troops in the Singapore garrison. On February 15, 1915, the 5th Light Infantry Regiment, a Muslim unit of the Indian Army, mutinied prior to its scheduled transfer to garrison duties in Hong Kong and the troops shot their officers. The mutineers took over their own barracks, except for the commandant's residence where some of the Europeans took shelter and resisted the mutineers. Although the 5th Light Infantry constituted the bulk of the Singapore garrison, the local Malay and Chinese volunteer force remained loyal to the Crown, as did the Police Force, which was largely Indian in composition. Those units, together with sailors from the Royal Navy vessels that were in port, formed a resistance that prevented the mutineers from entering the city of Singapore itself.[7] An immediate call for assistance went out over the wireless, and the French, Russian, and Japanese navies all responded. The IJN despatched HIJMS *Otawa*, and HIJMS *Tsushima* to Singapore, where the Japanese warships operated together with the FS *Montcalm*, and a Russian vessel, to help the British to restore order in the garrison.

The colonial government in Singapore also conscripted residents during the mutiny, including Japanese citizens who were resident in Singapore. The army mutiny was eventually put down with force, and quite a few of the mutineers were subsequently executed by the British, while those who did not surrender but who fled into the jungle were tracked down by Dayak head-hunters who were brought in from the British colonies on the neighbouring island of Borneo to hunt down the mutineers.[8]

The Japanese Navy rendered a significant contribution in maintaining allied control in the Pacific and Indian Oceans during the war. Japanese naval superiority served to frustrate any plans that von Spee might have formulated to play a significant role in the waters of the Far East, and forced the German East Asiatic Squadron to attempt a return to Germany.

Unquestionably the results of the Pacific Naval War of 1914-15 proved the value to the British Empire of the Anglo-Japanese Alliance. When the war started the Germans had powerful ships in the Pacific, and those ships had the ability to cause real havoc with allied shipping. In addition, the potential also existed for the Germans to interfere with the passage of allied troop convoys. However, the entry of Japan into the war as an allied belligerent restored overwhelming allied naval superiority in the Pacific Ocean.

Although the IJN did not directly engage the German navy, or the Austro-Hungarian navy, in battle (except at Tsingtao) its presence forced Admiral von Spee to abandon operations in the Pacific and to head south-east to Cape Horn in an attempt to return to Germany. Thus, the Royal Navy was able to keep its major forces concentrated in home waters, to face the threat of the German High Seas Fleet across the North Sea, while still maintaining naval superiority in the Pacific and Indian Oceans through the agency of the Imperial Japanese Navy.

The First Lord of the Admiralty, Winston Churchill, recognized the significance of the Japanese contribution to allied operations in the Pacific and Indian Oceans at the beginning of the war, writing to the Japanese naval attaché in London, Admiral Oguri Kosaburo on March 28, 1915, to commend the IJN for its sterling assistance to the allied cause.[9]

But Churchill was well aware the RN remained weak beyond India, and he wanted to ensure that the Japanese remained fully committed to the alliance. So he made a point of deliberately stating to the Japanese naval attaché Churchill's belief that if Great Britain required further assistance from Japan Britain could have confidence that Japan would provide that assistance.[10]

NOTES

[1] ANZAC is an acronym for the Australian and New Zealand Army Corps.

[2] Stephenson, 181

[3] Stephenson, 52, 183. SMS *Konigsberg* based in German East Africa (modern Tanzania) took refuge in the Rufiji River. Two RN monitors that were sent into the river managed to severely damage the cruiser, following which her crew scuttled her in the river.

[4] Clement, 83

[5] Christopher Dowling, "Clearing the Pacific" in *History of the First*

World War, Vo. 1, No. 12, BPC/Purnell, London/Bristol (UK), 1969, 338; Clement, 133

[6] Dowling, 340

[7] H H Wilson and J A Hamerton, "The Singapore Mutiny" in *History of the First World War*, Vol. 2, No. 14, BPC/Purnell, Bristol (UK), 1969, 824

[8] Wilson and Hamerton, 825. The cause of the mutiny remains obscure. This particular garrison regiment was made up of Islamic soldiers, although the British Indian Army did not normally create regiments from one religious faith alone. The entry of the Ottoman Empire into the conflict may have caused some of the Muslim Indian soldiers to identify with the cause of the Muslim Caliph, rather than with the Emperor of the British Raj, and the Islamic composition of the regiment may have allowed disaffection within the regiment to quickly spread. It is possible that the recent *Komagata Maru* incidents in both Vancouver, British Columbia, and in India, also may have contributed to the disaffection present among the Islamic Indian troops by emphasizing the existence of racial discrimination within the British Empire. Certainly, weak military leadership within the regiment itself was also present and contributed to the mutiny.

[9] Nish, *Decline*, 146

[10] Nish, *Decline*, 146

12. Conquering the German Pacific Empire

When World War One broke out Germany possessed a vast island empire stretching across Micronesia in the Pacific Ocean. Germany's possessions included the Mariana, Caroline, Palau, and Marshall Islands in the North Pacific. Germany also possessed the continental enclave of Kiaochow on the coast of China, which contained the important city and naval base of Tsingtao, the home base of the German East Asiatic Squadron. In the South Pacific, Germany possessed an even greater extent of island territories, including German Samoa, the Bismarck Archipelago, the German Solomon Islands, German New Guinea, which included the mainland Kaiser Wilhelmsland, Neu Pommern island (modern New Britain), and Neu Mecklenburg island (modern New Ireland), and Nauru island. All of the island territories, with the exception of German Samoa, were administered from German New Guinea, the oldest part of the German Pacific Empire. The fate of this great island empire, however, rested upon the control of the seas. Without the command of the ocean, the German Empire could not retain its oceanic possessions. As the naval theorist Captain Alfred Thayer Mahan explained in his seminal work:

> "Whatever may be the determining factors in strifes between neighbouring continental States, when a question arises of control over distant regions, politically weak, – whether they be crumbling empires, anarchical republics, colonies, isolated military posts, or islands below a certain size, – it must ultimately be decided by naval power, by the organized military force afloat, which represents the communications that form so prominent a feature in all strategy."[1]

The German government had established important naval support facilities in its North Pacific islands, particularly in the Marshall Islands, and the enormous expanse of Micronesia provided Germany with many opportunities to hide both warships and armed merchant cruisers.[2] The conquest of this Pacific island empire was a matter of military necessity from the outset of the war.[3] It was to Australia and the RAN that Great Britain primarily turned to ensure the occupation of the island territories of Germany in the Pacific, and Australia was game to conquer the German territories provided, however, that the first and most important objective remained the destruction of the German East Asiatic Squadron because of the danger that the German fleet posed to the transportation of Australian and New Zealand Army troops to the Near and Middle East, and to Europe.[4]

While the antipodean dominions organized themselves to begin the conquest of the German Pacific territories the Admiralty focussed its first efforts on the destruction of the German wireless network in the Pacific. Vice Admiral Jerram, commander of the RN's China Squadron, despatched the armoured cruiser HMS *Minotaur*, and the light cruiser HMS *Newcastle*, to the western Caroline Islands to destroy the wireless station on Yap Island. On August 12th the two cruisers arrived at Yap, and HMS *Minotaur* bombarded the wireless station, putting it out of action.[5]

Meanwhile, efforts were underway in New Zealand to occupy German Samoa. On August 15th two transports carrying approximately 1300 men departed Wellington, New Zealand for Noumea, Caledonia, a French possession lying north-west of New Zealand and east of Australia. There, the two transports rendezvoused with HMAS *Australia*, HMAS *Melbourne*, and FS *Montcalm*, which then proceeded to escort the troop convoy to Apia, in German Samoa, where the New Zealand troops landed on August 30th. While passing Tonga, they stopped to advise the King of Tonga that a World War had started, much to the King's surprise. The King promptly declared Tonga to be neutral.[6] At Apia, Samoa, the German Governor surrendered the colony to New Zealand without bloodshed when he was confronted with the allied invasion force, and New Zealand quickly established military control over the islands.[7] The occupation ended German control over the wireless station in Samoa. In addition, all German officials were removed from Samoa, and the German commercial establishments were subsequently taken over by New Zealand or were liquidated.[8]

On September 9th HMAS *Melbourne* arrived off Nauru and sent ashore a party of sailors who occupied the island, destroyed the Nauru wireless station, and captured the German administrator.[9] Next on the list was the wireless station at Angaur in the Palau islands, which HMAS *Sydney* visited on September 26th. A party from *Sydney* went ashore and destroyed the wireless station but Australia did not occupy Angaur or any of the other islands of Palau.[10]

The largest and most important German colony in the South Pacific was centred on German New Guinea, and its conquest was an important Australian military objective. On September 11th an Australian naval task force arrived at Neu Pommern island, part of the German New Guinea colony, and landed troops at Kubakaul to seek out and destroy the wireless station located on the island. German Imperial Army officers and local Melanesian troops were present on the island but the Australians, through a ruse, were able to capture the senior German officers that were present and to obtain valuable intelligence. A short, sharp, engagement was subsequently fought at the Battle of Bita Paka, where the superior numbers of Australian troops overwhelmed the German defenders and forced them to surrender. The wireless station at Bita Paka was then put out of commission by the Australian forces. The next day, September 12th, the Australians occupied the capital at Rabaul (Simpsonhafen) as well as Herbertshohe and captured the *Komet*, the Governor of German New Guinea's yacht, which the RAN then took over as HMAS *Una*.[11] The acting Governor, Dr Haber, played out negotiations for the surrender of the colony for a few days but the outcome was inevitable, and on September 21st he surrendered the colony and its dependencies to Australia.[12]

In the following months, Australia consolidated its control of Neu Pommern (renamed New Britain island) and occupied the major points of Germany's New Guinea colony, with landings on Neu Mecklenburg (renamed New Ireland), Madang on the New Guinea mainland, and the German Solomon Islands. However, a German officer in mainland New Guinea, Captain Hermann Detzner, remained in the field with about 20 Melanesian troops and he retreated to the interior where he resisted the Australian occupation until after the end of the war.[13] Detzner's surrender to Australian forces in January, 1919, was the last capitulation by the German army in the field in World War One. Australian casualties in the conquest of German New Guinea were light, only six dead and four wounded. However, on September 14th, the submarine HMAS AE-1 was lost with all hands during the occupation operation, adding 35 deaths to the Australian casualty count. The Germans suffered 31 deaths and 11 wounded, and all but two of the German casualties were among its Melanesian troops.[14]

Both Australia and New Zealand were determined to hold the conquered German territories in the Pacific once they were taken. To facilitate an orderly division of the spoils an accommodation was made between them. New Zealand was to retain any German territories east of 170 degrees of longitude, and Australia was to obtain any German territories west of 170 degrees of longitude.[15] This division of the spoils, however, did not take into account the desires of Japan.

In the North Pacific, the Australians were operationally constrained by the need to first deploy its naval units to protect the New Guinea Expeditionary Force because of the lack of intelligence concerning the whereabouts of Admiral von Spee, and his German East Asiatic Squadron. As a consequence, the commander of the RAN, Vice Admiral Patey, was forced to keep his major units close to Australian waters, and therefore he could not deploy a sufficient naval protection force for an expedition to conquer the North Pacific German territories, nor could Admiral Patey recommend that any expeditionary forces be sent north of the equator unescorted.[16]

Leaving the North Pacific islands unoccupied presented a quandary because the remaining German forces and civilians in the island territories were quite capable of repairing the damaged wireless equipment at Yap and to provide support for German naval forces hiding in the islands. Casting about for a solution to this problem, the British Admiralty noted that the IJN had begun extending its naval patrols in its search for Admiral von Spee, and the Admiralty, therefore, requested that Japan look in at Yap and assess the current condition of the wireless apparatus there. The Japanese Admiralty was quick to comply and a naval force under the command of Rear Admiral Matsumura Tatsuo arrived at Yap on October 7th and found a German naval survey ship, the lightly armed 650 ton SMS *Planet* at the island. The presence of the Japanese forced the German crew to scuttle their ship.[17]

Rear Admiral Matsumura discovered that the Germans had indeed made repairs to the Yap wireless station, following the earlier attack on it by HMS *Minotaur* and HMS *Newcastle*. To prevent any further German attempts to re-establish themselves at Yap, the Imperial Japanese Navy occupied the island.[18] The fact of the Japanese occupation was reported to the British Foreign Office in a communication from Ambassador Greene in Tokyo to the Foreign Secretary, Sir Edward Grey on October 10th, in which he reported that Japan was inquiring whether Australia intended to occupy Yap. If Australia did not intend to occupy Yap the IJN considered that the strategic importance of Yap required that it be occupied, and therefore Japanese forces would remain.[19]

Perhaps realizing that the German North Pacific islands might now fall into Japanese hands by default, and thus deprive the British Empire of war spoils, the British government pressed Australia to occupy Yap island. In addition, Sir Edward Grey advised the Japanese that Australia would occupy Yap Island, and the Japanese Government then advised that it would agree to hold Yap until the Australians came to occupy it, although the IJN wanted to occupy Yap and all of the other German islands in the North Pacific Ocean.[20]

Whitehall now urged Canberra to plan an expedition to conquer and occupy all of the German North Pacific islands. Not quite realizing the urgency of the British request, Australia responded by advising London that Australian troops were available for the mission but the continuing uncertainty about the whereabouts of Admiral von Spee, and his German East Asiatic Squadron, prevented the RAN from providing escorts for a troop convoy to Yap island. Australia suggested that an escort be obtained from the RN's China Squadron at Hong Kong, in lieu of an Australian escort. Australia also suggested that rather than mounting an expedition solely for the purpose of securing Yap Island Australia would prefer to take additional time to assemble a larger force that could effectively occupy all of the German islands north of the equator.

Meanwhile, the public and official opinion in Japan concerning the occupation of the German North Pacific islands began to crystallize around the position that Japan should take and keep the islands. Ambassador Greene cabled Sir Edward Grey on October 12th that Japanese public opinion was coalescing around the idea that Japan should acquire the German islands as part of an oceanic expansion strategy. Greene recommended that Britain should not press Japan to give up any islands that it took from Germany, at least for the present. Ambassador Greene's view corresponded with the views of Winston Churchill, the First Lord of the Admiralty, who wrote to the Colonial Secretary, Lewis Harcourt, on October 18th, advising the Colonial Secretary that the Admiralty did not have a cruiser available to support an operation against Yap and that it would be too difficult to rearrange current missions to make a cruiser available for an expedition to Yap.[21]

The unavailability of British, or Australian, naval vessels for operations in Micronesian waters, and the complete lack of long-range Canadian, or New Zealand, naval capacity meant that it would have to fall to Japan to carry out naval operations in Micronesia. Great Britain had already asked the IJN to occupy the important centre of Jaluit, the capital of the Marshall Islands, which was an important German administrative centre in the North Pacific, and a coaling station for the German East Asiatic Squadron. Vice Admiral Yamaya Tanin commanding the 1st South Seas Squadron with the battlecruisers HIJMS *Kurama*, and HIJMS *Tsukuba*, together with the armoured cruiser HIJMS *Asama*, proceeded to the Marshall Islands where Admiral Yamaya took Eniwetok atoll on September 29th, before arriving at Jaluit, where he informed the residents that Japan was provisionally seizing the island.

At that point, the Japanese government was still unsure whether it should actually take physical possession of the German islands, and therefore Admiral Yamaya quickly departed Jaluit but as the position of Japan's government began to harden on the question of occupying the German North Pacific islands he received new instructions from Tokyo to take and hold Jaluit. Therefore Admiral Yamaya returned on October 2nd and sent ashore an occupation force and removed all of the German colonial officials.[22] No resistance was offered by Germany to the Japanese occupation of the Marshall Islands.

The following week it was the turn of the Caroline Islands, which saw Japanese landings on Ponape (modern Pohnpei), Kosrae, and Truk (modern Chuuk). At Ponape, the main administrative centre for the Caroline Islands, the IJN sent ashore several hundred marines at Kolonia, the capital, and the Japanese marines meticulously searched every home for weapons (and then carefully re-packed everything the marines had disturbed) without finding any arms. At the time of the Japanese invasion, the local Administrator at Ponape had retreated into the interior of the island with a force of local Micronesian troops but after realizing that resistance was futile he emerged two days later with his troops and surrendered to the Japanese.[23] Admiral Yamaya subsequently left approximately 100 Japanese troops at each of the major islands in the Caroline chain that he occupied.[24]

Farther to the west, Rear Admiral Matsumura, in command of the Second South Sea Squadron, consisting of the older battleship HIJMS *Satsuma*, and two cruisers, proceeded to the Palau Islands, where Koror, the capital, was taken on October 7th, and Angaur, the location of an important wireless station that the RAN had earlier disabled, on October 9th. In the Caroline and Marshall islands the initial Japanese practice provided for the removal of all German officials, with many of the foreign traders opting to voluntary leave the islands. Normally, the existing missionaries were left in place to continue their work of proselytizing Christianity in the islands. In Palau, however, the local naval officer who was left in charge implemented harsher conditions. He threatened the local German population with firing squads, the Catholic mission was ransacked, and the local priest was beaten by the Japanese forces. The nuns at the mission fled to the neighbouring island of Babeldaob.[25] Later, in 1915, the German missionaries in Palau were accused of inciting rebellion and expelled. All of the remaining German missionaries in the Caroline, Marshall and Mariana islands were repatriated to Germany in 1919 after the war ended.[26]

The Mariana Islands, the most northerly of the Micronesian possessions of Germany were taken without bloodshed in October. The battleship HIJMS *Katori*, part of the 1st Battleship Squadron of the IJN proceeded to Saipan, the main island and administrative centre, and occupied the island on October 14, 1914.

Thus, before the end of October, the IJN had occupied all of German Micronesia, depriving the German navy of the ability to hide war vessels in its colonial islands. Australia, however, was still labouring under the impression that its forces would be needed to occupy German Micronesia but it was proceeding at such a slow pace that

Australia's preparations no longer mattered. On October 26th the Australians held a military planning conference to organize an occupation expedition to Micronesia without realizing that Japan had already successfully occupied the islands. By November 13th the Australians had organized an expedition force, and they were ready to proceed. However, when Australia suggested to London that it could now proceed to occupy Angaur, in the Palau Islands, London advised Canberra on November 21st that the Japanese were now in possession of Angaur, and that Australian forces were no longer needed. On the same day, Ambassador Greene cabled Sir Edward Grey to say that the Japanese wanted to retain Angaur for their own naval purposes but they were still willing to part with Yap based on the previous commitment made by Japan to withdraw from Yap if the British or Australians desired to occupy it.

The Australian government was nonplussed by the rejection of their offer to occupy Angaur, and Canberra sought clarification from the Colonial Office in London. On November 24th the Colonial Secretary, Lewis Harcourt, bluntly advised Canberra that Australia was not to proceed with any operations north of the equator.[27] That message was confirmed by Japanese Foreign Minister Kato in a communication to Ambassador Greene on December 1st, in which he stated that all of German Micronesia had been occupied by the IJN, and the islands should not be approached by any Australian military expeditions.[28]

Australia and New Zealand both cried foul over this development, asserting that the surrender at Rabaul by the Acting Governor of New Guinea, Dr Haber, had implied that all of the islands above the equator were also surrendered to Australia.[29] But this was a case where the facts on the ground dictated the result. Japan had taken the islands because neither Great Britain nor Australia, had sufficient naval resources in the war theatre to seize the islands when they became ripe for conquest. And, in several cases, Great Britain had asked Japan to assist in neutralizing the use of the islands for German military purposes. The German North Pacific

Islands would thus remain under Japanese occupation. On December 3rd the British government confirmed to the Australian government that Japan would occupy all of the German islands north of the equator, and Australia and New Zealand would occupy all of the German islands south of the equator. As part of this arrangement, Japan conceded to Great Britain that the question of sovereignty over the German North Pacific islands would ultimately have to be determined at the conclusion of the war but in that event, Japan expected that Britain, as Japan's ally, would loyally support any Japanese claim to the former German islands at a future peace conference.[30]

Australia and New Zealand were compelled to accept this *modus vivendi* to divide the German Pacific islands, which was subsequently confirmed by a secret agreement between Great Britain and Japan in February, 1917.[31] Thus, the Japanese participation in the war had conferred an important, and unlooked-for bonus on Japan, which continued to cast covetous eyes on the great expanse of China that lay to the west of the island empire.

Although taking the German Pacific territories was important to the allies, the great prize of the German Pacific empire was the German Concession of Kiaochow, located on the Shantung peninsula along the Chinese coast, and its important city and naval base of Tsingtao. Tsingtao was the home port and main naval base of the German East Asiatic Squadron, although Japan's entry into the war meant that Admiral Count von Spee could no longer base his fleet there because of the overwhelming naval superiority of Japan in Chinese waters. To have returned to Tsingtao from his summer cruise in the Pacific would have resulted in the German squadron being blockaded, with only a limited effect on the overall defence of the colony. As Captain Mahan had stated:

> "Seaports should defend themselves: the sphere of the fleet is on the open sea, its object offense rather than defence,

its objective the enemy's shipping wherever it can be found."[32]

Nevertheless, the possession of the Kiaochow Concession by a significant enemy naval power provided for the possible control of the Yellow Sea, and so its reduction and capture made it an important allied objective. It was also a national objective of Japan to increase its political influence in China, and the conquest of Kiaochow would facilitate that objective.

Great Britain was not prepared to concede that the reduction of the German enclave should be the sole responsibility of Japan however, and on August 12th, even before Japan entered the war, Sir Edward Grey pointedly stated to Japan that if an attack was made on Kiaochow it would have to be done in conjunction with the British Empire.[33] The arrangements for a joint operation against the Kiaochow Concession were set out in an agreement between the two powers on August 24th, although Britain conceded that any British Empire forces would serve under Japanese command, and the Japanese Army commander would hold the title of the Commander-in-Chief of the Allied Forces.[34]

Before the war Tsingtao had developed an excellent reputation as a desirable place to visit on the Chinese coast, owing to its pleasant climate. It was intended by Imperial Germany to be a colonial showcase, as well as a naval fortress, and so it possessed broad European-style tree-lined avenues, which were enhanced by public gardens, and beaches. Germany built attractive public buildings and schools, and the city was home to desirable cafes and beer gardens, with fine hotels for visitors. There was a good commercial harbour for ships and drydock facilities for ship repairs.[35]

The Kiaochow defences were equally impressive. Kiaochow was located on a peninsula and two ranges of hills ran close to the city of Tsingtao, with a wide valley lying in-between. Here, three ferroconcrete forts were built on hills, which were further protected by open batteries of four and six-inch guns. The Bismarck fort, located on the highest hill, was equipped with four 11-inch howitzers in armoured cupolas. At the Bismarck fort, the Germans had built a three-storey underground command post. The Iltis and Moltke forts located to the right and left of the Bismarck fort each held two 9.2 inch guns. Jutting out into the harbour on a spit of land was the Hsia-Ni-Wa fort containing two 9.2 inch guns, and three six-inch guns in revolving turrets, as well searchlights that could be raised or lowered. Lastly, the Germans scattered other open batteries consisting of 9.4 inch and 6-inch guns on adjacent hills near the city.[36] There was a weakness in this defensive line however because the defensive line was only two and one-half miles away from the city, and therefore a breach of this fortified line meant that the city would be lost. The close proximity to the city of the defensive line also rendered the city susceptible to enemy artillery bombardment.[37]

Further outwards from the city the Hai Po River, four miles away from Tsingtao, provided the best natural feature upon which to construct a preliminary line of defence. At the bottom of the slope that led to the river, the Germans constructed six concrete redoubts that were 200 yards in length, which held both field guns and machine guns. The redoubts were joined by trenches, with a reserve trench behind the forward trench, and a revetted escarpment lying before the trenches. A ten-foot-wide ditch at the base of the escarpment was filled with water, and obstacles were also placed there, along with a six-foot wall forward of the ditch. Forward of the wall was a minefield, with an electric wire running through the middle of the minefield that could be used to activate the mines.[38]

The farthest forward defensive work in the peninsula was a trench line constructed along a line of hills that was anchored by a large natural feature, the Prinz Heinrich Hill. This defensive line was too long to be held by the existing garrison, but skirmishers could use the line to delay the advance of an enemy force. The failure of the Germans to fortify Prinz Heinrich Hill, however, was a major omission by the Germans, and that failure undermined the utility of this forward line.[39]

The responsibility for the defence of the Kiaochow Concession in 1914 fell upon the Governor, Captain Zur See, Alfred Meyer-Waldeck. Meyer-Waldeck was a career naval officer who had joined the Kaiserlich Marine in 1884, and he had served in both sail and steam vessels, including, at one point, SMS *Geier*, which operated in the Pacific in 1914, before interning at Honolulu. He was appointed Governor of Kiaochow on August 19, 1911.

As early as July 27th, having been kept apprised by the KM of the deteriorating political situation in Europe, Governor Meyer-Waldeck, had taken steps to prepare the German colony for a siege. He recalled to Tsingtao the East Asiatic Marine Detachment, a German element of the foreign military forces assigned to protect western diplomats in Peking. The East Asiatic Marine Detachment consisted of four companies of infantry and included artillery.[40] Together with German reservists called up for service, and German volunteers who flocked to Tsingtao from all over China, Captain Meyer-Waldeck was able to put together a garrison force of somewhere between 4000 and 6000 men, including 3000 from the 3rd Marine Battalion, and the Marine Artillery. The Germans had 53 heavy guns, 77 light guns, and 47 machine guns to defend the fortress, in addition to the guns on the warships that remained at Tsingtao.[41] The Tsingtao fortress had sufficient stores for a full year, potable water from a pumping station and, in an extremity, wells and a distilling station within Tsingtao itself. On August 19th Berlin advised Captain Meyer-Waldeck to send out the women and children located in Tsingtao and to hold out to the last. Steps were accordingly taken before the hostilities to significantly reduce the civilian population.[42] The Kaiser also sent word to the Meyer-Waldeck, telling him in words that brought to mind his obsession with the so-called 'yellow peril' that it would be a greater shame to His Imperial Majesty if Kiaochow was surrendered to the enemy than if Berlin were to be surrendered[43] Presumably, the Kaiser meant that he could not bear to see a German surrender to an Asiatic race.

The process of isolating Tsingtao, and the surrounding Kiaochow Concession, actually began before Japan's declaration of war on August 23rd. On August 14th and August 24th the Royal Navy cut the undersea cables that connected Tsingtao to the world. However, even with the undersea cables cut it was still possible for the German enclave to communicate with Berlin by sending telegraphs through neutral China via Shanghai, or by sending messengers over the railway line that connected Tsingtao with China. Vice Admiral Jerram had been ordered to bring the RN's China Squadron to Hong Kong from Weihaiwei at the outset of the war, which had provided Captain von Muller of SMS *Emden*, as well as the auxiliary merchant cruisers SMS *Kormoran II* and SMS *Prinz Eitel Friederich* with an opportunity to escape from Tsingtao. However, the British did deploy a destroyer, HMS *Kennet*, to watch Tsingtao, and the *Kennet* fought an inconclusive action with German torpedo boat SMS *S-90* on August 23rd. After Japan's declaration of war, the IJN took immediate steps to blockade the port, and on August 27th a formal blockade of Tsingtao was declared by the Japanese.

The blockade of Tsingtao was established by Vice-Admiral Kato Sadakichi who had with him in the IJN Second Squadron the old battleship HIJMS *Suwo*, which had been originally captured from Russia when Japan took Port Arthur in the Russo-Japanese War. As well, he had HIJMS *Tango*, another old salvaged Russian battleship, HIJMS *Iwami*, originally the Russian *Orel*, and the only modern battleship captured by the Japanese from the Russians. Two older and obsolete ex-Russian vessels, the HIJMS *Mishima* and the HIJMS *Okinoshima* rounded out the core of the Japanese blockading squadron. Admiral Kato also had four armoured cruisers, HIJMS *Chiyoda*, HIJMS *Tokiwa*, HIJMS *Iwate* and HIJMS *Yakumo* plus the protected cruisers HIJMS *Takachiho* and HIJMS *Tone*, together with a few light cruisers. Finally, Admiral Kato also had at his disposal the seaplane carrier HIJMS *Wakamiya Maru*, which was equipped with four seaplanes. To this force was added from the Royal Navy HMS *Triumph*, the old pre-dreadnought British battleship stationed at Hong Kong, and HMS *Usk*, a destroyer.[44]

Against this powerful allied naval force, the Germans had a much weaker coastal defence squadron consisting of four ill-equipped gunboats (SMS *Iltis*, SMS *Jaguar*, SMS *Luchs* and SMS *Tiger*) and the minelayer SMS *Lanting*. The light cruiser SMS *Kormoran* was berthed at Tsingtao but its engines were out of service, and beyond repair, and its armament was stripped to arm the Russian merchant ship *Ryazan*, which had been taken as a prize by SMS *Emden* shortly after the start of the war between Germany and Russia. Once equipped, the *Ryazan* was commissioned into German naval service as the SMS *Kormoran II*. However, the SMS *Komoran II* left Tsingtao before the port was blockaded and it took no part in the defence of the fortress.

The more substantial defensive capability was provided by the torpedo boat SMS S-90, which was armed with torpedoes. A second torpedo boat, SMS *Taku*, was present but she was out of commission as a result of a collision that had occurred the year previously, in 1913. Germany also had three small river gunboats that protected German traders on rivers in the Chinese interior, SMS *Vaterland*, SMS *Tsingtau* and SMS *Otter*, but they were unable to sail to Tsingtao, and they were laid up in Chinese ports from whence some of their crews sought to travel overland to Tsingtao.[45]

Rounding out the squadron, and making it a joint squadron, was the old Austro-Hungarian protected cruiser SMS *Kaiserin Elisabeth*, which, although obsolete, could still be useful for coastal defence purposes because it was armed with two 9.4-inch guns, and six 5.9 inch guns. The SMS *Kaiserin Elisabeth* had been assigned to protect Austro-Hungarian interests in the Far East, where the Austro-Hungarian Empire's only foreign territorial interest was located, a small concession of approximately 0.6 sq. kilometres at Tianjin, which Austria-Hungary had obtained from China as compensation for its participation in the international relief mission during the Boxer Rebellion. With the outbreak of war, the SMS *Kaiserin Elisabeth* was extremely vulnerable, and the German naval port at Tsingtao was the only option open to her commanding officer, Commander Richard Makovicz. The *Kaiserin Elisabeth* arrived at Tsingtao in late July, a few days before the outbreak of the war and the kaiserliche und königliche Kriegsmarine (k.u.k. KM) in Vienna directed Commander Makovicz to place himself under the orders of the German Governor at Tsingtao for the defence of the Kiaochow Concession.

Severe storms in late August and September had an impact on military operations in the Kiaochow area. A severe storm on August 30th had forced a Japanese destroyer, HIJMS *Shirotaye* to ground on Lien Tau Island, south of Tsingtao. The Germans saw that the ship was aground and other Japanese ships were supporting it so the coastal battery at Hsiao-Ni-Wa[46] opened fire scattering the Japanese rescuers. Then, SMS *Jaguar* darted out and destroyed the *Shirotaye* by gunfire on August 31st.[47] Severe storms in September washed out the Shantung railway line and its accompanying telegraph line, further isolating the German concession.

The Japanese military had long been watching the Kiaochow Concession and had obtained good intelligence about the German defensive works. Knowing that the taking of the German colony would require a great effort the Japanese planned for an overwhelming assault, and actually trained for this operation before the war.[48] Beginning on September 2nd the Japanese Army under the command of Lieutenant General Kamio Mitsuomi began landing on the Chinese coast. The first Japanese landings occurred at Lungkow, and then later at Lau Shau Bay. Ultimately, General Kamio would have approximately 50,000 troops under his command for the assault on the Kiaochow Concession, 12,000 horses, 102 heavy siege guns and howitzers, and 42 field and mountain guns.[49] The

Japanese also mounted a railway battery of 11-inch guns on railway carriages.[50] The overwhelming majority of the allied force consisted of Japanese troops but the British Empire also sent a contingent consisting of British troops, and Sikh soldiers from the Indian Army, to participate in the siege.

The initial Japanese landings took place 90 miles away from Tsingtao at Lungkow because General Kamio had envisaged a methodical approach to the siege of Tsingtao. However, by landing so far away from the German colony the Japanese Army violated Chinese neutrality, and caused concerns as far away as Washington regarding the motives of Japan.[51] The allied advance began but it was impeded by storms that rendered the primitive roads impassable. Nevertheless, slow and steady progress was made. By September 17th the Japanese advance had completely cut off Tsingtao from the outside world. On the 19th another landing was made at Lao Shan Bay. On September 23 the Japanese were reinforced by the arrival of the British Empire contingent consisting of troops that had been assigned to Tientsin to protect the diplomatic personnel in China, under the Boxer Protocol of 1901. The British Empire contingent was escorted into the war zone by the battleship *HMS Triumph*, accompanied by the destroyer *HMS Usk*. British Army Brigadier Nathaniel Barnardiston commanded the Imperial contingent, and he served under the command of General Kamio. Likewise, the British naval commander, Captain Fitzmaurice of *HMS Triumph*, served under the command of Admiral Kato throughout the campaign.

The allies began a general advance on September 26th and the joint German and Austro-Hungarian naval force reacted by sailing into Kiaochow Bay from the harbour to bombarded the advancing allied force from SMS *Jaguar*, SMS *S-90*, and SMS *Kaiserin Elisabeth*.[52] The Germans also had a small aerial reconnaissance unit in the person of Lieutenant Gunther Plüschow and a Rumpler Taube aeroplane. He was able to advise the Governor by September 11th that the Japanese advance was progressing quickly.

The Japanese kept close tabs on the German aircraft and put one or more of their own aircraft from the seaplane carrier HIJMS *Wakamiya Maru* into the air each time they detected the German aeroplane in flight. The Japanese also mounted the first air-sea naval attack on September 27th on the ships of the German and Austro-Hungarian force bombarding Japanese troops from Kiaochow Bay, after the Austro-Hungarian protected cruiser joined in the bombardment with her 9.2-inch guns. The Japanese attack, which used bombs converted from artillery shells was unsuccessful but as the first occasion when ships were attacked by aircraft, it marked an important event in naval aviation.[53]

On the 28th of September, a surprise night attack by the Japanese Army resulted in the Germans being pushed off Prinz Heinrich Hill, the German anchor of the farthest trench lines. This was an ominous result and underscored the failure of the German military to fortify Prinz Heinrich Hill during peacetime. On the same day, the Germans scuttled SMS *Komoran I*, SMS *Iltis* and SMS *Luchs* after removing their remaining armaments for land defence. The next day, September 29th, the allies advanced in force and the Germans retreated from the forward trench line, abandoning equipment as they fell back to their interior fortification lines. To cover the retreat a German observation balloon and Plüschow's monoplane were used to spot the Japanese howitzers, and German guns bombarded both the Japanese and the British positions, forcing the British to move their camp. The Japanese targeted both the German balloon and the German aeroplane and succeeded in damaging the balloon cables. Subsequently, the cables parted, and the balloon floated away on October 7th. Although Plüschow tried to compensate with his Taube monoplane the Japanese pilots continually rose to challenge him whenever Plüschow was aloft, which greatly interfered with his ability to conduct aerial spotting.[54]

The Germans did have some success at sea, however. On September 30th the Japanese seaplane carrier HIJMS *Wakamiya*

Maru struck a mine and was badly damaged. She was no longer able to service her seaplanes, and they were removed and relocated to a base on land. The ship was beached but was afterwards repaired. Two Japanese minesweepers were also lost on the same day to mines, and the IJN concluded that some Chinese vessels behaving suspiciously in the vicinity of those losses were actually laying German mines. Accordingly, the Japanese warships sank them to stop further German minelaying.[55]

Meanwhile, the British Empire and Japanese forces had to adjust to serving with one another in a joint operation. After a few friendly fire mistakes, the Japanese Army issued Japanese overcoats to the British troops so that they would not be misidentified. The overcoats also helped the British to stay warm and healthy as the cooler autumn temperatures arrived.[56] The British experienced logistical problems, particularly with respect to rations. Although bully beef and biscuits were always available the bread supply was intermittent, and they rarely had jam or sugar. The Japanese tried to help by supplying some rice, and the British and Indian troops helped themselves to the Chinese sweet potatoes that they found in the fields, which they ate raw. On October 2nd an aide-de-camp to Emperor Taisho visited the British contingent and provided gifts of sake to the officers, and cigarettes to both the officers and the British and Indian Non-Commissioned Officers. The Emperor's aide expressed His Imperial Majesty's great satisfaction for the cooperation that existed between the Japanese and British Empire forces.[57]

In preparation for an all-out assault on Tsingtao, the allied commander, General Kamio, organized his assault forces from north to south as:

- Japanese 29th Brigade
- British Empire Expeditionary Force
- Japanese 24th Brigade
- Japanese 23rd Brigade.

He then proceeded to construct a line of assault trenches to provide for an infantry attack on the German fortifications. He also began bringing up and placing his siege artillery in order to reduce the German fortified positions.

On October 17th the Germans had a final naval success when SMS S-90, under the command of Lieutenant Helmut Brunner, while conducting a night patrol in Kiaochow Bay torpedoed and sank the older Japanese protected cruiser HIJMS *Takachiho* with a heavy loss of life. However, the IJN cut off the return of the S-90 to Tsingtao and the ship was forced to flee south. Brunner subsequently beached and destroyed his ship before moving inland with his crew.[58]

By October 29th General Kamio had put his siege artillery in place and a heavy bombardment of the German fortifications began. The final assault was now imminent. Seeing the handwriting on the wall, Governor Meyer-Waldeck ordered the scuttling of SMS *Tiger* on the 29th. On November 2nd, after firing all of her remaining heavy armament, the Austro-Hungarian protected cruiser SMS *Kaiserin Elisabeth* was scuttled in the Bay, and her crew joined the land defenders. With her went the floating dock and all of the smaller ships except for SMS *Jaguar*.

As the bombardment progressed, the German batteries continued counter-battery fire until they began running out of ammunition on November 2nd. The Japanese bombardment had damaged the electrical station and it was put out of action on November 3rd, causing the city's electric lighting to fail.[59] When the shell supply was exhausted the German and Austro-Hungarian gun crews destroyed their guns. On November 4th the Japanese Army took the pumping station, and the Tsingtao water supply was cut off leaving the garrison to rely solely on well water.[60] By November 5th the minefields and obstacles erected by the Germans had been destroyed by the siege bombardment.[61]

On November 5th Meyer-Waldeck prepared his final despatches to

Berlin, which he gave to Lieutenant Plüschow to fly out of Kiaochow to neutral China.[62] A final report from one of his subordinates on the condition of the defences told the Governor that the end was near.[63] Tsingtao was now doomed. The final infantry assault took place on the night of November 6-7, 1914. Desperate attempts were made by the Germans and Austro-Hungarians to hold the final defence line. SMS *Jaguar*, the last remaining naval ship, fired all of its remaining ordnance to support the defence. The redoubts failed under the force of the bombardment and the infantry attacks and were forced to surrender. The fortresses defences were breached, and the defence became hopeless. Governor Meyer-Waldeck hoisted the white flag as SMS *Jaguar* was scuttled in Kiaochow Bay.

Under the terms of surrender, the Kiaochow Concession was transferred to Japan effective November 10th, and all remaining German and Austro-Hungarian forces became Japanese prisoners of war. The Germans were forbidden to destroy any property in Tsingtao.[64] German and Austro-Hungarian prisoners were well treated by the Japanese, for the most part, and certain changes were made to their incarceration when the United States, as the protecting power for Germany in Japan, sent one of its diplomats, Sumner Welles, to investigate the conditions under which the prisoners were being held. Japan stated publicly that the Kiaochow Concession would remain under Japanese administration while the war lasted, and General Kamio stayed on as the Japanese-appointed Governor General of the territory.[65]

The campaign to conquer Kiaochow brought to the fore some of the hidden strains in the Anglo-Japanese Alliance. Great Britain harboured some mistrust over Japan's intentions with respect to China, a concern that was well-founded as events would show. In the field, at Tsingtao, there had been tensions between the Japanese Army and the British Empire forces, and the Japanese officers formed a low opinion of the quality of the British troops, although they thought somewhat better of the Indian Army troops that the Empire had sent to the campaign.[66] Partly, this attitude on the part of the Japanese may have reflected the close relationship between the Japanese Army and the German Army. During the westernization period in the late nineteenth century, Prussia had provided the trainers for the modern Japanese Army, and the Japanese Army retained a profound respect for its mentors. Indeed, right up until the end of the war the higher echelons of the Japanese Army expected Germany to prevail.

In reality, the British Empire forces did not particularly distinguish themselves during the campaign, and during the final struggle the British were actually pushed back by the Germans on the night of November 5/6, suffering 30 casualties.[67] In contrast to the relations between the allied armies, however, the relations between the IJN and the RN were much different. The IJN held the RN in high regard, and relations between Captain Fitzmaurice of HMS *Triumph*, and Admiral Kato were characterized by cordiality and professional respect throughout the campaign.[68]

The Tsingtao campaign was of great benefit to the British Empire, and its other allies. It is unlikely that Great Britain could have taken the Kiaochow Concession on its own, or even in conjunction with Russia and France, without a great expenditure of resources that it needed elsewhere in the world. Tsingtao was a potential threat to North Pacific shipping as a base for German raiders, and for the German East Asiatic Squadron.

The Tsingtao campaign, however, caused great concern in Peking, as the Chinese Government expressed alarm over the actual and potential infringement of its sovereignty by Japan. The Japanese took over the Shantung Railway as far as Tsinan, some 250 miles from Tsingtao and the Poshan mines. Naturally, China complained about the extent of the Japanese-declared war zone, and it asked for a reduction in size but Japan claimed military necessity required that it retain control of the railway, and Great Britain concurred with Japan in this regard.[69] The Foreign Office in London had been particularly perturbed by the German Charge d'affaires in

Peking, who had requested the United States, as the protecting power for Germany in Japan, to use its good offices to have the railway restored to its German owners.[70] The Foreign Office described that as a transparent attempt by the Germans to regain control of the railway, and as an impertinence.

With the fall of the Tsingtao, the German Pacific Empire was extinguished. The only remaining territorial presence of the Central Powers in the Asia-Pacific region were the extra-territorial concessions that Germany and Austria-Hungary continued to hold in Tianjin, China. Those concessions remained undisturbed until China issued its own declarations of war in 1917, after which the Chinese Government seized and extinguished the concessions.

NOTES

[1] Mahan, 416

[2] Strachan, 453

[3] Dua, 173

[4] Dua, 107

[5] Stephenson, 184

[6] Glen Barclay, A *History of the Pacific, from the Stone Age to the present day*, Sidgwick & Jackson, London, 1978, 151

[7] Christopher Dowling, "Clearing the Pacific," in *History of the First World War*, BPC/Purnell, Bristol (UK), 1969, 336

[8] Barclay, 151

[9] Stephenson, 184; "Capturing German Outposts," ANZAC *Portal*,

https://anzacportal.dva.gov.au/wars-and-missions/ww1/where-australians-served/captured-german-outposts [accessed June 9, 2020]

[10] Stephenson, 198

[11] Stephenson, 513

[12] Dowling, 337

[13] Strachan, 465

[14] Dowling, 337

[15] Strachan, 465

[16] Stephenson, 184

[17] The IJN raised the *Planet* from the depths in 1916.

[18] Stephenson 185

[19] Stephenson, 186

[20] Nish, *Decline*, 144

[21] Stephenson, 192

[22] Francis X Hezel SJ, *Strangers In Their Own Land; A Century of Colonial Rule in the Caroline and Marshall Islands*, University of Hawaii Press, Honolulu, 1995, 146

[23] Hezel, 150

[24] Hezel, 147

[25] Hezel, 150

[26] Hezel, 151

[27] Stephenson, 201

[28] Stephenson, 202

[29] Strachan, 481

[30] Stephenson, 204

[31] Strachan, 483

[32] Mahan, 453

[33] Nish, *Decline*, 134

[34] Nish, *Decline*, 136

[35] Terence Wise, "Tsingtao," in *History of the First World War*, Vol. 1, No. 12, BPC/Purnell, Bristol (UK), 1969, 321

[36] Wise, 321; Stephenson, 210

[37] Stephenson, 216

[38] Wise, 321

[39] Wise, 321

[40] Stephenson, 207

[41] Wise 321; Stephenson, 423

[42] Dua, 168

[43] Nish, *Decline*, 135

[44] Stephenson, 229-232

[45] Stephenson, 234

[46] This battery is also called the Hui tsch-en Huk battery in some works.

[47] Stephenson, 243

[48] Wise, 321

[49] Wise, 321

[50] Stephenson, 680

[51] Stephenson, 247

[52] Stephenson, 282-83

[53] Stephenson, 284

[54] Wise, 324

[55] Stephenson, 356

[56] Professor C T Atkinson, "The British at Tsingtao", in *History of the First World War*, vol. 1, no. 12, BPC/Purnell, Bristol (UK), 1969, 333

[57] Atkinson, 332

[58] Stephenson, 376

[59] Wise, 328

[60] Stephenson, 398

[61] Wise, 328

[62] Lieutenant Plüschow had an extraordinary series of adventures. After crashing in neutral China he travelled by river transport to Nanking where he was feted while preparations for his internment were made. After transport to Tientsin, he eluded the Chinese Army personnel assigned to guard him, and he escaped by train to Shanghai where a young woman he knew, the daughter of a

diplomat, helped him to escape on an American ship. He arrived in San Francisco where local Germans aided his passage to New York. Wary of internment, as he had no papers, he lay low until German confederates were able to assist him to obtain passage on a neutral Italian vessel. However the Italian vessel stopped at Gibraltar and he was made a prisoner by the British, who incarcerated him in England. But Pluschow was able to escape from his POW camp and he made his way to London where he languished around the Thames docks before managing to stowaway on a Dutch ferry that took him to Holland. From there he passed through the neutral Netherlands and arrived back in Germany. Plüschow was the only German POW in either of the two World Wars in the twentieth century to successfully escape from Great Britain.

[63] Stephenson, 406

[64] The surrender ceremony was an entirely Japanese affair. Although a British liaison officer was present, the British commander, Brigadier Barnardiston was not invited to the ceremony.

[65] Nish, *Decline*, 135

[66] Nish, *Decline* 137

[67] Atkinson, 333

[68] Nish, *Decline*, 138

[69] Stephenson, 433; Nish, *Decline*, 139

[70] Dua, 165

13. The Strains in a Wartime Alliance

By the end of 1914, the Central Powers were almost completely banished from the Asia-Pacific Region. Germany had lost all of its colonies to Japan, Australia, and New Zealand, and the Central Powers retained only their minor extra-territorial concessions within China.

In the North Pacific Ocean, Japan was the dominant naval power, and its navy exercised undeniable control of the ocean. The Anglo-Japanese Alliance had served its intended purposes. Japan had acquired new territory in China and a vast oceanic empire, subject to any final dispositions to be made at the post-war peace conference. For Great Britain, the alliance had provided it with the ability to establish naval safety for its possessions over the enormous expanse of the Pacific Ocean. Although the Royal Navy had been defeated at the Battle of Coronel, its subsequent victory at the Battle of the Falkland Islands had wiped clean the stain of that defeat, and the seas had been cleared of any significant German naval threat outside of the North Sea.

But the gains made through the alliance had not come without strains in the relations between the British Empire and the Japanese Empire. The limited assistance that Britain had initially hoped to obtain from Japan had been broadened by Japan's perceptions of its own national interests, and British efforts to restrain Japan had not been welcomed by the Japanese Government.

Great Britain now had to accept that Japan had control of a new enclave on the coast of China, and it was in an excellent position to consolidate its influence not only in Manchuria but farther afield within China. The potential for the displacement of British interests in China by further Japanese economic penetration was readily apparent to policy-makers in London. Furthermore, Great Britain had been forced to acquiesce to Japan's retention of the North Pacific islands that it had seized from the German Empire, much to the displeasure of Australia and New Zealand.

Now that Japan had established its dominance in the North Pacific Ocean, its attention turned back to its main foreign policy objective, which was to acquire paramount influence in China. On January 18, 1915, Japanese Foreign Minister, Kato instructed his emissary in Peking, Eki Hioki, to present the government of President Yüan Shih-k'ai with a list of 21 Demands from Japan. The Twenty-One Demands were listed in five separate groups with the first four groups constituting actual Japanese demands, while the final group was characterized as Japanese wishes, which implied that the last group was negotiable. All of the Twenty-One Demands were an affront to China's status as an independent country but Kato was determined to take advantage of China's weakness, and the inability of the European powers to intervene, in order to establish a predominant Japanese position in China.

The first group of demands required China to confirm that Japan had the right to arrange the future settlement of the status of the German Kiaochow Concession at whatever peace conference was convened at the end of the war. The second group required China to recognize Japanese hegemony in southern Manchuria, and in the eastern portion of Inner Mongolia. In addition, China was required to extend the Japanese lease on the Kwantung Peninsula, which Japan had acquired from Russia as a result of its victory in the Russo-Japanese War. The third group required China to give Japan joint ownership of the Hanyehping iron and coal works. The fourth group purported to prohibit China from alienating any harbour, or coastal region, to a foreign power (at this time Japan feared that the United States would seek a coastal base along the Chinese coast). The fifth and final group, which were characterized as wishes instead of demands, asked China to accept Japanese political and military advisors, to allow Japanese subjects the right to acquire property in China, and that China essentially accept Japanese supervisory control over China.[1] When he received these demands President Yüan was speechless, and he said that their acceptance meant that China would cease to be a country, and the Chinese people would become slaves of Japan.[2]

Japan moved quickly after defeating the Germans at Tsingtao to impose its will on China but it may have been prompted to act quicker than it originally planned because of China's announcement that the war zone China had declared around Kiaochow was to be terminated on January 7, 1915, a decision with which the Japanese government, and particularly the Japanese Army, did not concur. China also argued that Japan's occupation of the Kiaochow Concession must only be of a temporary duration.[3] Japan, however, argued that a reversion of Kiaochow to China could open a door for the return of the Germans to Kiaochow in a post-war settlement.

Primarily, Japan had now decided to take advantage of its temporary supremacy in the Far East to achieve its national goal of expansion into China. Japan noted that the European powers had been able to consolidate their own spheres of influence in a weakened China, with Russia dominant in Outer Mongolia, the British dominant in the Yangtze River valley, and the French dominant in the far south, while Japan had struggled to consolidate its influence in southern Manchuria. Now, in the aftermath of ousting the Germans from Kiaochow, Japan saw a new opportunity to achieve the territorial and economic goals that it had long sought, and which it had been unable to secure by earlier commercial penetration. Foreign Minister Kato was determined to establish Japanese control in the Shantung Peninsula, southern Manchuria, and the eastern part of Inner Mongolia and Kato expected that Britain, as Japans alliance partner, would support Japan in that effort.

For British Foreign Minister Sir Edward Grey the Twenty-One

Demands called for a careful and measured response. He had to balance Great Britain's commitment to the alliance with Japan against Great Britain's commitments to China. Writing to Ambassador Greene in Tokyo Grey advised the ambassador that he wanted Great Britain to be able to say that nothing Japan was doing in China was in conflict with the Anglo-Japanese Alliance, recognizing the reality that Japan's expansion into China was not significantly different from the activities of the European powers in China over the past quarter-century, and even earlier.[4] However, Grey certainly took the view that Japan had gone too far when it proposed to intrude on the British sphere of influence in the Yangtze River valley.

In China, President Yüan sought to develop a strategy to persuade Japan to moderate its demands. He engaged Japan with China in a diplomatic *pas de deux* from January to May of 1915, involving twenty-four separate meetings to discuss the Twenty-One Demands. Next President Yüan publicly leaked the Twenty-One Demands, which the Japanese had insisted should remain confidential, in order to bring the nature of the Japanese demands to the attention of other governments, and to the Chinese public. Thirdly, he sought support from foreign governments, and while the United States was of no great assistance to China,[5] Great Britain did offer some support, suggesting to Japan that the Group 5 'wishes', which were the most damaging to Chinese sovereignty, should not be imposed on China. Great Britain even went so far as to suggest that the Group 5 'wishes' went against the Anglo-Japanese Alliance. Yüan also sought to gain the support of the Japanese genro, or elders, who advised the Emperor, and who were risk-averse on foreign policy questions, including the Twenty-One Demands.[6] All of those efforts by President Yüan helped to moderate the severe impact of the Japanese demands upon China.

However, Kato remained determined to force a Chinese submission, and so he moderated the Japanese demands to render them slightly more palatable while still insisting that China must submit to Japan.

An ultimatum was presented to the Chinese Government on May 7, 1915, and two days later, following advice from Great Britain to accept them, President Yüan bowed to the inevitable, and accepted the modified Japanese demands. In the result, Japan established hegemony in southern Manchuria, and the economic rights that Germany had acquired in the Shantung Peninsula, as part of the Kiaochow Concession, were transferred to Japan. However, the question of the actual lease of Kiaochow was reserved for the peace conference that would be held at the end of the war. China also agreed to give Japan joint ownership of the Hanyehping works, and it agreed not to alienate any of its coastal territories to a third country.[7]

In the end, China was too militarily weak to defend its own sovereignty, and Britain and the other European powers were too engaged in the war in Europe to pay much regard to the developing relationship between China and Japan. However, the Twenty-One Demands did put a strain on the Anglo-Japanese Alliance. There was a clear divergence between the policies of Great Britain and Japan towards China. Japan's aggressive moves towards China gave Britain pause to ponder if Japan was a country that could be trusted. In the Far East, Britain's position during the crisis made it few friends. China viewed Britain as the ally of its nemesis, Japan, while in Japan there was resentment at the pressure brought to bear on Japan by Great Britain to abandon the Group Five 'wishes' that Japan had presented to China. Japanese resentment towards Great Britain led to new articles being published in the Japanese media alleging that the British troops at Tsingtao had been deficient, and even cowardly. The vitriol reached such a stage that the British ambassador in Tokyo was compelled to ask Kato to publicly defend the Anglo-Japanese Alliance.[8]

In Japan, Foreign Minister Kato was seen as having moved too quickly in the matter of asserting a superior Japanese position in China. He had alienated the genro, by failing to include them in the decision-making process leading up to the issue of the Twenty-

One Demands, and he had emboldened Imperial Army officers who now thought that force was the tactic most likely to achieve Japan's political and economic goals. He offended Japanese nationalists with his decision to draw back from insisting on the acceptance of the Group Five wishes, even though his resiling from the most egregious demands made it possible for Great Britain to advise President Yüan to accept to the Japanese ultimatum. In the result, Kato lost his political footing, and he resigned as Foreign Minister in the summer of 1915. He was replaced as Foreign Minister by Ishii Kikujiro.

President Yüan, despite his deft handling of the crisis, also lost stature. Although his strategy had moderated the Japanese demands, his resulting acceptance of the Japanese ultimatum was seen as a national humiliation in China, and the central government lost much public support. Yuan compounded his political difficulties by reverting to a monarchical government for China, with himself as the new Emperor of China. His brittle new monarchy was short-lived however, as Yüan, now the Hongxian Emperor, quickly lost support among the political class of China, and among the Chinese military, and by the spring of 1916 he was forced to re-establish the republic. After that debacle, Yüan came under strong pressure to resign, an outcome that was only forestalled by his unexpected death in June, 1916.

In Canada, the Twenty-One Demands played an important role in shaping public opinion. After a successful allied Pacific naval campaign against Germany, in which the IJN had provided substantive firepower in defence of Canada's west coast at the point in time when Canada was most vulnerable to a German attack, public opinion in British Columbia towards Japan had improved. But the Twenty-One Demands provided those who feared Japan with a new opportunity to berate Japan's potential threat to North America. Although nothing of the sort was possible, the prospect of potential Japanese aggression towards Canada lessened the positive views that had been created by the Imperial Japanese Navy's efforts to protect the British Columbia coast from Germany at the outbreak of the war.[9]

Meanwhile, in Europe, both Russia and France wanted Japan to become a full member of the Entente, in hopes that Japan could be persuaded to send troops to fight in Europe. On the European battlefields, defensive technologies had exceeded the offensive capabilities of the competing armies, leading to horrendous losses whenever offensive operations were mounted. The battlefield butcher's bill caused enormous distress in the belligerent countries, including Canada, and to both sides, an ultimate victory seemed far off.

Sazonov, the Russian Foreign Minister, pressed for Japan to join the Triple Entente but Japanese Foreign Minister Kato had hitherto refused. When Sazanov continued his efforts to raise the issue, Kato consulted with Sir Edward Grey, who stated that Japanese adherence to the Entente was desirable, but not imperative. However, Russia considered that it needed a peace guarantee from Japan so that Russia could transfer troops from Asia to Europe. For its part, France also hoped that Japanese troops could be deployed in Europe.

In Japan, however, the war was always viewed through the prism of advancing Japanese interests, and Japan had no intention of becoming embroiled in a European land war. Japan had consciously entered the war under the umbrella of its alliance with Britain, and that alliance was limited to the east, and not Europe. Although Japan was prepared to assist Britain in seeking out and destroying Count von Spee's German East Asiatic Squadron, and to protect allied shipping in the Pacific and Indian Oceans, as well as to reduce the German fortress at Tsingtao, that was the extent of the participation in the World War that Japan was initially prepared to make.[10]

Nevertheless, in light of the new suspicions that emerged after the

Twenty-One Demands were presented, Great Britain came around to the view that it was desirable to have Japan adhere to the Declaration of London, binding the allied belligerents to refrain from making a separate peace with Germany and Austria-Hungary. Foreign Minister Kato was not enthusiastic about it but he did not actively oppose it, although he still wished to avoid any formal alliance with Russia.

The Japanese Army command, in particular, remained opposed to sending troops to Europe on the grounds that Japanese troops, being conscripts, should only be deployed abroad in circumstances where the national interest of Japan was particularly engaged. An unstated consideration was also present in the consideration of the Japanese Army high command. The Prussian Army had originally trained the Japanese Army in the Meiji era, and there was a great deal of admiration for the German Army on the part of Japanese generals. It was one thing to fight the German Army in China, and quite another thing to send an expeditionary force to fight the German Army in Europe. There was also the low opinion of the Japanese Army officers of the efforts of the British Army during the Tsingtao campaign, and those negative viewpoints had not yet dissipated. Many Japanese Army officers continued to believe that the German Army would ultimately prevail on the European battlefield, and the Japanese generals did not wish to bind the army to the losing side of a war. Consequently, Japan remained unprepared to send troops to assist its allies in Europe.[11]

When Ishii succeeded Kato as Foreign Minister in the autumn of 1915, he took a different view of the matter and advised that Japan should adhere to the Declaration of London. Japan formally acceded to the Declaration of London on October 19, 1915, making Japan a full member of the Entente, and guaranteeing Japan a seat at the peace conference that would follow the war. Now that Japan was a full member of the Entente, Great Britain felt more secure in asking for Japanese aid. Early in 1916, Britain asked Japan to provide naval support to the allies in the Indian Ocean. Japan now saw an opportunity to further advance its interests and Japan replied on February 9, 1916, that it could provide four cruisers and four destroyers to supplement the allied forces in the Indian Ocean but that it would be desirable if Australia and Canada adhered to the 1911 Commercial Agreement between Great Britain and Japan, and if British Colonial officials in Malaya, and, more particularly, in the Straits Settlements, would recognize the medical credentials of resident Japanese doctors who had relocated there to serve Japanese expatriates.[12] Japan also wanted Great Britain to obtain relief from the racial discrimination that was evident in dominion immigration policies, and finally, Japan wanted Japanese-flagged vessels to be able to participate in the coasting trade within the British dominions.

Ambassador Greene wrote to Sir Edward Grey to warn him that despite the Japanese efforts to protect the British dominions in the Pacific Ocean there was still a prevalent feeling in Japan that Japan's efforts were not being fully respected by the British Empire. The Japanese Ministry continued to be attacked in the Japanese Diet over the prevailing racist attitudes in the immigration policies within the British dominions and British colonies.[13]

In Canada, national immigration policies during this period routinely discriminated on the basis of race, and the Federal government continued to discourage Japanese immigration. Despite the war, however, Japanese immigration to Canada had continued, although at lower levels than the pre-war levels of immigration. In 1914, a year in which Canada was at peace until August, 856 Japanese immigrants had been admitted as immigrants. However, in 1915, the first full year of the war, only 592 Japanese immigrants were received in Canada, and that number fell to only 401 during 1916, before beginning to recover in 1917 (648 Japanese immigrants admitted) and 1918 (883 Japanese immigrants admitted). There was a surge in Japanese immigration into Canada in 1919 following the return to peace, with 1,178 Japanese immigrants admitted before the numbers began to fall back again. The number of immigrants from Japan continued to be restricted by Canada, and the numbers of those who were admitted paled in comparison to the numbers of Japanese immigrants to Canada before Rodolphe Lemieux negotiated the Canada-Japan Gentleman's Agreement in 1908 (2042 Japanese immigrants in 1907 and 7601 Japanese immigrants in 1908). Despite Canada's alliance with Japan, the existing immigration restrictions remained in force throughout the war. However, Japanese immigrants were at least spared the head tax that Chinese immigrants were required to pay in order to immigrate to Canada. [14]

The Foreign and Colonial Offices examined the Japanese demands and presented the Japanese case to the dominion governments. In Canada, the Borden Ministry decided that it would adhere to the 1911 Treaty of Commerce and Navigation between the British Empire and Japan, provided that the treaty did not affect the existing immigration arrangements between Japan and Canada. Australia, however, would not agree to adhere to the 1911 treaty but it was prepared to offer some flexibility on the issues of immigration, and on Japanese access to the Australian coasting trade. At the end of March, Sir Edward Grey responded to Japan with the concessions that he had wrung out of the dominions, and Japan expressed its satisfaction with the results, and thereafter it sent its ships into the Indian Ocean as the allies had requested.

Japan also began to prosper from the war now that the North Pacific was cleared of German naval threats. The demand for war materiel boosted Japan's exports to Canada from 5,090,000 yen in 1913, to 22,318,000 yen by 1916, and even larger increases in trade occurred between Japan and other allied countries. Japan took full advantage of the fact that European trade with Canada was cut off by submarine warfare in the North Atlantic Ocean and the markets lost by European manufacturers were quickly taken up by Japanese suppliers. The increase in trade between Japan and other countries, including Canada, was well within the capacity of the Japanese merchant marine service, which also benefited from the absence of German surface or submarine raiders in the North Pacific. The safety of the North Pacific Ocean for allied merchant ships eliminated the need to employ a convoy system for merchant shipping in the North Pacific throughout the war.[15]

Through 1916, the Russian Foreign Minister, Sazonov, continued to press for a treaty of alliance between Russia and Japan, now that they were joined in the Entente as enemies of the Central Powers. Great Britain was not opposed to an alliance between Japan and Russia, and Foreign Minister Ishii was more open to the Russian initiative than his predecessor. Negotiations were undertaken by the two former adversaries, now adversaries of Germany and Austria-Hungary, and on July 3, 1916, a Russo-Japanese Alliance treaty was signed creating a defensive alliance between the two empires, which afterwards assisted in consolidating their respective positions in China. Only a few days later, on July 10th Sazonov, one of Tsar Nicholas II's most effective ministers, fell from power as the tsarist regime slowly headed towards disintegration.

The improved relationship between Japan and Russia led to an unusual mission for the IJN that also involved the RCN. In order to pay for war materiel, the Russian government needed to transfer gold reserves from St. Petersburg to the western countries but it was too risky to attempt a bullion transfer through the Baltic, owing to the local German naval superiority. As an alternative, it was decided to send the bullion across the North Pacific to North America. The IJN armoured cruisers HIJMS *Nisshin*, and HIJMS *Kasuga*, were used for this purpose. After the gold was shipped across European Russia, and Siberia, on the Trans-Siberian Railway the Japanese warships embarked the Russian gold at the Russian Pacific port of Vladivostok and then carried it across the North Pacific to Esquimalt, or Barkley Sound, where the gold was transferred into HMCS *Rainbow*. The *Rainbow* then took the gold to Vancouver and from there it was sent onward to the Royal Mint in Ottawa by a special Canadian Pacific Railway train camouflaged as a silk train, and under armed guard. Once the gold was safe in

Ottawa it could be used to pay Imperial Russia's war debts. A total of $140,000,000.00 in gold was transferred to Canada from Russia in three voyages in February, 1916, July-August, 1916, and February, 1917.[16]

In the broad North Pacific, any significant German naval threat had now been eliminated but the Japanese Navy still conducted long-range patrols to maintain allied naval security in the North Pacific. During 1915 and 1916, HMCS *Rainbow* also conducted patrols along the North American west coast as far south as Mexico, and Central America, searching for enemy ships and during its patrols the Rainbow captured two German-controlled schooners.[17] HMS *Newcastle* had also remained on the west coast of the Americas, and it conducted patrols as far south as the Chilean coast but with the diminished German threat to Canada's west coast it was eventually decided that there was no longer a need for the *Newcastle* to continue to be based out of Esquimalt, and she left the Canadian naval harbour in October, 1916, bound for Yokohama, Japan, and Hong Kong, en route to new duties in the Mediterranean Sea.

By the end of 1916, good relations between the allied powers had been restored and the Anglo-Japanese Alliance rested on firm ground. The British Admiralty, which was in need of further assistance from the IJN, took advantage of the prevailing good relations and for the first time began pressing Japan to send warships to Europe. Soon the Japanese naval ensign would fly in the Mediterranean Sea and, as well, new allies would appear in the Pacific Ocean with the entry into the war of both the United States and China, while another ally, Russia, would begin to take a path towards an exit from the war.

NOTES

[1] Strachan, 483

[2] Patrick Fuliang Shan, *Yuan Shikai*, UBC Press, Vancouver, 2018, 198

[3] Strachan, 484

[4] Nish, *Decline*, 154

[5] MacDougall, 508

[6] Shan,198; Strachan 486

[7] Strachan, 486

[8] Nish, *Decline*, 156

[9] Pringsheim, 21

[10] Nish, *Decline*, 150-51

[11] Nish, *Decline*, 152

[12] Nish, *Decline*, 171

[13] Nish, *Decline*, 172

[14] An example of how strictly enforced the racial immigration laws were at this period was provided by the SS *Harmattan*, a transport ship operating under the orders of the Admiralty off Canada's east coast. The *Harmattan* put into St. John, New Brunswick with a Chinese member of her crew suffering from acute appendicitis. He was treated at a hospital onshore but the Department of Immigration refused to allow the *Harmattan* to depart unless the ship's captain paid the $500.00 head tax for the landing of a Chinese person in Canada. The master had only $400.00, which he needed to pay the salaries of his crew, and the *Harmattan* had to sail

urgently to comply with wartime Admiralty orders. The immigration authorities were adamant about the collection of the head tax, however, and in the end, NSHQ in Ottawa was forced to intervene, and to assume liability for the head tax so that the *Harmattan* would be allowed to return to the war. (Tucker, 225)

[15] Tucker, 227

[16] Tucker, 280; HMCS *Rainbow*, Naval and Military Museum, Ship Histories https://web.archive.org/web/20100819014830/http://www.navalandmilitarymuseum.org/resource_pages/ships/rainbow.html [accessed February, 2021]

[17] Johnstone et al, 370

14. The Zimmermann Telegram

In late 1916 Germany approached a crossroads. Unable to break the Royal Navy's naval blockade of Germany, and facing growing shortages of food and the essential goods required for the war effort, the Supreme Command of the German military began to contemplate unrestricted submarine warfare. Hitherto, Germany had refrained from the indiscriminate sinking of merchant vessels in the North Atlantic Ocean because of the protests of the United States which, since the outbreak of war, had asserted the right of neutrals to exercise a right of innocent passage on the high seas.

However, historic rules on the manner of instituting and maintaining blockades, and the seizure of prizes on the high seas, did not fit very well with the submarine, which was a comparatively recent naval invention. The submarine was a stealthy killer, and the rules which required vessels to be stopped and boarded, in the case of neutrals, or to be given time to be abandoned before sinking in the case of belligerent ships, were ill-suited to submarine warfare. When the Imperial German Navy attempted to follow such rules the Royal Navy countered with Q-ships, camouflaged surface killers with a hidden armament that could swiftly overwhelm a submarine that surfaced to investigate a merchantman. The alternative for the submarine was the use of the torpedo in an underwater attack but that often left little chance for the passengers and crew to escape. The sinking of the passenger liner RMS *Lusitania* in 1915, by a torpedo from a submerged German submarine, almost ruptured diplomatic relations between the United States and Germany.

Germany resiled from underwater attacks, even to the point of withdrawing its U-boat fleet from British waters, in order to satisfy the strong American protests. Germany strove to maintain

American neutrality but the United States was never wholly neutral. American industry made vast profits from producing armaments and all manner of goods for consumption by the allies. At the same time, American trade with the Central Powers disappeared, owing to the supremacy of the Royal Navy and its European blockade, and there was bitter resentment in Germany as they watched America grow rich by producing the goods that sustained their enemies. By allowing American manufacturers and financiers to support the allied war effort President Wilson departed from his own formulation of neutrality, which he had expressed in 1913, in conjunction with the Mexican civil war, where President Wilson had said that he would forbid the export of arms and munitions from the United States to all of the warring factions in Mexico as a "best practice for a neutral party.[1]

In reality, American prosperity was too tightly tied to the allied war effort for Wilson to stop the passage of war materiel from American factories to European battlefields. The German Government was bitter but Chancellor Bethmann-Hollweg and Foreign Minister Jagow both concluded that America's entry into the war would mean defeat for the Central Powers, and they resisted demands from the military to unleash the U-boats.

The US did protest the high-handed manner in which the British instituted and policed its blockade of Germany. However, the British efforts, while contrary to long-established principles of neutrality in some cases, did not pose the same risk to American lives as the German U-boats did. As the President's close friend and advisor Colonel Edward M House later said, it was Germany's alienation of US affections by its reliance on submarine warfare that had precluded a strong American reaction to the control over US seaborne commerce that the allied powers insisted upon, through their control of the high seas.[2]

But with Germany's army stalemated on the European battlefronts the German high command resolved to put the submarine weapon to its full use in an attempt to starve Britain into submission. The navy boldly stated that it could force Britain to its knees if it could engage in unrestricted submarine warfare against both belligerents and neutrals, and sink passenger and cargo ships in addition to warships. The military leadership led by Field Marshal Hindenburg, and General Ludendorff, undermined the position of Foreign Minister Jagow and forced his retirement from office. He was replaced by Arthur Zimmermann, who sided with the military on the need for unrestricted submarine warfare.

Zimmermann realized that Germany's bold move to unrestricted submarine warfare was likely to bring the United States into the war on the side of the allies. Searching for some method to prevent the United States from bringing the full force of its power onto the European battlefields Zimmermann formulated a strategy of creating an alliance between Germany and Mexico, and then possibly encouraging Japan to switch sides and join a proposed German-Mexican-Japanese alliance. By doing so he hoped to tie down a large number of US forces in Mexico, and thus forestall their deployment to Europe.

Mexico had remained a recurring foreign policy problem for President Wilson. The year before the election that brought Wilson to power in the United States the Mexican dictator Porfirio Diaz was overthrown by reformers led by Francisco Madero. He, in turn, held office for only two years before reactionary forces under General Victoriano Huerta overthrew and slew Madero, and made Huerta the dictator of Mexico. Wilson was offended by the overthrow and murder of Madero, who was at least a democrat unlike the dictator Huerta, and Wilson sought to overthrow Huerta. In 1913 Great Britain recognized the unsavoury Huerta regime but not so the Wilson Administration, which continued to oppose Huerta. All of this created a great deal of instability in Mexico, and soon there were three men vying for political supremacy, General Huerta, Huerta's opponent General Venustiano Carranza, and a northern warlord and bandit, Pancho Villa. Huerta was briefly forced into exile in Spain but he emerged from exile to make one last attempt to regain power, travelling through the United States to the US – Mexican border where he was detained by US authorities, and where he died under house arrest on US soil early in 1916.

Meanwhile, Venustiano Carranza had become President, although his regime remained unrecognized by the United States. Diplomatic relations between Mexico and the United States were strained and remained especially so after Pancho Villa led a border incursion into the United States that resulted in the death of Americans. Villa's raid forced Wilson to send troops under the command of General John J Pershing into northern Mexico, in a vain attempt to corral Villa.

The troubles in Mexico occurred at a time when the American public was also expressing a growing sensitivity over the rising power of Japan in the Pacific Ocean. Racism against Asians played an important part in US west coast politics during the pre-war period, as it did also in British Columbia. Race-based fears of Japan made it easy for rumours of Japanese aggression in North America to quickly spread. In 1908, there were rumours that Japan had acquired a lease on Magdalena Bay, in Baja California, Mexico, as a future naval base. The rumour was completely unfounded but it carried some initial credibility because it was reported to Washington by the US Ambassador to Guatemala.[3] Even after the rumours of a secret Japanese naval base in Mexico had been refuted, stories continued to emerge of secret Japanese armies in Mexico that might cross the Rio Grande River, or conquer the (then building) Panama Canal.

After the World War broke out there were new rumours of Japanese incursions into Mexico in late 1914. The source of those rumours was the crew of the SMS *Geier*, the German gunboat that had been forced to intern in Honolulu when its engines failed, and ships from the IJN North American Squadron appeared off Hawaii seeking to sink or capture the *Geier*. The crew of the *Geier* spread rumours about Japanese incursions into Mexico via wireless and covered the sounds of their wireless transmissions, which were a clear violation of their internment status, by having their ship's band play afternoon concerts.[4]

New rumours of a Japanese penetration of Mexico came to the attention of the American public when the HIJMS *Asama* grounded on the west coast of Mexico, and several other Japanese warships came to her aid. The presence of the *Asama* was seen as proof in conspiracy circles that Japan was establishing a naval base in Mexico. The wartime German press supported such theories while Japan, of course, issued blanket denials.[5] The German propaganda machinery in the United States continued to spew out totally unfounded stories of potential Japanese aggression in Mexico and in that endeavour Germany was aided and abetted by the Hearst Company, which financed a serialized film starring actress Irene Castle as an American heroine caught up in the machinations of a Mexican-Japanese invasion of the United States.[6]

Germany's attempt to win over Japan to the cause of the Central Powers was not merely a propaganda exercise. German diplomacy also made a determined attempt to persuade Japan to switch sides and abandon the Entente. Contact was initiated between Germany and the Japanese Ambassador to Sweden in Stockholm. The Japanese ambassador held meetings with a German representative, and dutifully reported all of the contents of his discussions to Tokyo, and to Japan's allies.

In Peking, the German Ambassador, von Hintze, gave an important interview to a Japanese newspaper despite the belligerency between Japan and Germany. Von Hintze suggested that if Japan switched sides Germany could provide capital to assist in Japan's economic penetration of China and that Japan could keep Tsingtao after the conclusion of the war.[7]

Needless to say, all of Germany's attempts to persuade Japan to switch sides failed. Japan had placed its decision to go to war squarely within the framework of the Anglo-Japanese Alliance Treaty, which was the bedrock of Japanese diplomacy, and nothing Germany could offer Japan could dissuade the Japanese government from its adherence to its alliance with the British Empire. After the United States entered the war, Viscount Ishii told US Secretary of State Lansing that Germany had tried three times during the course of the war to persuade Japan to switch sides.[8]

Zimmermann, however, decided to embark on one last attempt to use Japan against the United States, in conjunction with Mexico, when the decision to mount unrestricted submarine warfare was taken. The decision to move to unrestricted submarine warfare despite the potential American objections was made by the Supreme Command, which foresaw that the German Army could not overwhelm the allies on the battlefield but that the naval weapon might provide an opportunity to bring Great Britain to its knees by starving it of essential supplies. The KM Admirals were adamant that they could bring the British to terms through unrestricted submarine warfare. Foreign Minister Zimmermann agreed with the Supreme Command, as did the Kaiser, although the Kaiser did not wish to overrule the Chancellor, who objected, and who held constitutional responsibility for Germany's foreign relations. On January 10, 1917, at the castle at Pless, which served as the German Supreme Headquarters, the fateful decision was taken to begin unrestricted submarine warfare against both belligerent and neutral ships in British waters commencing February 1, 1917.

Anticipating that the United States might treat unrestricted submarine warfare as a *casus belli*, Zimmermann sent a long telegram to Germany's ambassador in Washington, Count Bernstorff, requesting that he send along the message by a safe route to the German Ambassador, Eckhardt, in Mexico City. The fateful telegram read:

> "Berlin. Jan. 19. 1917. On February 1 we intend to begin submarine warfare without restriction. In spite of this it

is our intention to endeavour to keep the United States neutral. If this attempt is not successful, we propose an alliance on the following basis with Mexico: That we shall make war together and together make peace; we shall give general financial support, and it is understood that Mexico is to reconquer her lost territory of New Mexico, Texas and Arizona. The details are left to you for settlement. You are instructed to inform the President of Mexico of the above in the greatest confidence as soon as it is certain that there will be an outbreak of war with the United States, and suggest that the President of Mexico shall on his own initiative communicate with Japan suggesting the latter's adherence at once to this plan, and at the same time offer to mediate between Germany and Japan. Please call to the attention of the President of Mexico that the employment of ruthless submarine warfare now promises to compel England to make peace in a few month [sic]. -Zimmermann."[9]

Unwisely, Zimmermann sent the cable over a US State Department cable path that Germany's ambassador had obtained State Department permission to use in order to facilitate the transmission of President Wilson's peace proposals, following his re-election in November, 1916. What Germany did not realize, however, was that Great Britain had broken the German diplomatic code, and had intercepted Zimmerman's coded telegram, and deciphered it.

The British held onto the deciphered telegram until they could make arrangements to obtain the version that Germany's ambassador to the United States, Count Bernstorff, had sent onward to his counterpart in Mexico City. Skilful British intelligence operatives purloined a copy of the version sent to Mexico City by Bernstorff, and it was that version that the British Foreign Minister, Arthur Balfour, delivered to US Ambassador Walter Page in London on February 23, 1917, an event that Balfour later described as the most dramatic moment in his life.[10]

President Wilson was shocked, and indignant, at this evidence of German plotting against the United States while the United States was earnestly attempting to bring the warring parties to a peace conference to end the war. It was particularly chilling that Germany had sent the offensive cable over the US State Department cable system. Wilson acknowledged Britain's assistance in providing the US with intelligence on the Zimmermann Telegram by cabling his thanks and appreciation to the British Government.[11]

On February 1, 1917, Germany commenced unrestricted submarine warfare and President Wilson moved to break diplomatic relations with Germany. When it became apparent that Wilson still faced substantial resistance in the Senate to the arming of American merchant vessels to counter Germany's unrestricted submarine warfare, the Administration released the contents of the Zimmermann Telegram. When asked at a press conference if he would deny the telegram story, German Foreign Minister Zimmermann, guided by his conscience, said he could not deny it because it was true.[12]

The release of the Zimmermann Telegram was sensational, and it was received with great consternation by the American public. Americans were particularly offended by the Zimmermann Telegram's suggestion of an alliance between Mexico and Japan, which played directly into the ongoing fears of the American public, particularly in the western United States, of Japanese expansion. The more irresponsible elements of the American press continued to stir up fears of Japan.[13] The release of the Zimmermann Telegram greatly contributed to a pro-war shift in American public opinion in the weeks preceding the American entry into the war.[14]

Events now moved towards an inexorable American entry into the war. The torpedoing of American ships crossed a line that President Wilson could not allow to continue, and although he was very much a reluctant warrior he faced up to the German threat and the logical conclusion of the failure of Germany to respond to American protests and pronouncements on the rights of neutrals. On April 2, 1917, President Wilson appeared before the Congress of the United States and called for a declaration of war against Germany. Although the principle of the rights of neutrals to travel the seas was the overriding reason that drove Wilson to seek a declaration of war, Wilson also alluded to the Zimmermann Telegram in his speech to Congress by noting that Germany had tried to create an enemy out of America's neighbour, which was an allusion to the Zimmermann Telegram.[15] And so, to the great relief of the European Entente Powers, the United States entered the war on April 6, 1917, virtually guaranteeing that Germany would ultimately be defeated.

Meanwhile, the British Foreign Minister, Arthur Balfour, had interviewed the Japanese Ambassador about Japanese-Mexican relations and he was assured that Japan had no interests in Mexico.[16] Japan only hoped to allay American fears about a Mexican-Japanese combination, which was an invention of German propaganda, and exacerbated by the racial paranoia that was prevalent on the west coast of North America. For its part, Mexico was careful to reassert its neutrality.

Later, in November, 1917, Viscount Ishii travelled to Washington for talks with Secretary of State Lansing, and those talks led to the Lansing-Ishii Accord. Under that accord, Washington recognized that "territorial propinquity" created special relations between Japan and China, and thus the US accepted that Japan had special interests in China. At the same time, Japan pledged to uphold the Open Door Policy, a touchstone of US foreign policy, that permitted the continuation of American commerce with those areas within China in which Japan was now paramount.[17]

For Canada, the entry of the United States into the war was a great relief. Canada was now linked with both the country that held its sentimental affections, Great Britain, and with the country with which it had the closest social and economic relations, the United States. A closer wartime relationship now began between

Canada and the United States. Prime Minister Sir Robert Borden visited President Woodrow Wilson in Washington in 1917, after the US declaration of war. The two leaders quickly developed a productive relationship, with the United States agreeing to assist Canada economically, and a cooperative approach soon developed between the two countries. Military intelligence began to flow between the two countries, and some US aviators served under Canadian command at the east coast as part of reconnaissance efforts against the submarine threat.[18] Canada now began a slow pivot that would take much of the century to complete away from its Imperial security relationship with Great Britain, and towards a close security relationship with the United States.

The entry of the United States into the war also had practical consequences for the RCN at the west coast. The German naval threat in the North Pacific had long since receded. Japan maintained its overall responsibility for allied naval operations in the North Pacific, and the IJN continued to conduct patrols to maintain security on behalf of the Entente Powers.[19] However, the United States naval presence on the west coast of North America eliminated the need for the RCN to maintain an active defence in Canadian coastal waters at the west coast. Canada could now rely on US naval vessels at Puget Sound to provide guard ship capabilities. Furthermore, crews were urgently required by the RCN at the east coast for anti-submarine work. Accordingly, taking advantage of the entry of the United States into the war, the RCN paid off its workhorse at Esquimalt, HMCS *Rainbow*, in May, 1917, and transferred the ship's crew to Halifax.[20] Subsequently, the two submarines that British Columbia had bought for the RCN at the outbreak of the war, HMCS C-1, and HMCS C-2, were also transferred to Halifax, arriving there in October, 1917.[21]

Although the Germans unleashed the full fury of their submarines against the allies in European waters and did achieve great initial success, the allied navies reacted to unrestricted submarine warfare by instituting the convoy system and protecting the convoys with screens of destroyers. Those innovations were successful, and they held the allied losses of merchantmen below the replacement capacity of the allied shipyards. By the end of 1917, the German navy had lost the submarine war, and its only major consequence was the entry of the United States into the war against Germany.

NOTES

[1] Charles Callan Tansill, "War Profits and Unneutrality," in Herbert J Bass (ed.) *America's Entry into World War I, Submarines, Sentiment or Security?*, Dryden Press, Hinsdale (Ill.) 1964, 15

[2] Charles Seymour, "The Submarine and American Intervention" in Herbert J Bass (ed.) *America's Entry into World War I, Submarines, Sentiment or Security?*, Dryden Press, Hinsdale (Ill.) 1964, 10

[3] Barbara Tuchman, *The Zimmerman Telegram*, Bantam Books, New York, 1971, 31

[4] Tuchman, 55

[5] Tuchman, 59

[6] Tuchman, 61

[7] Tuchman, 58

[8] Tuchman, 218

[9] *The Zimmerman Telegram*, National Security Agency records, https://www.nsa.gov/Portals/70/documents/news-features/declassified-documents/cryptologic-quarterly/the_zimmermann_telegram.pdf [accessed February 26, 2021]

[10] Tuchman, 161

[11] Walter Millis, *Road to War: America 1914 – 1917*, Houghton Mifflin Company, Boston, 1935, 404

[12] Tuchman, 178

[13] Millis, 407; Tuchman, 170

[14] Link/Bass, 92

[15] Tuchman, 191

[16] Tuchman, 154

[17] MacDougall, 509

[18] Patrick McManus, *Stability and Flexibility: The Rush-Bagot Agreement and the Progressive Modernization of Canadian-American Security Relations*, University of Ottawa (PhD dissertation), Ottawa, 2009, 75

[19] The United States was not an allied power, as President Wilson wished to retain an independent foreign policy flexibility, and therefore the United States did not formally join the Entente. The United States became an associated power but that did not have any practical military effect. The allied and associated powers worked together in relative amity to ensure the defeat of the Central Powers.

[20] Tucker, 280

[21] Johnstone et al, 694

15. The Last Years of the War and the Siberian Intervention

The American declaration of war against Germany gave renewed hope to the Entente allies, whose populations were mortified by the enormous losses incurred on the static western front, where assault after assault on enemy positions resulted in a murderous defensive fire that mowed down the masses of attacking men. The technology of military defence had simply exceeded the capabilities of a military offence, leaving both sides unable to break through their enemy's front lines even though huge numbers of soldiers were flung against the defences of the enemy's trench works. The horror of the losses convinced some that a negotiated peace should be sought. Among them was Lord Lansdowne, the former Governor General of Canada, and the former Foreign Minister of Great Britain in Lord Salisbury's cabinet, who was one of the architects of the original Anglo-Japanese Alliance. Failing to convince his political colleagues of the need to consider a negotiated peace based on the principle of the *status quo ante bellum* in 1916, Lord Lansdowne released a public letter in November, 1917, later known as the Lansdowne Letter, that called for a negotiated peace. It fell on deaf ears, and Lansdowne was pilloried in political society for the temerity of even suggesting it. In all belligerent countries in Europe, including Great Britain, the tremendous sacrifices that had been made by the people, and the adamancy of the promises of victory that had been publicly declared by governments, rendered it politically unpalatable to consider any possible outcome other than a complete victory.

The entry of the United States into the war, and the almost simultaneous fall of Tsarist Russia, now cast the war as a struggle of the democracies against the autocracies. Despite this outward change in the complexion of the antagonists, the underlying imperialist motivations of many powers remained unaffected, and each side continued to seek to maximize gains from the enormous bloodletting of the war. Already, secret agreements had been entered into by the Entente Powers to divide up the spoils of any conquests made from the territories of the Central Powers. In the Near East, Tsarist Russia was to have obtained Constantinople, which would have achieved Russia's long-sought access to the Mediterranean Sea, leaving the remainder of the Ottoman territories in the Middle East to be divided between Great Britain and France according to the Sykes-Picot Agreement, a secret agreement negotiated by two Entente diplomats.

In the Pacific, the British Empire now acknowledged that the Japanese Empire would continue to hold the German Pacific Island territories north of the equator. Great Britain realized that Japan had no intention of releasing its hold on those islands at the conclusion of the hostilities. At the same time, the British Empire desired to hold the German possessions south of the equator, as both Australia and New Zealand looked to retain those territorial gains as compensation for the losses in manpower suffered by their armies during the war. Hence, the outlines of an agreement on the division of the Pacific spoils was already present when British and Japanese diplomats sat down to iron out a division of the German Pacific empire in 1917.

During this phase of the war, the Royal Navy continued to be much pressed by the German unrestricted submarine warfare campaign. The German unrestricted submarine campaign put the fate of the British Isles in the balance because it threatened Britain's essential food supply chain. The Royal Navy desperately needed assistance from the IJN, particularly with respect to destroyers, and therefore the British Government approached Japan for additional naval support outside of the Pacific theatre of operations just as the discussions about the fate of the former German territories received new attention from the Foreign Ministries of both countries. Now hard-pressed, the British Empire was in no position to contest Japan's desires concerning the future of the conquered German territories in the North Pacific. Nevertheless, Japan did not press its advantage to its fullest extent and merely asked that the British Empire support its claims to the Kiaochow Concession in China, and to the German Pacific Islands north of the equator. In both cases, Japan was, of course, already in actual possession of the ex-German territories.

Given the urgency of the British request for naval assistance, Japan agreed to provide two destroyer squadrons and a cruiser in the Mediterranean Sea even before the negotiations between Japan and Great Britain over the Pacific spoils of war were completed. The IJN was committed to assist in convoy duties in the Mediterranean, thus releasing additional Royal Navy destroyers for convoy escort duties in the Atlantic. Japan also promised Britain that it would provide two cruisers to be stationed at the Cape of Good Hope. In both cases the Japanese warships would remain under Japanese command but it was understood that the Japanese naval forces would cooperate with the local Royal Navy forces.[1]

Japan's faithfulness towards the alliance helped to smooth the path for an agreement between the Japanese Empire and the British Empire for a division of the spoils in the Pacific. There was some urgency in dealing with the question of the ex-German colonies because of the anticipated entry of the United States into the war. London preferred to keep the issue of territorial adjustments in the Asia-Pacific region between the two Anglo-Japanese Alliance powers, and not to admit other countries, particularly the USA, into the negotiations. The British Foreign Office realized that as the United States became a belligerent it would likely seek to intervene in the division of the conquered German Pacific territories.

British policy with respect to Tsingtao and Kiaochow was supportive of Japan, as there were no real conflicting British interests in north China. Although British foreign policy required that China be diplomatically supported, Great Britain had made no specific commitments to China concerning the future retrocession of the ex-German Kiaochow enclave.[2] As for the ex-German islands north of the equator, it was necessary to first canvass the opinions of the dominions, which the Colonial Office was tasked to do before acceding to the Japanese position.

Canada was not officially consulted about the future of the North Pacific islands, and it alone of the British dominions made no claim to any of the ex-German colonies. Australia had a claim to the German North Pacific islands based on the surrender of the German Acting Governor in New Guinea in 1914, whose surrender to Australian forces purported to include all of the German Pacific island territories, except German Samoa. However, both Australia and New Zealand ultimately concurred with the proposed division of the German territories with Japan, using the equator as the demarcation line between the British Empire and the Japanese Empire. For the British Empire, it was a *fait accompli*. The War Cabinet in London expressed its approval to the proposed resolution and, on February 16, 1917, Ambassador Greene in Tokyo advised the Japanese government that the British Empire agreed with the proposal to use the equator as the demarcation line for territorial acquisition, with Japan securing the former German colonial territories north of that line, and the British Empire taking the former German colonial territories south of the equator.[3] The Japanese approved the agreement on February 20th and subsequently obtained the concurrence of France, Italy, and Russia, on the condition that Japan support and encourage China to break with the Central Powers and enter the war on the side of the Entente, which was also agreeable to Japan.[4]

Although Japan had earlier opposed the entry of China into the war its position had changed by 1917, and with the United States now a belligerent there was a stronger encouragement for China's entry into the war by the Allies, who were increasingly concerned to prevent the Central Powers from manipulating political events in China. The United States, in particular, sought to enhance China's geopolitical position vis-a-vis Japan, and the US thought that Chinese belligerency would give China additional credibility with the allied powers in the post-war settlement.[5] It was also believed by the allied powers that German influence had led to a brief restoration of the Manchu monarchy in Peking in July, 1917, an event that was quickly overturned by republican forces. Shortly after the abortive monarchical restoration was put down by republican forces, the now weakened central government of China declared war on both Germany and Austria-Hungary, on August 14, 1917. Once China became a belligerent the existing German and Austro-Hungarian extra-territorial concessions in China were taken over by the Chinese Government, ending any territorial jurisdiction of the Central Powers in the Asia-Pacific region. As a result, German intelligence operatives could no longer operate with impunity within China.

The IJN continued to protect allied shipping in the Pacific for the remainder of the war. It ran patrols throughout the Far East and down to the Netherlands East Indies, and then across the Indian Ocean to the Cape of Good Hope. It also protected shipping along the east coast of Australia, and in the waters around New Zealand. The IJN organized regular cruiser patrols and deployed HIJMS *Idzumo*, HIJMS *Nisshin*, HIJMS *Tone*, HIJMS *Niitaka*, HIJMS *Akashi*, HIJMS *Yakumo*, HIJMS *Chikuma*, HIJMS *Tsushima*, HIJMS *Suma* and HIJMS *Yodo* plus three destroyer squadrons to carry out allied Pacific and Indian Ocean patrols.[6] In addition, the Japanese chartered significant Japanese merchant marine tonnage to carry allied supplies.

The pressing need of the Royal Navy for escort vessels to deal with the German submarine threat in the Atlantic not only forced Great Britain to ask for help from Japan, but it also propelled the Royal Navy to seek all available American vessels that were suitable for convoy escort duties in the Atlantic. Responding to the pressing need for escorts, the United States entered into an agreement with Japan whereby the IJN would protect American possessions in the

Pacific. In October, 1917, the armoured cruiser USS *Saratoga*, the American guard ship at Honolulu, was redeployed to the Atlantic, and its duties were assumed by the HIJMS *Tokiwa*, which, ironically, given what happened long afterwards, became responsible for the defence of the Hawaiian Islands, and of the important USN naval station at Pearl Harbour.[7]

The IJN also continued its long-range patrols across the North Pacific Ocean. The HIJMS *Asama* undertook a long-range North Pacific cruise in company with HIJMS *Iwate* between March 2nd, and July 6th, 1918. After cruising along the coasts of North and Central America the *Asama* sailed to Honolulu where it relieved HIJMS *Tokiwa* as the Hawaiian guard ship, and thereafter the *Asama* stayed in Hawaiian waters until February, 1919, when the IJN departed from Hawaiian waters upon the return in force of the USN.

Although German commerce raiders remained a potential threat throughout the war, in the later years of the war in the Pacific Ocean it was only in the South Pacific that Germany's commerce raiders made an appearance. The commerce raider SMS *Wolf*, although mostly active in the Indian Ocean did venture into Australian and New Zealand waters, where she managed to sink several allied vessels by minelaying. Perhaps the most colourful raider of the entire war, next to the SMS *Emden*, was the SMS *Seeadler* a steel-hulled square-rigged sailing ship that was captured by a German submarine early in the war and converted into a commerce raider – the only full-rigged sailing ship raider of the war. The *Seeadler*, under the command of Captain Count Felix von Luckner operated in the south-west Pacific in 1917, after a voyage from Germany that took the ship around Cape Horn. Count Luckner and the *Seeadler* had a fortunate cruise, taking 15 prizes, most of which were other sailing vessels. Few sailing ships were suspicious of another tall ship until it was too late to flee. However, the *Seeadler's* luck ran out in August, 1917, when it was wrecked at Mopelia Atoll, in the Society Islands. The German crew took possession of Mopelia, and von Luckner and a few men cast off in a small boat intending to sail as far as Fiji, where von Luckner hoped to steal another sailing vessel as a replacement for the *Seeadler*. Unfortunately for von Luckner, a local resident became suspicious after his small boat arrived at Fiji, and von Luckner and his boat crew were taken prisoner by the Fijian police. Meanwhile, the remaining German crew of the *Seeadler* left behind on Mopelia had seized a French schooner that stopped at the island and had sailed it to Easter Island, where the schooner was wrecked and the Germans were interned by the Chilean authorities. A number of von Luckner's prisoners from the ships that he had captured had remained on Mopelia, and an American mariner sailed in a small boat to Pago Pago, in American Samoa, and arranged for their rescue. With that, the impact of the Imperial German Navy in the Pacific in World War One ceased.

Although the German threat in the Pacific theatre was eliminated by 1918, a new concern now emerged on the Russian Pacific coast. In March, 1917, the Tsar of Russia had abdicated his throne, and a Provisional Government had been established in place of the monarchy. Political conditions in Russia rapidly deteriorated throughout the remainder of 1917, to the consternation of the other Entente Powers. Russia had suffered immense losses on the eastern front, and its population was war-weary, and unwilling to continue the struggle against the Central Powers. Seizing the moment, Vladimir Lenin and his Bolshevik Party took power from the failing Provisional Government in a coup in November, 1917, and established the world's first communist state, a development that alarmed the western powers, especially as the Bolsheviks sought an early and separate peace with Germany. By February, 1918, Russia was out of the war, and the prisoners of war that Russia had previously captured from the Central Powers were being released. The Entente Powers feared that this new source of manpower could be deployed against them on the western front and, in addition, large stockpiles of war materiel had been left at Vladivostok, in the Russian Far East, awaiting rail transportation to an eastern front that no longer existed. The western allies worried that if that war materiel could be captured or obtained by the Central Powers it could support actions against the allies in Europe, and in the Near East. [8] Additionally, the Entente Powers still hoped that an eastern front might be reconstituted if the Bolsheviks lost power and if Russia's western-oriented moderates were able to re-establish political control in Russia.

A particular concern was the fate of 4000 Czechoslovakian prisoners of war who had served in the Austro-Hungarian army but were now stranded in Siberia, along the line of the Trans-Siberian Railway. In June the Czechoslovakians took over the Trans-Siberian Railway and seized Vladivostok. The allied governments thereupon decided to intervene. The United States and Great Britain each agreed to send up to 7000 troops into Siberia, and Japan, being much closer geographically to Siberia, agreed to send 70,000 troops.

Canada was asked to provide a contingent of troops as part of a British Empire force, and Prime Minister Borden readily agreed to provide Canadian troops. Borden's rationale for intervening in Siberia was that Siberia might become important if it established a separate political identity from Russia after the war, and Canadian participation in the allied intervention force could assist Canada in establishing a future political relationship with Siberia.[9]
Ultimately, Canada supplied three-fourths of the total British Empire contingent including two battalions of infantry, as well as medical and administrative units. The first Canadian troop convoy sailed from Vancouver for Vladivostok on October 11, 1918, and the last convoy left Vancouver for Vladivostok on March 27, 1919.[10] Although the armistice in November 1918, removed any outstanding Entente military concerns relating to the Central Powers, Canada continued to support and reinforce its presence in Siberia even after the conclusion of the World War. Some 3500 Canadian troops were actually sent to Siberia after the end of World War One.[11]

The Canadian contingent was organized as the Canadian Siberian

Expeditionary Force (CSEF) and it included a British battalion within it. The CSEF was under the command of Canadian Major-General J H Elmsley and it reached brigade strength, consisting of more than 4000 Canadians, in addition to its British battalion. In Siberia, the CSEF came under the operational command of the Japanese Army, and thus the Siberian intervention became the only joint military operation undertaken by Canada and Japan while the Anglo-Japanese Alliance was in force. General Elmsley reported to the Japanese Army commander, General Otani Kikuzo. When the Canadians arrived they found that Vladivostok and its environs had already been secured by the Japanese Army, and by the troops of the US Army, both armies having arrived earlier than the Canadians. As a result, by the time that the CSEF arrived, there was no actual fighting for the CSEF to do.[12]

Japan provided the backbone of the allied intervention forces in Siberia, sending 70,000 Japanese troops into the country. The next largest contingents were from the United States, which sent 12,000 Americans, and Poland, which also sent 12,000 troops. China provided 5000 troops and Canada provide 4,200 troops to which the 1,500 strong British contingent was attached. Other contingents included 4,000 Serbs, 4,000 Romanians, 2,000 Italians, and 1,850 French troops.[13] The CSEF formed part of the allied garrison at Vladivostok, and it assisted in the occupation of the surrounding coastal areas. Actual duties were light, and the Canadian troops enjoyed soccer games against Royal Navy crews and baseball games against American army troops. While the bulk of the Canadians stayed put at the coast, a small contingent of administrative personnel, consisting of eight officers and 47 other ranks, went west as far as Omsk, in Siberia, to provide administrative support for ongoing allied operations.[14]

By the beginning of 1919, the Russian Civil War had broken out and the Red (communist) and White (monarchist-capitalist) forces were contending for control of the giant Russian and Siberian landmass. Allied government sympathies were entirely with the Whites, and in

Siberia the White Supreme Ruler, Admiral Kolchak, received support from the allied governments. However, the Whites never succeeded in attracting the sympathies of the Russian, or Siberian peoples, and over time support for the White cause withered, although for a brief period it did appear that the White forces might prevail in the Russian Civil War.

Meanwhile, there was increasing resistance in Ottawa to the presence of the Canadian troops in Siberia. After the armistice ended the war in Europe, in November, 1918, the Cabinet wanted the CSEF withdrawn but Prime Minister Borden, who was temporarily in Great Britain attending the Imperial War Cabinet, refused to permit it. Borden felt that, at least initially, the presence of the CSEF would encourage political stability in the country, and the Canadians could be useful in training Admiral Kolchak's forces.[15] However, the Cabinet continued to press Borden to agree to withdraw. Finally, the exasperated Prime Minister said that the Cabinet could order a Canadian withdrawal if it left behind sufficient personnel to train Kolchak's forces.

Ultimately, the Cabinet in Ottawa compromised by maintaining the CSEF in place as the Prime Minister wished but with a proviso that individual soldiers could opt to come home one year after the signing, on November 11, 1918, of the armistice with Germany. The Prime Minister expressed satisfaction with that resolution. But then the Cabinet began to worry that US and Japanese troops might clash in Siberia, and the CSEF might be caught in the middle of a conflict. If that happened, the Cabinet felt that the Canadian population would naturally wish to side with the Americans in the event of any Japanese-American conflict in Siberia, but the Anglo-Japanese Alliance committed the entire British Empire, including Canada, to support Japan. The Cabinet fretted over whether Great Britain would ask Canada to remain neutral in the event of a Japanese-American conflict. The Prime Minister, still stuck in Britain, continued to be exasperated by the wallowing of the Cabinet on the Siberian intervention, and he essentially gave it permission to do as it liked. The Cabinet decided to restrict the movement of the CSEF from any movements further westward in Siberia, and to prevent it from engaging in any active military operations without Cabinet approval. The restrictions that Ottawa placed on the CSEF prompted sharp cables from the War Office in London to the Canadian General Staff in Ottawa, and also prompted protests from General Elmsley, the CSEF commander in Vladivostok.[16]

By now however, Prime Minister Borden had realized that there was no future political value in maintaining the CSEF in Siberia given the likely outcome of the Russian Civil War, and he turned his mind to extricating the CSEF. Borden proposed that an international conference be convened to arbitrate a settlement in Siberia. Although allied opinion favoured the proposal it was not supported by the White Russian authorities in Siberia. Facing intransigence in Siberia Canada decided in early February, 1919, to withdraw the CSEF, and Canada advised its allied partners of its decision. Between April and the end of June, 1919, the CSEF was slowly withdrawn from Siberia.[17] The Canadians suffered no losses due to enemy action during the Siberian intervention, but three personnel were killed by accidents, and 16 died of disease.[18]

In the end, the only active military operation that the CSEF carried out came in April, 1919, even as the Canadian contingent began preparing for its government-ordered withdrawal from Siberia. General Otani ordered the suppression of a Bolshevik force that had taken over a village north of Vladivostok. General Elmsley sent a company of the 259th Canadian battalion to attack the Bolsheviks but when the Canadians took up positions outside the occupied village they found that the Bolsheviks had already withdrawn from the area, and there was no attack to be made. Returning to Vladivostok the Canadians found that their disappointment at missing out on a firefight was somewhat lightened by General Otani, who had sent the CSEF, as presents, 96 bottles of wine, 18 bottles of whiskey, and 3 casks of sake, in recognition and thanks for the service of the CSEF under his command. General Otani obviously knew how to maintain cordial inter-allied relations.

The British withdrew their remaining forces in Siberia in the autumn of 1919, after finding it too difficult to continue once the Canadians had withdrawn the Canadian administrative personnel that served in the CSEF. White resistance in Siberia began to crumble thereafter. Admiral Kolchak was captured by the Bolsheviks, and he was executed in February, 1920. The United States withdrew its forces in April, 1920, and the Japanese withdrew in October, 1922, ending the allied intervention.[19]

Although the Siberian intervention was not a geopolitical, or military success, it did give the Canadian Army an opportunity to work together with Canada's Japanese partner in the Anglo-Japanese Alliance, and relations between the Canadian and the Japanese forces had remained cordial throughout the mission. With the conclusion of the Siberian intervention active Canadian military operations in the First World War period came to an end. Now the bitter realities of the peace would have to be faced, and important questions about the continuation of the Anglo-Japanese Alliance answered.

NOTES

[1] Nish, *Decline*, 206

[2] Nish, *Decline*, 206

[3] Nish, *Decline*, 207

[4] Nish, *Decline*, 210

[5] Dua, 82

[6] Timothy D Saxon, *Anglo-Japanese Naval Cooperation, 1914-1918*, Naval War College Review, Winter 2000, Vol III, No. 1, 9

[7] Saxon, 11

[8] John Silverlight, *The Victor's Dilemma: Allied Intervention in the Russian Civil War*, Weybright and Talley, New York, 1970, 16, 22

[9] Nicholson, 519

[10] Allan Donnell, "The Campaign in Northern Russia" in *Canada in the Great World War*, Vol. VI, United Publishers of Canada, Toronto, 1921, 238

[11] Donnell, 239

[12] US forces had fought under Japanese command in the Ussuri Valley north of Vladivostok, in August, 1918. By October, when the Canadian Army began to arrive the area had been pacified.

[13] "Why Siberia," *Canada's Siberian Expedition*, University of Victoria, http://www.siberianexpedition.ca/story/index.php.html [accessed March, 2021]; Silverlight, 236

[14] Nicholson, 522

[15] Nicholson, 520

[16] Nicholson, 521-22

[17] Nicholson, 522

[18] Donnell, 239

[19] Silverlight, 351

16. The Versailles Settlement

The Peace Conference that followed the conclusion of World War One was held in Paris in 1919, and formalized at the historic royal palace of Versailles, outside of the City of Light. Hostilities had only ended with an armistice, and not with a formal Peace, and so it was important to finalize the terms of peace as quickly as possible. Although the Central Powers thought that President Wilson's Fourteen Points would be the just basis for a peace agreement, such was not the understanding in the minds of the European allied leaders whose countries had suffered so much in the war.

Germany, in particular, received a shock when it was disabused of the expectation that a just peace based on the Fourteen Points was in the offing. For the Austro-Hungarian and Ottoman Empires, the peace of Versailles meant imperial dissolution. After Versailles, the political landscape of Central Europe, and of Asia Minor, was changed forever.

Both Canada and Japan went to Paris with a goal of recognition in mind. However, it was two very different forms of recognition that each country sought. For the Canadians, the sufferings of the war, in which 51,727 servicemen and 21 servicewomen were killed by enemy action, had been psychologically devastating, but the war had instilled increased Canadian pride, and nationalism, within a weakened British Empire. Prime Minister Sir Robert Borden was determined that Canada would take its place in Paris as a country in its own right, although he envisaged Canada remaining a country within the British Empire, or British Commonwealth, as the empire now began to call itself in the post-war era. As a country, Canada, and most of the other British dominions, insisted on full national representation in Paris. That posed a significant dilemma for Great Britain because constitutionally the British dominions remained subordinate to Britain, and thus the ultimate sovereignty over their territories was held by Great Britain. Would the other sovereign participants at Paris concede equal rights of representation to the British dominions?

For Japan, the issue of recognition revolved around race and nationality. The Japanese came to Paris seeking a racial equality and national non-discrimination clause in the structure of the new world order that President Wilson remained determined to promote. Racial discrimination towards Asians in general, and towards the Japanese race in particular, was rampant in many western societies and Japan quite rightly asserted that if the Japanese were equal to their Caucasian brothers and sisters in wartime, they should be equal to them in peacetime as well. But race was a difficult subject to broach in many Occidental societies, particularly those that had experienced a high level of pre-war immigration from Asia, and in those societies which harboured overt, or latent, white supremacist ideologies. It was by no means clear that a Japanese demand for racial and national origin equality would be accepted by the other conference participants in Paris.

When it came to the representation of the dominions at the Peace Conference both President Wilson and Premier Clemenceau of France were dubious, seeing the claims of the British dominions as a subtle attempt by Great Britain to increase its voting power at the Peace Conference. But the contribution made by the dominions to the ultimate victory of the allies could not be denied. Therefore, it was agreed that the dominions could have one representative each but that proved to be unacceptable to Prime Minster Borden, and to the leaders of most of the other dominions.

Eventually, the US and France agreed that Canada, Australia, South Africa, and India could each have two separate delegates, New Zealand could have one delegate, and that the British dominions could also be represented in rotation on the five-person British Empire delegation, which suited the dominion of Newfoundland.

Alone among the dominions, Newfoundland did not aspire to a separate status at Paris.

There was a division of perspective between some of the dominions on one significant issue pertaining to the empire as a whole, and that was the need to maintain a close political relationship with the United States of America. Canada was obviously quite concerned to maintain a cordial relationship between the British Empire and the United States, with Prime Minister Borden actually hoping for the establishment of a partnership between the two great English-speaking world powers. However, Prime Minister Billy Hughes of Australia did not necessarily see a closer relationship develop between the British Empire and the United States as essential, a point of view that would also be played out in the subsequent negotiations over the Anglo-Japanese Alliance.[1] For his part, President Wilson returned the Australian sentiments – Wilson did not like Billy Hughes.

Canada feared a collision of interests between the British Empire and the United States over the question of the division of the former German territories that had been taken by the allies early in the war. Both Australia and New Zealand wanted to retain the South Pacific territories that they took from Germany, and South Africa was anxious to retain German South-West Africa (later to become Namibia) which it had conquered in 1915. On this issue, Japan was of a like mind to the antipodean dominions, as it wished to retain the North Pacific islands, and the Kiaochow Concession, which Japan had taken (with British and Indian assistance in the case of Kiaochow) in 1914. Only Canada had no territorial ambitions arising from its participation in the war.

President Wilson was entirely opposed to a parcelling out of the conquered German territories, and he sought a peace without territorial acquisitions. The difficulty for Wilson was that the United States had come into the war quite late, and only after the German colonies had already been taken by the Entente allies.

The losses that some of the allies had suffered in the war made it politically difficult for them to deny themselves territorial aggrandizement at the expense of the Central Powers.[2]

Canada worked within the British Empire to mediate the differences between the opposing viewpoints. Great Britain wanted the British Empire to retain the territories it had earmarked for acquisition, as a result of the Central Powers defeat, but as British Prime Minister David Lloyd-George told Australian Prime Minister Hughes, the United Kingdom would not go to war with the United States over the issue of who would control the German Solomon Islands.[3]

The solution that was ultimately arrived at was to forswear the taking over of the former German territories outright but to create mandates within the framework of the new League of Nations, and to assign the mandated territories taken from Germany to one or the other of the allies. The mandatory powers would be obligated to assist their mandates to reach the level of self-governing states within the community of nations at some unspecified future date. To ease the concern of the allies who wanted to maximize their control over the ex-German territories the Peace Conference created three classes of mandates, A, B, and C. Class A mandates were almost completely self-governing, and would proceed to independence within a few years. Those were mostly found in the Middle East, being former Ottoman Empire territories. Class B mandates would be separately governed by the mandatory power, with independence far off in the future. The Class C mandates were territories that would be administered integrally with the mandatory power, and that class included the South Pacific territories of German Samoa, taken by New Zealand, German New Guinea, and the German Solomon Islands, taken by Australia, and the German North Pacific Islands that were now held by Japan. This three-class mandate system was subsequently applied to all the former German African colonies, and to the former Ottoman territories of Palestine, Syria, and Iraq.[4]

While that outcome was pleasing to the antipodal dominions it did not stop them from getting into a dispute over which dominion would take control of the phosphate-rich island of Nauru, a German island located just below the equator. To resolve the impasse between Australia and New Zealand, Britain assumed the formal mandate over Nauru, with participation in the mandate by Australia and New Zealand.[5]

Japan came to the Peace Conference as a major power. Its delegation was headed by a genro, Prince Saionji Kinmochi. However, Prince Saionji left most of the heavy lifting at the conference to the professional Japanese diplomats, preferring to remain in the background of events. At the end of the war, Japan had the third-largest navy in the world and a respectable army. Canada's Prime Minister Borden considered Japan to be one of only three great powers to emerge from the wreckage of the war.[6]

The Anglo-Japanese Alliance was not a subject for discussion at the Peace Conference but it lurked in the background. For Japan, the alliance remained an important touchstone proving that Japan was one of the great powers of the world. Canada remained concerned about the relationship between the British Empire and the United States, and how the Anglo-Japanese Alliance could affect that relationship in the future. Apart from sentiment, a recurring Canadian diplomatic nightmare was the thought that the Anglo-Japanese Alliance could pull Canada into a war between Japan and the United States, with potentially disastrous consequences for Canada.[7]

In the Versailles settlement, there were two major objectives that Japan sought to achieve. Firstly, Japan wished to retain the territories that it had taken from Germany during the war, and secondly, it wished to ensure that a racial equality clause was inserted into the League of Nations covenant. Japan feared that following the end of the war a race-based alliance of the western powers against Japan might emerge, and that is why an expression of racial equality was important to Japan. Furthermore, racial equality was the one subject upon which Japan could make a common cause with China against the western powers.[8]

Japan feared that its formal Entente allies, Great Britain, France, and Italy, would renege on the agreements that they had made concerning the Japanese claim to the German North Pacific territories but none of them did.[9] In the end, the western allies adhered to the agreements that they had made with Japan leaving only the United States as a holdout. American admirals were concerned about Japan's conquest of the German North Pacific Islands because Japan's possession of the former German islands placed Japan in a commanding strategic position in the Pacific from where it could interrupt the American lines of communication to the Philippine Islands.[10]

In the end, President Wilson decided not to contest the Japanese possession of the German North Pacific islands because he thought that it was more important to pressure Japan to leave Kiaochow, and the President knew that he could not hope to succeed in removing the Japanese from both German China, and the German North Pacific together. Although Wilson went along with the conferral of League of Nations mandates on Japan for the former German North Pacific islands, he did contest Japan's right to hold Yap Island because it was an important transit point for international cables. The United States called for international control over Yap but in vain. Yap went to the Japanese as a mandate along with all of the other former German islands in the North Pacific.[11]

Kiaochow was more difficult. China had entered the war in 1917, with American encouragement, and China expected to recover the entire Shantung peninsula now that Germany had been defeated. Of course, Japan had other ideas. It wished to retain Kiaochow for itself, and in that desire, Japan had the backing of Great Britain and the other Entente allies. Although the Entente allies did wish to restore Chinese sovereignty over the ex-German territory, China's position on recovery of Kiaochow had been compromised by treaties that China had entered into with Japan during the course of the war.[12] Japan had taken advantage of China's weakness to obtain China's agreement to Japan's post-war retention of Kiaochow, an agreement that admittedly went against the general public opinion in China. The United States remained particularly opposed to Japanese expansionism in China, and US Secretary of State Lansing began to refer to Japan as "Prussia".[13]

Although Japan sought to have the Kiaochow Concession treated as part of a package including the North Pacific islands, the Allied Supreme Council demurred, and instead insisted that Kiaochow be treated as a separate issue. China was clearly opposed at Paris to Japan's retention of the enclave, arguing that the entire area was very important to Chinese culture because it was the homeland of the great Chinese philosophers Confucius and Mencius.[14]

Meanwhile, the Japanese delegation had been promoting its second objective, which was the insertion of a racial equality clause in the League of Nations Covenant. That effort provoked a backlash from many of the Anglo-Saxon delegations, where racial discrimination policies were prominent in both immigration and social policy. Although China agreed with Japan on the principle of a racial equality clause, Japanese hopes for strong Chinese support were dashed by the Japanese recalcitrance at returning Kiaochow to Chinese sovereignty.

Race played an important role in the formulation of British Empire policy towards the Japanese demand. Great Britain itself should have had no difficulty with the clause that Japan proposed because the British presided over a world-girdling empire that contained many different races and cultures within it. The problem the British faced was the attitude of the British Empire's settler dominions, which maintained closed immigration policies discriminating in favour of Caucasian immigrants, and against immigrants from Asia or Africa. The dominions were adamant that they did not want to grant equal immigration access to the Asian races.[15]

The racial equality clause that Japan sought to insert in the League Covenant was concerned with prohibiting discrimination on two grounds, race and nationality. The proposed clause read:

> "The equality of nations being a basic principle of the League of Nations, the High Contracting Parties agree to accord, as soon as possible, to all alien nationals of States members of the League equal and just treatment in every respect, making no distinction, either in law or in fact, on account of their race or nationality."

To attempt to resolve the impasse within the British Empire, the British convened a private meeting on March 25, 1919, that included representatives of Great Britain, and the British dominions, together with Japanese diplomats in order to search for a way forward. Australia and New Zealand continued to express strong opposition to the racial equality clause, and the two antipodean Prime Ministers, Hughes of Australia, and Massey of New Zealand formed a team to block any initiatives to resolve the impasse.[16]

Prime Minister Borden of Canada was much more flexible on the issue, and he proposed a compromise, but Hughes refused to agree. The meeting broke up without a positive result but the participants came together again on March 30th and on that occasion both Prime Minister Borden and Prime Minister Smuts, of South Africa, tried to mediate the differences between Japan and Australia over the racial equality issue, shuttling back and forth between the two delegations. Although Prime Minister Hughes did show some flexibility, ultimately the question of Asian immigration could not be resolved on any terms that he could favour. Hughes was adamant that the 'White Australia' immigration policy that was applied in his dominion must be maintained, and Hughes feared that approval of the racial equality clause could, over time, erode Australia's immigration policy. In his report to Tokyo on the failure of the Peace Conference to embrace racial equality, Prince Saionji blamed the British dominions for the result.[17] There is little doubt that the Japanese were shocked that Great Britain could no longer control the diplomacy of its settler dominions, and they took particular umbrage at Australia, and at Prime Minister, Hughes, whom Baron Kato described as a mere peasant.[18]

Prince Saionji may have been a little harsh in fixing blame solely on the British dominions for the failure of the racial equality clause but only slightly so. The other party at the Peace Conference that opposed the racial equality clause was the United States, where race played an important role in domestic politics and social policy. President Wilson's advisor, Colonel House, slyly spoke against racial discrimination to the Japanese delegates but did nothing when they asked him for help with the British Empire's objections. In private, Colonel House was gladdened by the fact that the British delegation was at the forefront of opposition to the clause because it allowed the United States to posture sanctimoniously – at least until the Japanese insisted on the US taking a stand on the question. When the Japanese delegation insisted on a formal vote on the adoption of the racial equality clause President Wilson, who was serving as the Conference Chairman, complied with their request. But when the racial equality clause was passed by a majority vote of 17 to 11, Wilson ruled from the Chair that racial equality was a matter of principle, and as such it must be passed unanimously in order for the resolution approving the clause to be carried. Since the racial equality clause did not attract unanimity, it was deemed by Wilson, as the Chair of the Conference, to have failed. It was a dubious ruling but the Japanese were unwilling to directly challenge Woodrow Wilson.[19] The failure of the racial equality clause would have consequences for the future, however. It was one of the factors, along with the subsequent failure of the Anglo-Japanese Alliance, that led Japan to turn away from the West and to embrace an aggressive nationalism that would ultimately lead to another world war in the Pacific Ocean.[20] The Japanese were dignified in defeat but unmistakably bruised by this encounter with racial prejudice.

Why did the Japanese not contest Wilson's ruling on the racial equality clause? The practical reason was that the final outcome of the Kiaochow issue remained outstanding. The Japanese now glimpsed the outlines of a deal in which Japan would give way gracefully on the racial equality clause, and in return receive a satisfactory resolution regarding the Japanese desire to retain possession of the Kiaochow Concession. Japan insisted that they must have Kiaochow, as they had incurred lives lost in taking it from the Germans, and public opinion in Japan expected Japan to retain possession. Japan was also quick to remind the allies that Japanese efforts in the Pacific during the war had kept open the Pacific and Indian Ocean shipping lanes.[21]

Japan was adamant that it could not accept losses on both the Kiaochow issue and the racial equality clause. If that happened, Japan would not sign the Peace Treaty. That ultimatum put the other allied powers in a difficult position because Premier Orlando of Italy had already walked out of the Peace Conference over a dispute concerning Fiume, which was a part of the former Austro-Hungarian Empire that Italy wanted to possess. If the Japanese also left the Peace Conference it would seriously diminish the aura surrounding the Peace Conference in the eyes of the world. Thus, there was a begrudging acceptance on the part of the western allies of Japan's entitlement to the former German enclave in China, even though allowing Japan to keep it went against the pro-China sentiments of several of the western allies.

For its part, Japan smoothed the way for a Kiaochow accommodation by giving a verbal promise that it would eventually return Kiaochow to Chinese sovereignty.[22] In addition to conceding Chinese reversionary sovereignty, Japan also promised to limit its control of Kiaochow to the German economic privileges that had been associated with the territory, together with the right to a settlement at Tsingtao.[23] A formal announcement of those Japanese intentions was made in August of 1919. The western allies left Paris skeptical that Japan would ever return Kiaochow but in fact, the Japanese were as good as their word, and the enclave was returned to China in 1922, largely because the Japanese concluded that it was an uneconomic venture. It would fall again to Japanese arms in World War Two.

Having obtained most of what it sought at the Peace Conference, Japan signed the Versailles Peace Treaty and entered the League of Nations. Canada and the other dominions also separately signed the Peace Treaty, giving Canada and the other dominions their first international recognition as autonomous countries within the British Commonwealth. For Canada, however, there remained one last battle and that was to obtain full membership rights in the new League of Nations. At first, the major powers were averse to giving the British dominions full membership rights in the new League but Prime Minister Borden fought to obtain a separate membership for Canada and, with Great Britain's support, on May 6, 1919, the United States, Great Britain, and France, agreed that the British dominions could become full members of the League of Nations, and they could be selected, or named, as members of the League Council.[24] Canada's separate signature on the Paris Peace Treaty in the Hall of Mirrors, in the Palace of Versailles, at the end of June, 1919, initiated an evolving recognition of Canada as a state with an international legal personality that was separate and apart from that of Great Britain.

Almost as an afterthought it seems, the Canadian Government next turned its attention to its diplomatic representation in the United States. Canada had long used the agency of the British Ambassador to the United States to represent the country diplomatically in Washington but the wartime relationship between Canada and the United States made it imperative, from the Canadian perspective, to achieve a more direct level of diplomatic communication between

Ottawa and Washington. A solution was arrived at after negotiations between Ottawa and London to create a hybrid diplomatic model within the British embassy in Washington. In May, 1920, it was announced that a Canadian Minister would be appointed to represent Canada in the United States as part of the British Embassy in Washington, and the new Canadian Minister would operate as the British Ambassador's next-in-command within the embassy, and would actually manage the embassy, and the diplomatic relations between the British Empire and the United States when the British Ambassador was absent, or the post was vacant. However, on purely Canadian issues the Canadian Minister would negotiate directly with the American government based on instructions from the Canadian government, and without reference to the British government.[25] In the official joint announcement by the British and Canadian governments, great care was taken to assure the public in both countries that the new arrangements would not impair the diplomatic unity of the empire. But the reality suggested otherwise. The separate signature of the Canadian government on the peace treaty, the recognition of Canada's separate membership in the League of Nations, and the pending appointment of a separate Canadian diplomatic representative in the United States all pointed to an inescapable conclusion. The imperial dominions, and Canada in particular, had their own separate and distinct foreign challenges and they now had to craft their own foreign policies, commensurate with their new standing in the world.

Unfortunately for the future of the Anglo-Japanese Alliance, neither Prime Minister Borden, nor his successor, Arthur Meighen, perceived the logical result of the direction in which they were taking the country. Thus the tension between Canadian autonomy, and Imperial interests, would come to the fore in 1921, at the Imperial Conference, at which time the renewal of the Anglo-Japanese Alliance would become the major subject for consideration.

NOTES

[1] Margaret MacMillan, *Paris 1919: Six Months That Changed the World*, Random House, New York, 2002, 93 [afterwards: MacMillan, 1919]

[2] Despite President Wilson's aversion to territorial conquests, it is notable that, in 1917, the United States pressured neutral Denmark to sell the Danish Virgin Islands to the United States, ostensibly to prevent them from being used as a base for German U-boats, or German surface raiders. When the Danes appeared to be recalcitrant, the Wilson Administration told Denmark that the United States might occupy the Danish territory without Danish approval, if Denmark refused to sell the islands to the United States.

[3] MacMillan, 1919, 103

[4] In Africa, part of German Tanganyika was carved out and a new territory of Ruanda-Urundi was created and given to Belgium as a mandate, and a small slice of Tanganyika (German East Africa) was also given to Portugal for incorporation into its colony of Mozambique. German South-West Africa went to South Africa as a League mandate.

[5] Later, in 1923, Australia would replace Great Britain as the formal mandatory power, with a subsidiary role assigned to both Great Britain and New Zealand.

[6] MacMillan, 1919, 306

[7] MacMillan, 1919, 47

[8] Nish, *Decline*, 269

[9] Imperial Russia had also signed a treaty with Japan but it no longer existed in 1919, having been replaced by the USSR, which was then in the throes of a civil war. The United States entered the war as an associated power and was never formally part of the Entente.

[10] Stephenson, 437

[11] MacMillan, 1919, 316

[12] Nish, *Decline*, 272

[13] MacMillan, 1919, 330

[14] MacMillan, 1919, 334

[15] Nish, *Decline*, 269

[16] MacMillan, 1919, 318-319

[17] Nish, *Decline*, 270 fn

[18] Nish, *Decline*, 271

[19] Nish, *Decline*, 270

[20] MacMillan, 1919, 321

[21] MacMillan, 1919, 315

[22] MacMillan, 1919, 338

[23] Nish, *Decline*, 273

[24] Allen, 193

[25] Roger Graham, *Arthur Meighen Vol II And Fortune Fled*, Clarke, Irwin and Co., Toronto, 1963, 56 [afterwards: Graham, *Fortune Fled*]

17. The Anglo-Japanese Alliance in the Balance

The Great War was over and as the British Empire picked its way through the wreckage of the old pre-war world the future of the Anglo-Japanese Alliance hung in the balance. During the war tensions had emerged in the alliance on both sides, leading to suspicion and recriminations but nevertheless, the alliance had held through to the general peace.

Within Great Britain there was gratitude for what Japan had done in the war but that feeling was tempered by a suspicion that Japan had not done as much as it might have done for the allies, and there was an underlying concern that Japan had taken advantage of the war to greatly extend its reach, and influence, in the Far East and the Pacific Ocean. The Twenty-One Demands Japan had presented to China, and the unequal treaties that Japan had subsequently foisted on the weak republican government of China rankled the British, who saw that Japan had taken advantage of the absence of the European powers from the Orient to extend its influence throughout China. The Yangtze River valley that pre-war Britain had regarded as its own special sphere of influence was now an active area of commercial penetration by Japan. Australia and New Zealand also worried about the commanding position that Japan now held in the Pacific, and how that might affect their own future national security.

In Japan, there had been pronounced pro-German sympathies throughout the war in the Japanese universities, and in the Japanese Army, which had been trained by Prussian officers in the aftermath of the Meiji Restoration. Japanese army officers admired the Prussian-German approach to army command and control, and they had spoken disparagingly of the courage and efficiency of the

British Empire forces that had served under Japanese command at the siege of Tsingtao. The Japanese had thought that the metropolitan British units were reluctant to fight, although they expressed a somewhat better view of the Indian Army contingent that served within the British force at Tsingtao. So great was the respect of the Japanese Army for the German Army that many Japanese Army officers were surprised and disappointed, by the sudden collapse of the Central Powers in 1918. The Imperial Japanese Navy, on the other hand, had received its initial training from the Royal Navy after the Meiji Restoration and it was always a pro-British service. Its respect for the professionalism of the Royal Navy ensured that the Japanese navy's sympathies would lay with Great Britain. During the course of the war the British, Australian, New Zealand, and Canadian naval forces had worked together amicably with the Japanese naval forces, and there was mutual respect amongst the services of those countries.

However, Japan had resented the stopping of Japanese merchant vessels by Royal Navy warships in 1916, when the British engaged in ship searches for Indian political activists who were agitating for Indian independence, a group that the Japanese, as fellow Asians, quite naturally sympathized with. Furthermore, the failure of the racial equality clause at Versailles also caused deep consternation in Japan especially as the failure was attributed, in no small measure, to the British dominions, which continued to oppose the flow of Japanese immigrants into their countries.

Before the war ended there was both a recognition, and a concern, in London about the fraying of the relationship between the British and Japanese Empires, and a special effort was made to counteract the drift in the alliance by employing an old pre-war practice that, even in 1918, seemed anachronistic. The British government decided to confer the rank of a Field Marshal in the British Army on Japanese Emperor Taisho, as a sign of respect, and alliance, between the two island empires.

Prior to the First World War, it had been quite common for monarchical states to confer honorary military ranks on foreign sovereigns. For instance, the German Kaiser, Wilhelm II, had been made an Admiral in the Royal Navy in the pre-war era. Now, London decided to confer the military rank of a Field Marshal on the Japanese Emperor, and in keeping with the pre-war protocol necessary on such occasions, a special embassy was despatched to Japan to extend the honour to the His Imperial Majesty Emperor Taisho. To lead that special embassy, the former Governor General of Canada, His Royal Highness Prince Arthur, the Duke of Connaught, was selected to go to Tokyo. He was accompanied on this mission by several senior British army officers who had obtained significant field experience with the British Army during the war.

At a court ceremony in Tokyo on June 19, 1918, the Duke of Connaught, accompanied by senior British officers dressed in wartime khaki dress, black boots, and carrying canes, presented themselves to the Emperor Taisho, who was attended by senior Japanese Army officers dressed in their full ceremonial dress uniforms. The Duke of Connaught presented the baton of a Field Marshal to Emperor Taisho on behalf of his nephew, His Majesty King George V, Emperor of India. The British ambassador, who was present for the ceremony throughout, considered the ceremony to be a diplomatic success because it helped to counteract the pro-German sympathies held by Japanese generals, and it reminded the Japanese generals of the importance to Japan of the Anglo-Japanese Alliance.[1] Afterwards, the Duke of Connaught left Japan on the Japanese battleship HIJMS *Kirishima*, and sailed to Canada and, after crossing Canada by train, he sailed across the Atlantic returning to Britain to report to the King-Emperor on the success of his royal mission.[2]

Subsequently, Japan reciprocated the British courtesy by sending Admiral Prince Higashifushimi to London to present the baton of a Japanese Field Marshal to King George V. The Japanese prince was met by His Majesty the King-Emperor in person at the railway station in London, and the Prince stayed at Buckingham Palace during his visit. These symbolic ceremonies, redolent of a bygone era, marked an attempt by both empires to inject a new life into the historic friendship between the British and Japanese empires. Marquis Inouye, the Japanese Ambassador in London, hailed the exchanges as an "unprecedented event" and noted that it was a form of chivalry that was very much appreciated by the Japanese.[3] Japan's Prime Minister Hara echoed those sentiments by stating that the Anglo-Japanese Alliance was the "leading factor" in Japanese diplomatic relations, and for his part the Duke of Connaught, while in Japan, had hailed the important role that the IJN had played during the war in maintaining world trade in the Pacific and Indian Oceans, and the anti-submarine assistance that the Japanese Navy had provided in the Mediterranean Sea.[4]

But what were the true facts of the matter? From the outset of the war, Japan had placed its participation in the war effort against the Central Powers within the framework of the Anglo-Japanese Alliance, which meant that it had limited its sphere of operations as a belligerent to the territorial scope of that treaty relationship. Despite the entreaties from France, and Russia to take on a stronger role as a member of the Entente, Japan had largely restricted its efforts to the Asia-Pacific theatre of war operations. Yet, within the framework of the Anglo-Japanese Alliance, the contributions that Japan made to the allied victory were significant. The mere fact of Japan's entry into the war had condemned Tsingtao as a wartime naval base and had forced Admiral Count von Spee to take his German East Asiatic Squadron out of the Pacific war theatre to avoid a crushing defeat at the hands of the superior Japanese navy. During the initial stages of the war at sea, the IJN had despatched reinforcements to Canada to guard against the possibility of an attack by German cruisers and had maintained a North American covering force to protect against Admiral von Spee putting his whole squadron on the west coast of North America to attack

Canadian and other allied shipping. The Japanese Navy had also played an important role in the protection of the ANZAC convoys through the South Pacific, and Indian Oceans, during a period of time when von Spee was active, and his whereabouts were unknown. Japan had also assisted in the suppression of the Indian Army mutiny in Singapore.

The German North Pacific island colonies were conquered by Japan, and the remaining German naval units in Micronesian waters were either forced to scuttle, or compelled to intern themselves in neutral US ports in the Pacific. The taking of the North Pacific islands, and the Kiaochow Concession, had permanently disrupted German communications in the Pacific Ocean. Japan played the predominant role in the siege and conquest of the German fortress port of Tsingtao, and afterwards, the Japanese routinely patrolled the North Pacific sea lanes between Canada and the Far East, enforcing allied command of the North Pacific Ocean. Later, after the United States entered the war the IJN assumed the protection of the Hawaiian Islands, and of the US naval station at Pearl Harbour until the end of the war.

The Japanese navy had also played an important role in keeping open the Indian Ocean sea lanes, and it actively participated in the search for the German raider SMS *Emden*. Later in the war, the IJN sent a squadron of destroyers and a cruiser to work with the allied navies in the Mediterranean Sea, where the Japanese force was much needed, and the Royal Navy offered high praise for the Japanese contribution in the Mediterranean. At the end of the war, Britain invited the Japanese Mediterranean squadron to visit Great Britain and to be feted before sailing home to Japan.[5]

Japan was also instrumental in keeping Imperial Russia in the war for as long as possible by shipping war materiel to the ramshackle Russian Empire throughout the war, helping to stave off for a time a Russian collapse on the eastern front. Japanese artillery was shipped to Russia for its defence of Warsaw when Warsaw was attacked by General von Hindenburg's eastern armies in 1915.[6] Japan's timely intervention, with the United States and Canada, and other allies, in Siberia in 1918 was undertaken at a time when there were still allied fears that a German and/or Bolshevik Russian front might be established in Asia.

Although the Germans put out peace feelers to Japan several times throughout the war, and there were actual discussions between Japan and Germany in Stockholm mid-way through the war, the Japanese remained loyal to the Anglo-Japanese Alliance and reported to Great Britain all of the overtures made to Japan by Germany.

Nevertheless, despite the important role performed by Japan during the war the changed conditions of the post-war world required a reassessment by the Royal Navy of future threats. The Royal Navy had ended the war with 40 dreadnought battleships, and the fleets of Germany and Austria-Hungary had ceased to exist. The Royal Navy was now supreme in European waters but the enormous power of the United States had been revealed by the war, and British policy-makers were adamant that Great Britain would never contest America for maritime supremacy. Consequently, the British decided that in the post-war world they would not build capital ships to match the United States.[7]

A defence review undertaken at the end of the war concluded that if the Anglo-Japanese Alliance was continued Britain would have no security concerns about their eastern empire but if the alliance was terminated Great Britain would have to consider the possibility of an eventual war with Japan in the Far East and to prepare for that eventuality. In that case, it would be essential to find a different base for a British battle fleet in Far Eastern waters because Hong Kong was too exposed to a potential Japanese attack. After considering the options, the Royal Navy proposed that Singapore should become an alternate base for the eastern fleet. By October, 1919, following the Versailles settlement, the Royal Navy was becoming even more certain that the Anglo-Japanese Alliance would fail, and the Admiralty advised the British Cabinet that the navy now had serious concerns about its strength in the Far East.[8]

In Tokyo, the Japanese military was also looking toward the future to ascertain where the coming threats to Japan might arise. The Japanese military was impressed by the demonstrated military and economic strength of the United States but closer to home the military remained uncertain about where Russia's path would lead it, and despite its current prostrate condition the Japanese generals and admirals knew that great strength lay in the Russian steppes, and Russia might soon rise up again. The conclusions reached in Tokyo were that Japan should prepare for a potential land conflict with Soviet Russia, and a potential maritime conflict with the United States.[9]

The United States remained deeply suspicious of Japan and was particularly concerned about Japanese aggrandizement towards China. Like the IJN, USN officers foresaw the possibility of a future conflict between the United States and Japan over maritime supremacy in the Pacific Ocean. Gradually, the American navy began to see the Japanese navy as its most likely enemy, rather than its historic adversary, Britain's Royal Navy. In that view they were increasingly supported by American public opinion, which remained deeply suspicious, and hostile, towards the Anglo-Japanese Alliance, viewing it as inimical to US interests in the Pacific Ocean.[10]

From London, the future of the Anglo-Japanese Alliance was clouded but on the whole, Whitehall retained a positive impression of the relationship with Japan and in the immediate aftermath of the war, there was no thought at the political level of ending the alliance. However, challenges to the alliance were clearly evident, and Great Britain had to ponder the value of the alliance against the antagonism expressed towards it by the United States, and the deep unease that the three settler dominions in the Pacific, Australia, New Zealand, and Canada, felt towards the rising power of Japan in the Pacific. There was still strength in Great Britain to hold the empire together but Britain had been badly weakened by the war, and now there were nationalistic strains not only in the settler dominions but in India and Ireland as well. The changing political and constitutional landscape within the empire was an important factor to be taken into account in deciding the future intentions of the British Empire towards the Anglo-Japanese Alliance.

In Japan, the alliance had provided the country with significant diplomatic cover for its expansion into China and stretching Japan's control of adjacent seas across the island chains of the North Pacific. Japan was now an oceanic, as well as an Asiatic empire, and the result had been popular in Japan. Japanese public opinion thought that Japan had made an enormous contribution to the allied war effort through the alliance with Great Britain, and therefore Japan was deserving of the territorial gains that it had acquired during the war. Japanese policy-makers were aware that the decline of the British Empire had been advanced by the economic shock of the war, and that, diplomatically, Japan was no longer as restrained by the alliance as it might have been in the pre-war years.[11]

Nevertheless, Japan had not been able to obtain the recognition that it had sought at Versailles, and the rejection of the racial equality clause was a particularly bitter blow. The United States posed a potential future threat to Japan, and even though Great Britain had long made it plain that the Anglo-Japanese Alliance could not be invoked by Japan in the event of a Japanese-American war the alliance with Britain could still provide Japan with useful avenues of diplomacy for the problem posed by the prospect of an American challenge. On balance, therefore, it was desirable for Japan to maintain the Anglo-Japanese Alliance.

Thus, as the tenth year of the third alliance approached the political leadership of both empires began to contemplate the negotiations that would be necessary to renew the Anglo-Japanese Alliance but as yet neither party even remotely contemplated that their alliance might fail.

NOTES

[1] Nish, *Decline*, 248

[2] Nish, *Decline*, 247

[3] Dua, 182

[4] Dua, 183

[5] Nish, *Decline*, 254

[6] Dua, 186

[7] Nish, *Decline*, 284

[8] Ian T M Gow, "The Royal Navy and Japan, 1900-1920: Strategic Reevaluation of the IJN", in *The History of Anglo-Japanese Relations 1600-2000, vol. 3, The Military Dimension*, Chihiro Hosoya, Ian Nish ed. Macmillan Press, New York, 2000, 48

[9] Nish, *Decline*, 283

[10] Nish, *Decline*, 281

[11] Gow, 47

18. Canada's Opposition to the Japanese Alliance

With the conclusion of the Great War, and of the Paris Peace Conference, a number of departures of high officials took place in the now peaceable kingdom atop the North American continent. Prime Minister Sir Robert Borden, worn out by his years as Canada's wartime leader, retired from office on July 10, 1920, and Arthur Meighen succeeded him as the leader of the Unionist Party, and as Prime Minister of Canada. Borden was followed into retirement by Admiral Sir Charles Kingsmill, the commander of the Royal Canadian Navy, who retired on December 31, 1920, and was succeeded in office as the country's naval commander by Commodore Walter Hose. Much of Commodore (later Rear Admiral) Hose's time in command of the navy would be spent fighting rear-guard actions in connection with both the naval budget and the naval organization, as Canada transitioned into peacetime and successive governments looked to obtain economies by cutting military expenditures.

As the RCN moved into peacetime mode there was a review of Canadian naval requirements, and a particular focus of that review concerned the future of the Anglo-Japanese Alliance. The navy had reported its conclusions in stark terms to the government in May, 1919:

> "By the elimination of Germany from the Pacific the Alliance, however, appears to have lost its main value for us, and may even be looked upon more in the light of an encumbrance, as it is a potential means of embroiling us with the United States. We are, therefore, confronted with Japan as a possible and even probable future enemy. This problem of the Pacific may be approached from other points of view but

always it leads to the same conclusion, namely, that Japan is the enemy."[1]

For Canada, the principal consideration, as always, was the country's relations with the United States. World War One had, for the first time, placed both of the North American countries together in an alliance instead of facing off against each other defensively, with each seeing the other as a potential hostile threat. From Canada's perspective, the United States had remained a potential enemy throughout most of the nineteenth century, and several times British troops had to be sent to Canada to protect it from incursions by filibusters, or to ward off American invasion or the threat of an invasion. The last major threat had occurred only a quarter-century before during the border dispute between Venezuela and British Guiana, which had caught Canada in the middle of an Anglo-American dispute over South American borders. The Great War alliance represented a positive development in the relations between Canada and the United States and Canadian civilian and military officials were strongly motivated to encourage that positive relationship to continue on national security grounds.

The Canadian perspective also found some resonance within Britain's Royal Navy but for a different reason. All militaries need to have a potential challenger in order to focus their activities and to justify the public expenditures that are required to support large military establishments. The Royal Navy was no exception to that rule. At the end of the war, the Royal Navy was dominant in the Atlantic and Indian Oceans. The German High Seas Fleet had essentially been jailed by the Royal Navy for the duration of the war, and then afterwards it was interned at Scapa Flow. Now, it was gone – scuttled on the eve of the signing of the Peace Treaty at Versailles by loyal German sailors who preferred to see their ships on the bottom of the ocean rather than in the hands of the victorious allied navies. The Royal Navy no longer had a potential antagonist to defend against in the Atlantic, as both France and Italy were allies, and British policy-makers had determined that a future war with the United States was unthinkable and must be avoided at all costs. That left Japan as the only potential challenger to British naval supremacy anywhere in the world, and within the navy, there was an increasingly jaundiced eye cast on the British Empire's Far Eastern ally. Lord Jellicoe, the victor at Jutland, was sent around the empire in the aftermath of victory to discuss the future of Imperial naval defence. He stopped in India, Australia, and New Zealand, and then finally in Canada and held talks with the colonial and dominion governments within the British Empire. The future of the Anglo-Japanese Alliance was an important topic for consideration in those discussions. In Canada, Lord Jellicoe diplomatically noted that future relations with Japan were unpredictable.[2] In reality, from 1920 onward, the planning for future naval conflict within the British Admiralty focussed on Japan as the likely enemy of the British Empire.[3]

At the political level in London, however, there was still support for renewing the alliance. Japan had proven to be a faithful ally for the British Empire during the war. Without Japan's assistance, Great Britain could have potentially lost local control in the Pacific and Indian Oceans at the outset of the war. Now, in peacetime, the Imperial government in London was faced with uncertainty in the far reaches of the empire. The peacetime navy would not be able to maintain the forty dreadnoughts that it had at the end of the war, and peacetime economies would be necessary. The British Empire had been victorious but the economic and demographic cost had been tremendous. Great Britain itself was no longer in a position to sustain or protect, its far-flung empire by force. The Royal Navy was inferior to the Japanese, and the Americans, in the Far East and in the Pacific. There was uncertainty about the future even in Europe, and it was considered possible that a Soviet-German understanding could eventually emerge. The assessment of the political actors in London, led by Prime Minister David Lloyd George, was that while Great Britain needed good relations with the United States, and British and American interests were aligned, or could be aligned, in the Orient and in the Pacific, there was still a great benefit in maintaining the Anglo-Japanese Alliance.

Japan had been a faithful ally during the war and had met its obligations under the alliance to assist Great Britain. Japanese statesmen were honourable men who could be counted upon to uphold their commitments, and the failure of the alliance might force Japan into future arrangements with the Soviet Union and Germany that would be contrary to Britain's interests. While a comprehensive worldwide alliance between Great Britain and the United States, France, and Weimar Germany would probably be an ideal outcome, American isolationism would not allow for such an arrangement and consequently, the renewal of the alliance with Japan was the next best course of action to follow.[4] The Admiralty partially came around to the government's way of thinking and advised that it was now neutral on the question of renewing the alliance. While the Admiralty thought that renewal of the alliance was unnecessary, and perhaps not desirable, the Admiralty stated that it did hope for the achievement of a broad understanding between Britain and Japan.

As it became clearer that Great Britain was leaning towards a renewal of the alliance, Canada ramped up its opposition. Prime Minister Meighen and the Ottawa bureaucracy opposed the renewal of the alliance for several reasons. Meighen took the view that there was no longer a rationale for the alliance following the defeats of both Russia and Germany in the world war and that Japan now posed a threat to the territorial integrity and sovereignty of China. But most importantly, the Prime Minister was concerned about the possibility that the alliance with Japan could embroil the British Empire in a war between Japan and the United States in which, according to Meighen's view, Canada would occupy the place that Belgium had occupied at the outbreak of the recent world war – a lesser country caught between warring giants. Meighen urged on the imperial authorities Canada's claim that it had a special role to play in determining whether there should be a renewal of the Anglo-Japanese Alliance.[5]

While the politicians and military analysts were contemplating the future of the alliance, the calm deliberations necessary for determining the right course of action were nearly upended by the lawyers at the Foreign Office in London. Officials there had been examining the Anglo-Japanese Alliance for its congruence with the League of Nations Covenant and had found it to be wanting. As a result, the British and Japanese Governments decided, based on legal advice, to jointly advise the League of Nations that the "British Government and Japanese Government have come to the conclusion that Anglo-Japanese Agreement of July 13th, 1911 now existing between their two countries though in harmony with [the] spirit of [the] Covenant of League of Nations is not entirely consistent with the letter of that Covenant which both Governments earnestly desire to respect." As a consequence, Great Britain and Japan recognized that "if said agreement be continued after July 1921 it must be in a form which is not inconsistent with that Covenant."[6] The advice to the League Office was also transmitted to Ottawa, and Canada responded to London through the Governor General, the Duke of Devonshire, to express its agreement with the approach suggested by the two signatories to the alliance.

What the politicians in London did not realize, however, was that, according to a subsequent opinion rendered by the Foreign Office legal advisors, that declaration made to the League of Nations by Great Britain and Japan operated as a notice of termination of the alliance under Article 6 of the 1911 treaty. Neither Great Britain nor Japan had the slightest intention of consciously giving a notice of termination of their alliance. Japan was not even told about this legal opinion from the Foreign Office, nor was the British Foreign Minister, Lord Curzon, adequately briefed by his officials about the matter.[7] In the meantime, the Imperial government in London decided to postpone the scheduled Imperial Conference by one year, from 1920 to 1921, and during that delay, the notice period for termination of the agreement quietly continued to pass according to the interpretation placed on it by the Foreign Office's legal advisors.

Japan did remain worried about the British attitude towards the renewal of the alliance. The Japanese government wished to continue the alliance with Great Britain but it now recognized that the evolving constitutional structure of the British Empire was a major complication in effecting the renewal of the alliance. Based on their experience at Paris, the Japanese believed that a renewal of the alliance would encounter substantial opposition within the British Empire from Australia and New Zealand. They did not expect that substantial opposition would come from Canada. For Japan, the alliance was important because Japan obtained an important status in the world from its alliance relationship with the British Empire. The alliance was thus a marker of its entry into the world as a great power. Furthermore, the alliance prevented Japan from becoming politically isolated. Political isolation was dangerous for Japan both from an international perspective, and from a domestic perspective, as events would subsequently show. Yet both Japan and Great Britain had to recognize that with Germany and Russia prostrate from the war, there was no longer a challenger to focus the energies of the alliance upon, with the result that the alliance now lacked a common purpose in the Far East.

As for the United States, it was now the paramount power in the world, although it shrank from leadership on the international stage. Its retreat from world affairs masked the fact that it had supplanted the British Empire as *primus inter pares* in the world. Historically, Great Britain had always leaned against the greatest power of the age, first Spain, then France, and most recently Germany. The United States was now in the position of being the greatest power of the age but for the first time, Britain shrank from standing against a rising power. There were a number of reasons for that development. For the first time, the rising power was outside of Europe, and Britain had always been concerned to balance power in Europe by frustrating the dominant country on the European continent. The fact that the United States posed no threat to Europe meant that Britain did not have to stand against it to preserve the European balance of power. But more importantly, there were deep and strong cultural and social ties between Great Britain and the United States that had not been present when other great powers had arisen in Europe in the past.

The world had become more complicated for Great Britain. Britain's hold on its empire was declining. There were nationalist forces at work in India, in Ireland, and in the dominions that threatened the future integrity of the world-girdling empire that Britain had built. Great Britain increasingly lacked the strength to hold the mantle of command across the broad sweep of the globe, and it realized that it must look to an understanding with another power. Which was it to be? The United States with its chequered past relationship with Great Britain in the Americas, or Japan, Britain's occasionally competitive but generally faithful ally in the Orient?

Japan was well aware of the increasing hold of the United States on British foreign policy and it too worried about the potential of a collision with the rising power on the other side of the Pacific Ocean. In order to save the alliance, it was necessary to placate the United States and with that view in mind, both Great Britain and Japan released notes pledging that the Anglo-Japanese Alliance was not directed against the United States.[8]

However, Canada, after reviewing the statements issued respectively by the British and Japanese Foreign Ministers, came to the conclusion that Japanese Foreign Minister Uchida had not explicitly, and publicly, stated that Article IV of the 1911 Agreement, which exempted alliance members from assisting the other party to the alliance where an arbitration agreement with another power existed, had released Great Britain from its potential participation in a war between Japan and the United States, as Japan's ally.[9]

Uchida was probably legally correct in remaining ambiguous on the question of whether a conciliation treaty met the legal test for constituting an international arbitration within the specific meaning of the existing Anglo-Japanese Alliance Treaty. Yet, it was surprising that Canada did not take Great Britain at its word in such a case, rather than attempting to parse the language of the Japanese declaration, but that no doubt reflected the strengthening of Canada's objections to continuing the alliance with Japan.

As time moved towards the convening of the Imperial Conference in 1921, the Canadian government kept up its pressure on London to forego a renewal of the alliance with Japan. On February 21, 1921, Prime Minister Meighen sent a message to British Prime David Lloyd George through the Governor General, the Duke of Devonshire:

> "We feel that every possible effort should be made to find some alternative policy to that of renewal. Admitting that the Alliance has been useful in the past, it nevertheless seems true that the conditions have been so altered that the old motives no longer hold, while the objections have been greatly increased. It is unnecessary to elaborate those points at the moment but I would emphasize the need of promoting good relations with the United States. In view of her tendency towards abandonment of attitude of isolation generally, her traditional special interest in China which is as great as ours, and of the increasing prominence of the Pacific as a scene of action, there is danger that a special confidential relationship concerning that region between ourselves and Japan to which she was not a party would come to be regarded as an unfriendly exclusion and as a barrier to an English speaking concord.
>
> Consequently we believe we should try to attain our objects in the Far East in another way. Specifically we think we should terminate the Alliance and endeavour at once to bring about a Conference of Pacific Powers – that is Japan,

China, the United States, and the British Empire represented by Great Britain, Canada, Australia and New Zealand – for the purpose of adjusting Pacific and Far Eastern questions. Such a straightforward course would enable us to end the Alliance with good grace and would reconcile our position in respect of China and the United States. It would be a practical application of the principles of the League of Nations. Should it eventually result in a working Pacific Concert the gain to the stability of British-American relations is obvious..."[10]

Here in a nutshell was Prime Minister Meighen's approach to the question of the renewal of the alliance with Japan. Meighen wanted to ensure that the alliance relationship that Canada and Britain had developed during the course of the war with the United States would not decay because of the alliance relationship with Japan. Meighen used expressions such as "an English-speaking concord" and "a working Pacific Concert" to describe his wish for an understanding between the British Empire and the United States. At all costs, Meighen wished to avoid any potential for a future conflict between the British Empire and the United States in the Pacific that would involve Canada. The British insistence that there was no obligation on the part of the British Empire to come to the aid of Japan in the event of the latter's entering into a war with the United States was surprisingly unconvincing in Ottawa. The Canadian government remained suspicious of Japan and carefully parsed Japanese diplomatic language to conclude that Japan did not really think the conciliation treaty that Great Britain had with the United States was adequate as a foundation for an exemption under the existing 1911 Agreement. In Meighen's view, the only way to ensure that Canada did not get sideswiped by a conflict between Japan and the US was to terminate the Anglo-Japanese Alliance.

The mere recital of Prime Minister Meighen's views was not unduly alarming in Whitehall – the British already knew that Canada was having grave reservations about the renewal of the alliance. What did alarm London however was a practical suggestion made by Meighen to accomplish the object he set out in his telegram to the British Prime Minister. Meighen suggested a direct approach to the US Government by Canada, stating: ". . . we suggest that a representative of the Canadian Government should get in touch with the new President and his Secretary of State as soon as possible after their inauguration and discover through informal confidential conversations whether any such policy is feasible. For this purpose I would nominate Sir Robert Borden who is willing to act."[11]

The Imperial government in London quickly responded to Meighen's initiative by cabling back on February 26th through the Colonial Secretary, Winston Churchill, to suggest that the Canadian focus was much too narrow, and that the matter required a more fulsome discussion, and consideration, by all of the dominions as well as by the Imperial government:

> "In the first place we have throughout felt nothing should be done to prejudice complete liberty of action of forthcoming Imperial Cabinet in regard to Anglo-Japanese Alliance. Question affects all the Dominions and especially Canada, Australia and New Zealand. It affects India and British possessions in the Far East. We fear formulation, from an official quarter in however tentative and informal a form, of a proposal to the United States (that a) round table conference of all Powers concerned should be summoned to discuss Pacific question, could hardly fail to tie the hands of the Conference next June especially if it was favourably regarded by Washington. In any case we think that the other Dominions would have to be consulted before such a proposal was approved. In the second place we think while there is much to be said for a conference of this description as a possible ultimate solution there are very many questions to be settled before the decision to make such a proposal could be reached. Questions at issue affect

international position of Great Britain and the general foreign policy of the Empire. They are inseparably bound up with disarmament, naval shipbuilding, future of League of Nations and its disarmament programme. Various expert committees have been sitting for some months in this country considering various political, economic, military and naval issues involved with [the] object of placing members of Imperial Cabinet in possession of all the considerations necessary to enable them to arrive at a judgment. We think that these are very strong arguments for having a full discussion of whole problem between the various Governments of the British Empire in light of information now being collected before making any official approaches however informal to the United States of America."[12]

Prime Minister Meighen waited a long time before responding to Churchill's message. When he did respond there was no question that despite the diplomatic language, the Prime Minister was miffed by the British attitude, and by what he perceived as a lack of recognition of Canada's unique circumstances, lying next door to a behemoth. Responding again through the Duke of Devonshire to Prime Minister David Lloyd George, Meighen stated that:

"... if the Alliance is to wait upon the settlement of questions of disarmament, naval shipbuilding, and the future of the League of Nations we fear it will wait a very long time. Nor are we able to appreciate the exact connection between these questions and the question of the Alliance. . . .

We consider it essential once more to emphasize the very special Canadian position in this matter. Of the Canadian people more than of any other people whatever it is true that their welfare and security are intimately involved in any question vitally affecting the relations between the British Empire and the United States. They will expect every effort to be made toward a policy of co-operation and will attach great importance to the present question as involving the first definitely significant step in post-war British American relations. In spite of occasional differences their whole experience has been favourable to principle of co-operation and they would recoil from anything to the contrary. They have had special opportunities through intercourse and association to understand and deal with the Americans and they will feel that the advantages of this consideration should not be overlooked. They will be unlikely to be convinced by the conclusions of committees which must necessarily be lacking in the intimate experience and association essential to a judgment upon the political conditions of this hemisphere.

From [the] Canadian view point it might become necessary to consider an alternative solution by which only those parts of the Empire desiring to do so should join in renewal, on the analogy to the abortive Anglo-Franco-American Reinsurance Treaty concluded at Paris; but it seems desirable to avoid the implications of such a solution if possible. We therefore are still strongly of the opinion that steps should be taken as soon as possible along the lines of our proposal."[13]

Prime Minister Meighen clearly put the Imperial government on notice that at the forthcoming Imperial Conference he would be contesting the renewal of the Anglo-Japanese Alliance. Meighen even went so far as to suggest to the Imperial government the possibility that Canada might resile from the renewal, thus breaking the diplomatic unity of the political Empire. That it was largely an empty threat did not necessarily make it less meaningful for the purpose of developing an Imperial policy on the subject of the alliance. Meighen's views, while boldly stated, probably reflected the trend of Canadian public opinion at the time.[14]

Later in April Churchill responded to Prime Minister Meighen with an attempt to quell the rebellious Canadian initiative to involve the United States directly in the formulation of Imperial foreign policy:

> "Your Government may rest assured that renewal of Alliance in any form is a question which will be left entirely open until June Meeting of Imperial Cabinet.
>
> . . . Meanwhile we would strongly urge Canadian Government should not approach Government of United States independently at this stage. Later on, if consultation with America becomes necessary we shall be very glad to profit by offer of services of your Government, when definite policy has been decided upon."[15]

Meanwhile, the Government of Japan had not been idle. Recognizing that there was dominion opposition to the renewal of the alliance, Japan decided to send Crown Prince Hirohito to the United Kingdom in an effort to bolster ties between the two island empires. It was the first time that the heir to the Japanese throne had been sent abroad, and the visit was symbolically significant, as it reflected the strong Japanese desire to continue the Anglo-Japanese Alliance. Hirohito was given all the great honours that his position demanded. He was met by the Prince of Wales, the future King Edward VIII, at Portsmouth when he arrived in Great Britain, and he was met by King George V at the railway station upon his arrival in London.[16] While his visit was accounted a success, Prince Hirohito's visit does not seem to have had a major impact in London on the course of foreign policy, or on the question of the renewal of the alliance.

In the South Pacific, there had been a change of heart about the Anglo-Japanese Alliance. While New Zealand was always prepared to accept the lead of London, and to see the alliance renewed, Australia had initially balked at renewal. However, Prime Minister Billy Hughes had undergone a conversion, realizing that without a renewal of the alliance, a weakened British Empire might not be able to successfully defend Australia against a potentially hostile Japan.[17]

The festering legal problem of whether the joint declaration issued by Great Britain and Japan to the League of Nations in 1920 constituted a notice of termination of the Alliance treaty now came forward when Britain proposed a three-month extension of the agreement to Japan, in order to carry the continuation of the alliance past the forthcoming Imperial Conference, which was to be held in the summer of 1921. The Japanese were aghast at the idea that the joint declaration of the previous year amounted to a denunciation of the treaty of alliance and Japanese lawyers employed in the Foreign Ministry in Tokyo were immediately set to work to review the opinions of the British Foreign Office lawyers. Predictably, the Japanese lawyers came to a different view, holding that the declaration made to the League Office was not tantamount to a notice of termination. The British Foreign Minister, Lord Curzon, gave the issue over to the Law Officers of the Crown, the most senior legal advisors to the British Government, who regrettably contributed more muddle to the situation. Ultimately, the Prime Minister had to put the matter before the Lord Chancellor, whose august office encompassed both judicial and political functions. The Lord Chancellor dealt with the issue deftly, essentially finding a way to agree with the Japanese lawyers, although the legal issue was still active when the Imperial Conference convened in 1921, and the Lord Chancellor's resolution remained a secret until Prime Minister Lloyd George decided to make it known to the dominion leaders. Needless to say, the Japanese were not amused by all these legal antics, which caused them to question the sincerity of the British intention to renew the alliance.

As the Imperial Conference approached in 1921, the British government finally committed to proceed with a modified renewal of the alliance. Churchill was of the view that the Canadian government was opposed to the renewal but it was biddable if the British supported a Pacific Conference, as Prime Minister Meighen had suggested.[18] The final position of the British government heading into the Imperial Conference was to renew the Anglo-Japanese Alliance but to modify it to conform to the League Covenant, and to shorten its duration to four years from the previous ten-year term. At the same time, Britain was prepared to agree with the Canadian suggestion that a Pacific Conference be convened, and Britain would even be amenable to the US President convening the conference. In this way, Great Britain hoped that the policy of the Imperial government could be reconciled to the desires of the Canadian government, and thus keep peace in the Imperial family of nations.[19]

NOTES

[1] Naval War Staff, *Occasional Paper* No. 1, May 28, 1919, Library and Archives Canada File RG 24, vol 5696, quoted in Johnstone et al, 744

[2] Tucker, 316

[3] Johnstone et al, 745

[4] Nish, *Decline*, 298

[5] Johnstone et al, 745

[6] Department of External Affairs, *Documents on Canadian External Relations*, Vol. III, 1919–1925, edited by Lovell C. Clark, Ottawa, Queen's Printer for Canada, 1970, No. 203, p. 156 [afterwards: DCER Vol. III]

[7] Nish, *Decline*, 303

[8] Nish, *Decline*, 316

[9] Nish, *Decline*, 318

[10] DCER vol. III, No. 209, p 162 at 163

[11] DCER vol. III, No. 209, p 163

[12] DCER vol. III, No. 210, p 163 at 164

[13] DCER vol. III, No. 213, p 166

[14] Johnstone et al, 745

[15] DCER vol. III, No. 216, p 168

[16] Nish, *Decline*, 323

[17] Nish, *Decline*, 325

[18] Nish, *Decline*, 329

[19] Nish, *Decline*, 330

19. Arthur Meighen

Arthur Meighen was born on June 16, 1874, at Anderson, near St. Mary's Ontario, the son of a farm couple of Irish Protestant stock. He was a quiet, intelligent, child who did not enjoy sports much but who excelled at debate and oratory. Arthur would memorize his speeches as a child, reciting them aloud in the local woods as a form of practice, and his oratorical skills impressed all of the adults who heard the precocious youngster. Although Meighen possessed a clear and logical mind, his sense of humour was somewhat limited. As a young man, he had a lean build, and a serious mien, joined to a clear mind, and a superior capacity to debate and to argue.

After completing his provincial secondary education he entered university at the University of Toronto, where he subsequently graduated with a degree in mathematics. Meighen then attended an Ontario teachers college, and afterwards he taught school for a year at Caledonia, Ontario, before deciding in 1898 to move to Manitoba to pursue a career in the law. Meighen was called to the Bar of Manitoba as a barrister and solicitor in 1903, and he established a law practice in Portage La Prairie, where he continued to practice law until 1915.

In 1908, when he was 34, Meighen stood for election as a Conservative in the Federal general election that was held in that year and was he elected to the House of Commons in Ottawa. The story is told that when Robert Borden was first elected as the leader of the Conservative Party in 1900, he stated that he would only serve as the leader of the Conservative Party until another man could be found to lead the party. In 1908, when Arthur Meighen rose in the House of Commons for the first time and made his maiden speech in Parliament, the Liberal Prime Minister, Sir Wilfrid Laurier, turned to those around him and said "Well, Borden has found a man!" Despite his obvious talents as a parliamentarian, Meighen had to pay his dues as a backbencher before he could hope to ascend to the Cabinet. His years in Ottawa from 1908 to 1913 were spent in the political wilderness on the Tory backbenches in Ottawa, first as a member of the opposition, and then, after 1911, as a government backbencher.

In 1913, Borden, now the Prime Minister, appointed Arthur Meighen to be Solicitor General of Canada, a perfect fit for a barrister with a clear and logical mind. The Solicitor General was one of the Law Officers of the Crown, and the office assisted the Minister of Justice and Attorney General with the legal business of the government. However, at this point in Canadian political history the Solicitor General, although a member of the Canadian Ministry, was not summoned to sit in the Cabinet, and so Meighen remained a Minister of the government outside of the Cabinet, which set him somewhat apart from the centre of politics.

With the outbreak of the war, the demands on Prime Minister Borden increased exponentially, and as time passed Borden more and more began to rely upon his brilliant Solicitor General to get things done. Meighen proved himself to Borden as absolutely loyal and possessed of a sharp mind, an ability to concentrate on the problems at hand, calmness under pressure, and the energy and determination to do the things that were politically unpopular, but that had to be done in order to govern effectively.

As a result, Borden invited Meighen into the Cabinet in 1917, and assigned him to the dual portfolios of Secretary of State, and Minister of Mines. Shortly afterward, he promoted Meighen into the more important position of Minister of the Interior. However, none of Meighen's wartime Cabinet responsibilities placed him into portfolios that had a direct impact on the war effort, and he acquired little managerial experience in the departments that were most closely connected to foreign or military affairs. Yet, that did not stop Prime Minister Borden from using Meighen to tackle some of the most difficult wartime files that faced his government.

Foremost among the problems the government faced as the war dragged on was the shortage of manpower in the army, leading to a decision to impose wartime conscription on young males. Meighen's task was to draft the resulting Military Service Act and to see it through Parliament. Although he successfully managed that important project the resulting political furor ruined the Unionist Party for the foreseeable future, particularly in Quebec, where there was strong and active opposition to conscription. The conscription bill actually shook the pillars of Confederation, and the army had to be used to suppress public dissent.

Meighen was also responsible for the War Time Elections Act, which extended the electoral suffrage to female relatives of Canadian soldiers who were serving overseas, and removed the franchise from naturalized subjects who had immigrated to Canada from Germany, or the Austro-Hungarian Empire, after March 31, 1902. The effect of that bill was to enfranchise people who were likely to support the government and to disenfranchise those who might not support the government. A companion Military Voters Act also allowed the government to assign the votes cast by soldiers overseas to ridings where the government needed additional votes to win in that riding – a clearly undemocratic initiative. While the electoral legislation was popular in the short term, it rendered long-term damage to the fortunes of both the wartime Unionist Party and the Conservative Party, especially among those who were denied the right to vote, and particularly in Quebec where conscription remained very unpopular.

When the financial pressures of the war caused the collapse of the Canadian Northern Railway, the Grand Trunk Railway, and its subsidiary, the Grand Trunk Pacific Railway, the government moved to nationalize the bankrupt railways, and Meighen was put in charge of the file. Nationalization of the railways meant that Meighen had to face the wrath of the bondholders and the shareholders of the now-bankrupt companies, who stood to lose their investments. Then, in the immediate aftermath of the war, the Winnipeg General

Strike of 1919 found the Borden Ministry in a major conflict with labour, and Meighen was named as the point man for the government in the suppression of the Winnipeg strike, an assignment that besmirched Meighen's name amongst organized labour.

By the time that Borden was ready to retire and pass the reins of government on to a successor, Meighen, though respected, was politically toxic. He had been politically damaged by conscription, which angered Francophone voters, and farmers; voting restrictions, which upset immigrants; railway nationalization, which put out the bondholders who lost their investments; and the suppression of labour during the Winnipeg General Strike turned organized labour against him. Nor was Meighen very popular in Parliament, where opposition members had not enjoyed experiencing Meighen revel in debating victories over them, and many opposition members remained bitter at the tongue-lashings they had received from Meighen. Many in the Unionist Party, the Conservative-Liberal wartime coalition that was formed in 1917 when Anglophone Liberals broke with Sir Wilfrid Laurier over the conscription issue, wished for Sir William Thomas White to become the new leader of the party but he was disinterested. Ultimately, there was no one else who was seen as suitable in the Unionist ranks, and Meighen followed Borden into the leadership of the Unionist Ministry. In July, 1920, Meighen became the ninth Prime Minister since Confederation in 1867.

Across the aisle in the House of Commons Arthur Meighen now faced off against his diminutive and pudgy opponent, William Lyon Mackenzie King, the leader of the Liberal Party, who, despite appearances, was a wily parliamentarian, and who knew how to dissemble, and how to muddle through successfully. King, unlike Meighen, had the political skills to make compromises, and to balance the regional and national interests of the disparate empire that formed the Canadian union. Despite Meighen's intellectual gifts, King would best him on the hustings over the course of the next several years, and he would deny Meighen tenure as an elected Prime Minister of Canada.

For now, however, Meighen held power, and in the winter and spring of 1921, Meighen began preparing for the Imperial Conference which was to be held in London that summer. Although Prime Minister Borden had taken Meighen to Britain with him in 1918 to attend the meetings of the Imperial War Cabinet, and Meighen had met all of the leading figures in British politics, including David Lloyd George the Prime Minister, Lord Curzon the Foreign Minister, and Winston Churchill, now the Colonial Secretary, Meighen recognized that he did not have any special expertise in foreign affairs. Meighen's role at the meetings of the Imperial War Cabinet had been minor, and he spent most of his time in Britain dealing with the financial impacts of Canadian railway nationalization on British investors.

Despite his limited exposure to foreign affairs, however, Meighen held a firm attachment to Great Britain as Canada's mother country, and he continued to believe in a common foreign policy for the British Empire. Nevertheless, Meighen also recognized the growing importance of the United States to Canada, and he viewed Canada as a North American country that was linked by sentiment to Great Britain, but by geography and economy to the United States.[1]

The Prime Minister's political opponent in the House of Commons, Mackenzie King, approached the matter of Imperial unity differently than Meighen. King was a Canadian autonomist in his political philosophy, and he did not favour lock-step imperial unity in foreign affairs. King held that each dominion should be free to set their own course on foreign policy, and the diplomatic unity of the empire that had hitherto prevailed might now work against the individual interests of the dominions, and hamper their freedom.[2] King had worked in the United States, and he knew many influential people in America and he was well aware of the growing economic importance to Canada of its linkages to the United States, as well as the strong American antipathy to Japan, and to the Japanese race.

At this juncture in Canadian political history the Department of External Affairs, Canada's nascent foreign ministry, did not have a permanent Minister assigned to it, and it was the Prime Minister who actually conducted the country's foreign relations, as a sideline to his other duties. Prime Minister Meighen, knowing that he lacked extensive foreign policy knowledge, or experience, relied heavily on the advice he received from Loring Christie, a senior official in the Department of External Affairs.

Loring Christie was a protégé of Sir Robert Borden and a solicitor who possessed a lucid mind. He had been educated at Acadia University in Nova Scotia, and at Harvard, where he studied law. After his call to the New York Bar, Christie practised in New York before joining the US Justice Department in Washington as an attorney. Returning to Canada in 1913, he joined the Department of External Affairs with the title of legal advisor, but he quickly became the primary foreign policy advisor to Borden, and he was even more important to Borden than the Deputy Minister of External Affairs, Sir Alexander Pope.

Christie soon realized that Canada needed to understand the current thinking in Washington about the Anglo-Japanese Alliance before the Imperial Conference convened in London in 1921. It was Christie who had worked up the Canadian approach to London by suggesting that Canada should approach the United States, possibly through former Prime Minister Borden, to ascertain the American reaction to a renewal of the alliance. Without clear knowledge of where America stood on the question of renewal, Christie reasoned, the Empire's Prime Ministers would be faced at the conference with a binary choice, either to renew, or not to renew, the alliance.

While the reaction to the Canadian proposal had been negative in London, the Canadian government had not given up on the initiative. Newton Rowell, a Liberal who had broke with Sir Wilfrid

Laurier to join Borden's wartime Unionist Ministry as President of the King's Privy Council for Canada had continued as a backbench Unionist Member of Parliament following the formation of Meighen's Ministry in 1920. Now, in early 1921, Rowell visited Washington, where he had talks with several prominent men who were close to President-elect Harding, and he reported back to Meighen what he had heard in Washington, all of which was unfavourable to the continuation of the alliance. William Gardiner, an American associated with the Navy League in the United States, and who was also a close friend of influential US Senator Henry Cabot Lodge, visited Ottawa to quietly express the negative sentiments of American policy-makers concerning the renewal of the Anglo-Japanese Alliance.[3] It seems quite likely that American policy-makers had discerned that Canada was now able to advance an independent position on foreign policy issues in the Imperial forum, and the Americans reasoned that if Canada took a firm position on the non-renewal of the Anglo-Japanese Alliance Britain might be forced to succumb to that position or see the diplomatic unity of the British Empire publicly sundered. Another person who also had the ear of Prime Minister Meighen in the months leading up to the Imperial Conference was Bertram Lennox, a British advisor to the Chinese Foreign Office who visited Ottawa in early 1921, and who sought to make the case that Japan had taken advantage of China to the detriment of the Chinese. Lennox lobbied hard in Ottawa on behalf of China against the renewal of the alliance.

Fears by some Canadian policy-makers that a full-blown naval arms race could occur in the Pacific were exaggerated. Although there were legitimate concerns about a naval armaments contest in the Pacific, the reality was that in the post-war environment economic considerations tolled against any substantial expenditure on naval assets similar to what had occurred in pre-war Europe between Great Britain and Germany. Neither the United States, Japan, or Great Britain, were anxious to devote greater public funding to naval armaments in the post-war period. More important to Canada however, was the general attitude of the United States, where there was a strong dislike of Japan, almost amounting to paranoia about Japanese intentions in the Pacific. And yet it was also understood in Ottawa that the Imperial government would have to consider the loyalty of Japan to the alliance during the war, the long history of their alliance, and most importantly, the security of the southern dominions, and of the British possessions in Asia. Searching for a way through this foreign policy maze, the Meighen government landed on the idea of a multi-lateral conference of the powers with interests in the Pacific, in hopes thereby of negotiating a multilateral treaty that would satisfy the security concerns of all the principal actors in the Pacific.[4]

In the run-up to the Imperial Conference of 1921, there was a foreign policy debate in the House of Commons concerning the foreign policy and constitutional issues that the Canadian government would face at the Imperial Conference. Most of the debate concerned whether Canada should espouse a national, as opposed to an imperial approach to foreign policy, and the larger question of Canadian autonomy within the empire. Here, there was a contrast between the two main antagonists in the House of Commons, Arthur Meighen, the Prime Minister, and Mackenzie King, the Leader of the Opposition.

Meighen did not wish to publicly break with the traditional position that the British Empire spoke with one voice in international affairs, and he considered that diplomatic unity within the empire was a paramount consideration. However, Meighen did believe that a common foreign policy for the British Empire must be worked out through consultations between the Imperial government in London, and the governments of the self-governing dominions, among which Canada was the senior dominion, and therefore possessed of a national voice that ought to carry weight in the Imperial councils.

King, on the other hand, accepted that at the particular stage of political development that Canada had reached it must begin to follow a nationally-grounded foreign policy that addressed Canadian interests. King acknowledged that Imperial considerations were still important, but increasingly they would now become secondary to Canadian national concerns. Thus, the diplomatic unity of the empire did not concern King. In a general sense, Meighen looked to the past, and Mackenzie King looked to the future, in the formulation of Canadian foreign policy and the conduct of Imperial relations.

Although Prime Minister Meighen felt that the diplomatic unity of the empire was important it is curious that his logical mind did not discern that the development of a national approach to foreign policy was a logical evolution of the Borden Ministry's efforts to secure separate Canadian recognition in the Versailles Peace Treaty, and Borden's insistence on Canadian representation in the League of Nations that would be separate from the representation of Great Britain. Borden had also secured an agreement, shortly before he stepped down as Prime Minister, for the appointment of a Canadian diplomatic Minister to Washington to be the overall second in command at the British Embassy in the American capital, but who would also separately represent Canadian interests directly to the American government. The so-called diplomatic unity of the British Empire had become, at best, a fiction.

In the Foreign Policy debate in the House of Commons that preceded the Imperial Conference of 1921, there was little attention or controversy over the renewal of the Anglo-Japanese Alliance, although it was actually the main foreign policy issue to be determined at the conference. One reason why the alliance was not extensively debated in the House of Commons was that there was little to differentiate the approach of the Meighen Unionist Government and the Liberal Opposition under Mackenzie King. Meighen told the House that, "the importance of [the Alliance] to us arises, in a very great degree, out of the very great interest of the United States in the renewal or non-renewal thereof."[5] And Newton Rowell spelled out the issue even more clearly, stating, "The

Government of this country cannot ignore the feeling that does exist in the United States in reference to this alliance . . . this treaty should not be renewed, at least in its present form."[6]

In his main speech to Parliament Rowell chose to lay out nine conditions for the formulation of Imperial foreign policy from a Canadian perspective in the post-war period:

1. No territorial ambitions or aggressive intentions
2. Promote the peaceful resolution of international disputes
3. Full support for the League of Nations
4. Promote and support disarmament
5. Avoid special or exclusive alliances with other states
6. Promote international cooperation
7. Obtain recognition of a Canadian special interest on all questions that touch upon relations between the British Empire and the United States
8. No settlement of important questions between the British Empire and the United States without Canadian consultation
9. Canada's views should be conclusive on any question that is purely one of the Canadian interests.[7]

The Liberals did not say much about the renewal of the Anglo-Japanese Alliance in the House of Commons debate, but in the country at large the Liberal news media were invariably opposed to its renewal. The Liberal Party shared the government's view on the desirability of abandoning the alliance with Japan. As well, the Canadian public was indifferent to the continuation of the alliance, another reason why it did not receive much attention in the House of Commons debate. There was no public constituency in Canada that favoured the renewal of the alliance, and the perspectives of the general public of the era retained a strongly transatlantic focus where foreign policy issues were concerned. With no constituency in Canada strongly favouring the continuation of the Anglo-Japanese Alliance, and with serious political concerns about a negative American reaction to the renewal of the alliance, it was clear that Canada would go to the 1921 Imperial Conference opposed to its renewal.

On June 7, 1921, Meighen, with his wife, mother, and secretary, C H A Armstrong, joined Loring Christie aboard the Canadian Pacific liner RMS *Empress of Britain* for the voyage across the Atlantic, where Prime Minister Meighen would arrive as the youngest, newest, and perhaps the most adamant of the dominion Prime Ministers. The voyage, however, would provide a temporary respite from the cares of state, and Meighen, relaxed and convivial for once, was popular among the other passengers.[8] Awaiting Meighen in Britain would be the man who would become his nemesis at the Imperial Conference on the issue of renewing the Anglo-Japanese Alliance, the irrepressible Billy Hughes of Australia, small in stature, but large in voice, and in political courage.[9]

NOTES

[1] Graham, *Fortune Fled*, 55-56

[2] Graham, *Fortune Fled*, 55

[3] Graham, *Fortune Fled*, 75

[4] Graham, *Fortune Fled*, 70

[5] *Debates of the House of Commons* (1921), Vol. III, The King's Printer, Ottawa, 1921, 2639

[6] *Debates of the House of Commons*, (1921), Vol. III, 2657

[7] Thomas P Socknat, *Canada, imperial foreign policy and the*

abrogation of the Anglo-Japanese alliance, 1921, Thesis Submission, University of Nebraska, Omaha, 1967, 14, fn45.

[8] Graham, *Fortune Fled*, 79

[9] Roger Graham, *Arthur Meighen, Vol. I, The Door of Opportunity*, Clarke, Irwin and Company, Toronto, 1960, 199 [afterwards: Graham, Door]

20. The Imperial Conference of 1921

After arriving in Great Britain, Prime Minister Arthur Meighen found himself enmeshed in social engagements, an activity that did not generally appeal to the remote, cerebral, Prime Minister. However, major social engagements could not be avoided, and Meighen and his wife found themselves attending a state dinner with His Majesty the King-Emperor at Buckingham Palace, and subsequently a state ball, again at the palace. Later, there were luncheons with His Royal Highness, Prince Edward, the Prince of Wales, and also with His Royal Highness Prince Arthur, Duke of Connaught, the former Governor General of Canada. Meighen also dined with Winston Churchill, the Colonial Secretary in the Imperial government, and with General the Baron Byng of Vimy, who had recently been selected to replace the Duke of Devonshire as the next Governor General of Canada. Amidst his hectic social schedule, Meighen also found time to be sworn into the Imperial Privy Council, an honour that was always extended to the dominion Prime Ministers, and Meighen also received the Freedom of the City in both London and Edinburgh.[1]

Finally, the social engagements gave way to the business of the day. At noon on June 20, 1921, the Imperial Conference formally opened with the Prime Ministers of Great Britain, Canada, Australia, South Africa, and New Zealand in attendance, together with a representative of the Government of India. The Prime Minister of Newfoundland chose not to attend the 1921 Imperial Conference. British Prime Minister Lloyd George opened the proceedings with a state of the world address, in which he commented particularly on Japan, noting its loyalty during the war, as well as China's hopes for fair dealings from Japan in the future. Lloyd George also acknowledged that it was imperative for the British Empire to stay on good terms with the United States of America, and he tried to convey the sense that the British Empire was united politically, as well as culturally.

The Conference continued with opening statements from each of the dominion Prime Ministers and Prime Minister Meighen, the leader of the senior dominion, spoke first but said little. After the opening statements were completed the British Foreign Minister, Lord Curzon, a masterly advocate in the "Roman manner"[2] attempted to convey a sense of urgency to the proceedings by informing the Prime Ministers that the Anglo-Japanese Alliance would fail if it was not extended within the next 16 days because of the legal opinion that had been delivered by the Foreign Office lawyers the year before. That legal opinion, which interpreted the earlier Anglo-Japanese Joint Statement to the League of Nations to be a formal denunciation of the treaty of alliance, meant that the treaty would end exactly one year after the date the Joint Statement had been registered with the League, a date that was now quickly approaching.[3]

Afterwards, it was the turn of the dominion Prime Ministers to respond. Meighen, as the leader of the most senior dominion, went first. His initial statement on foreign policy dealt primarily with the processes that were necessary for formulating a unified foreign policy for the empire in an era of equality between the dominions and metropolitan Britain. Meighen set out three principles that he thought should guide the future formulation of the foreign policy of the empire:

> "1. There should be regular, and so far as possible, continuous conferences between the responsible representatives of Britain and the self-governing Dominions and India with a view, among other things, of determining and clarifying the governing principles of our relations with foreign countries, and of seeking common counsel and advancing common interests thereupon.

2. That while in general final responsibility rests with the Ministry advising the King, [i.e. the British Cabinet] such Ministry should, in formulating the principles upon which such advice is founded and in the application of those principles, have regard to the views of His Majesty's Privy Council in other Dominions and of the Representatives of India.

3. That as respects the determination of the Empire's foreign policy in spheres in which any Dominion is peculiarly concerned the view of that Dominion must be given a weight commensurate with the importance of the decision to that Dominion. Speaking for Canada, I make this observation with particular reference to our relations with the United States."[4]

Prime Minister Meighen emphasized to his counterparts that a dominion should be able to refuse to be bound by a foreign policy decision of the empire if that foreign policy was created without the consent of the dominion. To render his intentions unmistakable Meighen asserted that because of its geographical position Canada's views must be determinative with respect to any broad foreign policy issue between the British Commonwealth and Empire, and the United States.[5]

Meighen's proposed redesign of the foreign policy apparatus of the British Empire was disconcerting (to say the least) to the operators of that apparatus in London. There were several practical and constitutional contradictions inherent in Meighen's formulation for determining the future foreign policies of the empire. Firstly, how could the British government in London be held responsible to the British Parliament if it had to espouse a foreign policy that it might not agree with, simply because a dominion government had primary responsibility for an issue? How could a British Cabinet advise the King-Emperor on an issue of foreign policy if it did not agree with the advice that was being given to the monarch? How could 'continuous conferences' be maintained between the constituent parts of the empire when it could take weeks for documents sent out from England to reach their recipients in the far-off dominions and India? More importantly, how could the empire determine which dominion should take priority for particular files? When would Britain itself take priority?

The alliance with Japan was a case in point. Canada saw itself as the primary conduit for relations between the British Empire and the United States, and therefore Meighen asserted that Canada should exercise primacy on the question of renewing the Anglo-Japanese Alliance. As Meighen eloquently put it to the conferees:

> "Canada is a neighbour of the United States across a boundary of nearly 4,000 miles. We share with them a great portion of the American continent. Their trade with us is second in magnitude in comparison of their trade with the countries of the world, and may easily become the first. We have almost every form of international negotiation with them. The course of the United States' policy in every field affects Canada. Their numbers are many times the numbers of the Dominion in population; their decisions, their lines of policy, consequently affect us in profound degree. We live in constant and vital touch with this problem from day to day. The maintenance, and if it is by any means possible, the betterment, of relations between the British Empire and the United States of America should be, as the Foreign Secretary has well said "the pivot of Britain's world policy." To no country does this truth appeal with such tremendous force as it does to Canada."[6]

And Canada was very aware that the United States was averse to the rise of Japan as a great power, clearly seeing the Far Eastern island empire as its potential rival for supremacy in the Pacific Ocean. Good relations with the United States, in Meighen's view, required that the Anglo-Japanese Alliance be abandoned.

Prime Minister Meighen's viewpoint quickly generated opposition from the Prime Ministers of Australia and New Zealand, both of whom feared that the abandonment of the alliance with Japan could jeopardize their own national security. To that, Meighen naively said that everything could be worked out in due course, in conference, by well-meaning representatives of the respective countries.[7]

The Prime Minister also advanced the view that everything should be done to support the League of Nations, which was unobjectionable in itself, and aligned with both British foreign policy and the foreign policies of the other dominions, but Meighen also emphasized that the empire should avoid holding onto diplomatic legacies that were out of step, and disharmonious, with the objectives of the League.[8] Clearly, he meant the Anglo-Japanese Alliance.

On June 28th the Conference specifically turned its attention to the Anglo-Japanese Alliance and the question of whether it ought to be renewed. Prime Minister Meighen immediately challenged the proposal of Lord Curzon that the alliance be renewed. In rising to the challenge against the renewal of the alliance in any form Meighen knew that he was on solid political ground back home. He was in control of the Unionist Ministry, the Conservative-Liberal coalition that governed the country, and so he could ensure that the members of his caucus supported his lead on this important foreign policy issue. Furthermore, Meighen knew that the Liberal opposition in the House of Commons was generally aligned with his views about the continuation of the Anglo-Japanese Alliance. The Liberal press had come out against the renewal of the alliance. Both the *Toronto Globe* newspaper and the Liberal editor of the *Winnipeg Free Press*, John W Dafoe, were opposed to the renewal of the alliance.[9]

Meighen began his argument for non-renewal by stating that the alliance had served its purpose. Originally it had been intended to frustrate the ambitions of Imperial Russia but the menace of Russia had been eliminated by Japan's crushing victory in the Russo-Japanese War of 1905. Later, the alliance had assisted the British Empire in contesting the rising might of Imperial Germany but the Great War had ended all German pretensions to over-lordship in the Asia-Pacific region. Now there was no remaining threat to the British Empire in the Far East, and therefore the alliance was no longer required.

Secondly, Meighen focussed on Japan's relationship with China, and he stated that the 1911 alliance renewal treaty had committed the British and Japanese Empires to the "preservation of the common interests of all powers in China by ensuring the independence and integrity of the Chinese Empire . . . ," something that Japan had failed to do. Rather, the Japanese had penetrated deeply into China, and now in the aftermath of the war, Japan controlled southern Manchuria and the Shantung Peninsula. Meighen recalled the address to the conference by Lord Curzon, who said of the Japanese to the Prime Ministers, "They are people who must expand. They have done so in so far as this was open to them during the last twenty years, and they have done it, if not with an excess of scruple, at any rate with fairly successful consequences."[10]

Meighen called Curzon's statement a "formidable indictment" of a country that was ostensibly pledged to uphold "the independence and integrity of China" and to maintain the widely acknowledged Open Door policy. Meighen held that Japan had exceeded its rights, and had violated the covenant of the treaty relating to China. Lord Curzon tried to defend the alliance by pointing out that China had only protested the renewal of the treaty of alliance between Great Britain and Japan in its current form but he had proposed that a new version must conform to the requirements of the League of Nations. However, Meighen merely retorted ". . . on what ground [do] you expect under the Treaty to curb the rapacity of Japan in China?"[11]

Thirdly, and most importantly in Meighen's estimation, was the question of relations between the British Empire and the United States. Good relations between the empire and the US were essential, as was generally agreed. However, those good relations would be threatened by the renewal of the alliance, even with a proviso that the British Empire would never honour its alliance in the case of a war between Japan and the United States, an announced British position that both the United States and Japan were well aware of. Meighen argued that even if the British Empire remained neutral in such a war, the Japanese would quite rightly expect the empire to extend benevolent neutrality towards it, an attitude that, if followed, would be favourable to Japan, and unfavourable to the United States.[12][13] That course, argued Meighen, would be unacceptable to the United States.

In fact, Lord Curzon already knew from Britain's Ambassador in Washington, Sir Auckland Geddes, that the US Secretary of State, Charles Evans Hughes, was strongly opposed to the renewal of the Anglo-Japanese Alliance.[14] It was quite possible that relations between the British Empire and the American republic would suffer if Britain maintained its historic alliance with the Japanese.

Meighen asserted that Canada's views about the alliance emanated from the perspective of British Empire – USA relations and Canada's views must be seen as paramount by the other conference participants. He told the conferees:

> "But as regards this aspect, its effect on British-American relations, we do feel that we [i.e. Canada] have a special right to be heard. We say that because we know, or ought to know, the United States best, and because in the continuance and improvement of our relationship with them we have a vital concern. If from any cause, or from the initiation of any disastrous policy, we should become involved in worse relationships than we are now, Canada will suffer most of all. And if, in the last awful event – God forbid

it should ever come! – we reach the penalty of war, Canada will be the Belgium."[15]

Meighen's comparison of Canada's position vis-a-vis the United States under the Anglo-Japanese Alliance to that of Belgium, in the context of the pre-war European alliance system, was, of course, sheer hyperbole. Later, he said, "... the very existence of that Treaty [of Alliance] has undoubtedly injured British-American relations. Its continuance will do so even more . . ."[16] But Canada had "got along with the United States for 100 years" and Meighen was convinced that "we can still get along."[17] The Prime Minister was so adamantly opposed to the alliance with Japan that he refused to accept even the limited three-month extension to the 1911 treaty that Lord Curzon had proposed in order to allow for a fulsome consideration of the alliance by the various governments of the empire. Meighen accused the Imperial government in London of not advising Ottawa that the dominion Prime Ministers would be asked at the Imperial Conference to consider extending the alliance temporarily for three months.[18] A few minutes later, however, British Prime Minister Lloyd George forced Meighen to withdraw that accusation when Lloyd George pointed out that he had referred to the possibility of a three-month extension of the alliance in a cable that was sent to Ottawa on April 26, 1921.[19]

Meighen now proposed to the Imperial Conference that instead of renewing the treaty of alliance with Japan the British Empire should propose a multi-nation Pacific conference to focus on the reduction of naval armaments in the Pacific Ocean. In the interim, Meighen said that he would remain opposed to the renewal of the alliance for any purpose, including the proposed three-month extension to keep the alliance alive while the Imperial Conference proceeded, and the dominions considered their positions. In Meighen's view, it was time for the alliance to die.

After Meighen finished his oration the Conference turned next to the man who would become Meighen's nemesis at the Imperial

Conference, Australian Prime Minister William (Billy) Hughes. Short of stature but fierce in temperament, Billy Hughes stood in direct contrast to the tall, cool, cerebral Arthur Meighen. Hughes was a rough man but an eloquent one, a member of the Australian labouring class who had been toughened by life's circumstances. He was "a full-blooded fighter . . . asking no quarter and giving none",[20] a perfect contrast to the "icily unyielding"[21] Arthur Meighen. Remarkably, Hughes, like Meighen, was a member of the King's Privy Council for Canada, a unique honour for a foreign leader that Sir Robert Borden had arranged for Hughes during the war. Now, these two members of the King's Privy Council for Canada squared off against each other at the 1921 Imperial Conference over the question of the renewal of the empire's alliance with Japan.

Hughes tore into Meighen's arguments, accusing Meighen of speaking for the United States at the Conference, rather than for Canada, a wounding remark. Hughes emphasized that Japan had been the loyal ally of the British Empire during the recent war and that it should not now be rejected. While he agreed with Meighen that friendship between the British Empire and the United States should be an important consideration that did not mean that the foreign policy of the British Empire should be designed to obtain approval in Washington.[22] Prime Minister Hughes dismissed Meighen's arguments as merely the United States speaking through Canada to the conference. He urged that the British Empire needed a friend in the Pacific, and that friend should be Japan. Japan had been a loyal ally in the war, and Hughes feared that Japan would seek revenge if it was insulted by the rejection of the British Empire.[23]

Hughes undoubtedly realized that spurning Japan by rejecting the renewal of the alliance was unwise because it exposed the antipodean dominions to a potentially hostile power. That was the weakness in Meighen's position. Meighen had emphasized that the alliance was no longer needed because the threats posed to the British Empire by Russia and Germany had now passed, with the former's revolution, and the latter's defeat in the late war. However, the power of Japan remained, and its power had now been enhanced by its territorial acquisitions as a result of the war. Therefore, if the choice was to have Japan as an ally, or Japan as an adversary, it was much more preferable, in Hughes view, to keep Japan as an ally, and thereby mitigate any potential threat to the empire, especially to Australia and New Zealand. As for Canada, it was protected both by the Royal Navy (in the Atlantic Ocean) and in the Pacific by America's Monroe Doctrine, which rendered it inconceivable that Japan could physically threaten Canada without provoking an American response.

As for Meighen's plea for the protection of China against Japanese encroachments it seemed disingenuous that Canada had suddenly discovered sympathy for the Chinese. At this point in history, and for 35 years previously, Canada had maintained a Chinese head tax which by 1921 had reached $500.00 per person applicable to every Chinese person landed in Canada. The purpose of the head tax was to discourage Chinese immigration to Canada generally and to particularly discourage the immigration of Chinese women, whose immigration into Canada would secure the foundation of new Chinese communities in Canada.[24]

Canada's concerns about Chinese independence and sovereignty expressed at the Imperial Conference tracked the similar concerns expressed in the United States, however. America was sympathetic to China, a country where American missionaries had been prominent for some time, and where the overthrow of the monarchy, and the establishment of the republic, had created a superficial sense of alignment with the historical narrative of the United States. Nevertheless, the United States also discriminated against Chinese immigration, and, in fact, American immigration laws were even more discriminatory towards Chinese immigrants than the Canadian laws of 1921.

Reversing the logic of Lord Curzon, and the British Government, Prime Minister Meighen argued that a renewal of the alliance would, far from operating as a brake on Japanese ambitions in China, actually encourage further Japanese aggrandizement there. But in reality, there was no real evidence, either way, to judge whether Tokyo policymakers viewed the treaty of alliance as a support to Japanese imperialism in China, or whether it made the Japanese more cautious in implementing their designs. What was certain, however, was that the existence of the alliance treaty gave the British government a special entrée to speak to the government in Tokyo, and to remonstrate with it about the actions of Japan in China whenever those actions exceeded the international norms acceptable to the western powers.

Prime Minister Hughes was especially irked by the sense that Washington was pulling the Canadian strings at the Imperial Conference, and Hughes considered that the Canadian attack on the alliance was actually a smokescreen behind which was the United States interfering in the British Empire's relations with Japan. Hughes and others present at the conference were certainly aware that after much talk from Washington in the late war years, and at the Paris Peace Conference about a new, and more just world order, the United States had effectively abandoned any pretension to international leadership and had defected from its earlier idealism by refusing to join the League of Nations. The United States had left behind, in the aftermath of the war, a rudderless international system as the United States itself retreated into isolationism, much to the consternation and confusion of its wartime partners.[25]

Underlying all of Prime Minister Hughes' concerns was the potential threat of a Japan untethered by a treaty with the empire. Hughes himself had initially been averse to continuing the alliance, and he had expressed such sentiments during the peace process in Paris. The Japanese had fully expected that Prime Minister Hughes would be the main opponent of renewing the alliance at the 1921 Imperial Conference. However, Prime Minister Hughes had since had an epiphany concerning the alliance, and he now saw it as essential for the protection of Australia and New Zealand. Japan as a friend was much more desirable than Japan as an enemy, even though Hughes still firmly maintained his adherence to a whites-only immigration policy for Australia, and he refused to consider Japanese immigration. Australians, like Canadians (and Americans), were the prisoners of the racial prejudices of their times.

For British Prime Minister David Lloyd George the intransigence in the conversations between Canadian Prime Minister Arthur Meighen, and Australian Prime Minister Billy Hughes, portended the potential downfall of the conference, a conclusion that could shatter Imperial unity, and expose the fault lines of the British Empire for all other countries to see. Lloyd George correctly sized up Prime Minister Meighen as an obdurate man, who would not bend for the sake of the interests of the empire as a whole but who remained wholly fixated on his own country's national interests. Thus, although Prime Minister Lloyd George believed, along with Prime Minister Billy Hughes, and Prime Ministers William Massey of New Zealand, and Jan Smuts of South Africa, that the alliance with Japan should be renewed on the grounds of British imperial interests, the British Prime Minister calculated that from a political perspective time had run out for the Anglo-Japanese Alliance. The interests of Imperial unity, which was then an important political concern for every British Prime Minister trumped the continuation of the alliance. The dominion Prime Ministers were now treated to a master class in British diplomatic manoeuvrability, even sleight-of-hand, as one Imperial foreign policy (the alliance with Japan) was replaced by another (foreign policy alignment with the United States) to maintain the unity of the empire in the face of Canadian intransigence.

Prime Minister Lloyd George now released to the dominion Prime Ministers the legal advice of Lord Birkenhead, the Lord Chancellor. The office of the Lord Chancellor, one of the great offices of the state of long historical pedigree in Great Britain, combined both executive and judicial functions. The Lord Chancellor was both a

Cabinet Minister in the British government, as well as a judge who sat as the presiding judicial lord in the House of Lords, the highest appellate body in the judiciary of Great Britain. As such, his views about the law superseded even those of the Law Officers of the Crown (the Attorney General, and the Solicitor General) and thus obviously far outweighed the advice of the ordinary legal advisors in the Foreign Office.

Lord Birkenhead, had been called upon by Prime Minister Lloyd George to settle the dispute over whether the Joint Declaration of Great Britain and Japan that had been filed with the League of Nations in 1920, was a true denunciation of the treaty of alliance within the meaning of the alliance treaty. After considering the matter, the Lord Chancellor ruled that the Anglo-Japanese Joint Declaration was not a true denunciation of the treaty, and thus reached the same conclusion that the Japanese government's legal advisors had reached earlier. In releasing the Lord Chancellor's legal opinion to the dominion Prime Ministers Lloyd George undercut the strategy of his own Foreign Secretary, Lord Curzon, who had tried to use the imminent demise of the treaty as a pressure tactic to promote an agreement among the dominion Prime Minister to renew the alliance, at least temporarily. Curzon now cut a sorry figure at the Conference because his negotiating position was shown to have been based on a false premise. But Curzon's arguments had been ineffectual on Meighen anyway, and Lloyd George decided that he had to bid for time to avoid a crisis in Imperial unity. Politics is a ruthless business.

Lord Birkenhead's legal opinion had now taken the pressure off of the question of renewing the Anglo-Japanese Alliance because there was no longer a looming artificial deadline. That allowed Arthur Meighen to return to the attack when the Imperial Conference reconvened on July 1st, Canada's Dominion Day, its day of national celebration. Meighen was still smarting from the pummelling he had taken from Australian Prime Minister Hughes, and he now sought to dismiss all of Hughes' accusations against him, and at the same time blame Lloyd George for supporting Hughes, by stating; "I did, however, listen to a rather forceful attack, not on the position that Canada really took, but on a caricature of that position stated by the Prime Minister of Australia, and, I am afraid I must say, apparently acquiesced in by the Prime Minister of Great Britain."[26]

Meighen stuck to his position that friendship with the United States was a paramount consideration for Canada, and for the empire, and that there should be a conference of Pacific powers to deal with all of the issues concerning the interests of the great powers in the Pacific Ocean. Prime Minister Hughes remained adamant about renewing the alliance but the intervention of the Lord Chancellor had altered the position of the other Prime Ministers, as Lloyd George probably knew it would. Now that there was no need for an immediate decision on the renewal of the alliance Massey, Smuts, and Lloyd George could all agree with Meighen that there should be a Pacific Conference of the powers that had interests in the Pacific, to work towards harmonious relationships in the region. Prime Minister Hughes now found himself isolated on the subject of the renewal of the alliance.

A consensus was crafted that the question of the renewal of the alliance with Japan should be deferred in favour of a proposed Pacific Conference. If that conference succeeded, the alliance with Japan would be terminated but if it failed then the alliance with Japan would be renewed. Even that was too much for the haughty Canadian Prime Minister, who expressed his disagreement with this result because he considered that it gave Japan too much power to determine the success or failure of the proposed Pacific Conference, and thus of the renewal of the treaty of alliance. Meighen said: "the thing is madness in my mind. Japan would have the key to the situation, they would be the arbiters of the whole Conference."[27] But the other Prime Ministers supported this compromise, and there was nothing more that Meighen could accomplish by continuing to contest the consensus of the British and other Commonwealth prime ministers.

Nevertheless, Meighen had succeeded in his main objective at the Imperial Conference because he had prevented the renewal of the Anglo-Japanese Alliance. If he had not objected, and if he had not strenuously maintained his objections to the alliance throughout the Imperial Conference, the renewal of the alliance would have been accomplished because all of the other Prime Ministers had come into the conference favouring its continuation. Meighen's objections to continuing the alliance had forced the deferral of the question of renewal and, as it turned out, the decision to defer renewal would ultimately prove to be tantamount to a refusal to renew the alliance.

Meanwhile, in Washington, Secretary of State Charles Evans Hughes had got wind of the possibility that Great Britain would be seeking an international conference to limit armaments in the Pacific. Coincidentally, a recent US Senate resolution had called upon President Harding to convene a general disarmament conference but the Harding Administration had not yet acted on the Senate resolution. Now, Secretary Hughes became concerned that an invitation to an international arms limitation conference issued by Great Britain would prevent the US President from reaping any political credit for a disarmament initiative that would be popular with the increasingly isolationist US electorate. Secretary Hughes hastened to the White House to recommend to President Harding that he invite representatives from all of the major powers to come to Washington to discuss the subject of naval disarmament. The President quickly agreed, and formal invitations were expeditiously issued to Great Britain, France, Italy, and Japan, inviting them all to send delegates to Washington. The conference that President Harding called for was not the Pacific Conference that had been suggested by Prime Minister Meighen, and contemplated by the Imperial Conference in London. Rather, the American proposal suggested a much broader conference, with a general disarmament focus rather than one that would be narrowly focussed on Pacific issues.

When Lord Curzon finally got around to speaking with the American Ambassador about a specific conference of Pacific powers the original intention of a British invitation had become transformed into something much larger as a result of the invitation quickly issued by Washington. Therefore, a supplemental invitation was issued to all of the powers that had interests in the Far East to also discuss Pacific issues at Washington. Essentially, there were two separate but intertwined conferences that convened in Washington in November, 1921, one of which dealt with the size of the navies of the great powers, and the other conference which dealt with Pacific and Far Eastern issues.

The conference process suited Prime Minister Meighen, who had successfully prevented the renewal of the Anglo-Japanese Alliance by his firm and unyielding stance at London. The British Government had given in to Canadian demands and would soon find at Washington that American pressure on Great Britain to surrender the alliance was no less firm than the Canadian pressure at the Imperial Conference. Perhaps the best that can be said of the Pacific Conference process was that it provided a mechanism for terminating the alliance with Japan without giving a direct diplomatic offence to the Japanese.[28]

For Arthur Meighen, the Imperial Conference of 1921 was less of a personal triumph despite some of the accolades he received in the British media for the stance that he had taken.[29] Back home in Canada, Lord Atholstan, the proprietor of the *Montreal Gazette*, and an arch-Tory took Arthur Meighen to task and severely chastised the Prime Minister for failing to protect the interests of the British Empire by preferring instead the interests of the United States. His paper, the *Montreal Gazette*, asserted that it had been the Prime Minister's duty to cooperate with the Imperial government in the task of the protection of the empire, a duty that, according to Lord Atholstan, Meighen wholly failed in when he argued the case against the alliance from an American perspective, and thus exposed the antipodean dominions, and the British possessions in the Far East, to the risk of making Japan a future enemy of the British Empire.

Meighen returned to Canada before the official end of the Imperial Conference on August 5, 1921. He could have subsequently waited another year, until the end of 1922, before calling a general election but the strains in his Unionist government, which was a wartime Conservative-Liberal coalition holdover, rendered it unlikely that Meighen would be able to retain the confidence of the House of Commons until then. Meighen decided that it was better to take his political chances as soon as possible, and he obtained the Governor General's consent to call a general election for December, 1921.

Meighen tried to hold the Liberals who had joined with the wartime Conservative Government to form the Unionist Ministry by briefly renaming the Conservative Party the National Liberal and Conservative Party but most of the Unionist Liberals decided to return to the Liberal Party fold for the election, marking the end of the Unionist Party. Meighen presented himself to an electorate that was upset with the Conservatives over their highly unpopular wartime conscription policy and worried about the sharp, recession of 1920-22. Meighen's strong stand against the Anglo-Japanese Alliance had put him on the political outs with most of the right-wing Tories in his party. With his leadership challenged on both the left and right of his formerly Unionist Ministry, and with the economy in trouble, it was hardly surprising that the result of the election held on December 6, 1921, was a defeat for Meighen, and his Conservative party. The Conservatives were turned out of office and replaced by a strong Liberal minority government headed by William Lyon Mackenzie King, who would now begin a long tenure that would eventually see him serving as Canada's Prime Minister, with interruptions, for a record 21 years. The western-based Progressive Party came second in the polls in the 1921 election and the Conservatives were relegated to a dismal third place in the House of Commons. Meighen, himself, was defeated for re-election in his own riding. Shortly after Christmas, the Liberals returned to office, and Mackenzie King took the reins as Prime Minister.[30]

Of Arthur Meighen, it was said that although he was brilliant and gifted intellectually, he was also dogmatic and rigid, too sure of his own views, and reluctant to listen or consider the opinions of others. An unyielding man, especially when faced with opposition, he was unable to see the true aspirations of Canadians in the post-war period and therefore he could not succeed politically. Although he would become Prime Minister a second time in 1926, he would only hold office briefly before losing another general election, following a defeat on a vote of confidence in the House of Commons. He remained prominent in politics into the Second World War period but he faded thereafter and is little remembered a century after he made his mark at the Imperial Conference in 1921.

His legacy in foreign policy was among the least distinguished of Canadian Prime Ministers. His refusal to countenance the renewal of the alliance with Japan because of the antipathy of the United States towards Japan began a process of isolating Japan internationally. Ultimately that led to Japan becoming an enemy of the British Commonwealth and Empire in World War Two, when Japan, as an Axis ally, overran the vast territories of the British Empire in Asia and the Pacific Ocean, and took vast tracts of China, while simultaneously threatening the security of both Australia and New Zealand.

In the 1920's, as the Opposition Leader in Parliament during the Chanak Crisis, Meighen demanded that the King Ministry heed the British government's call for dominion troops to support the British military position in Turkey, as the new Turkish Republic rose from the ashes of the Ottoman Empire and repudiated the prior Ottoman treaty commitments. Canada had not played a substantive role in the defeat of the Ottoman Empire, and it had no foreign policy interests in Turkey. Predictably, Canadian public opinion considered Meighen to be politically tone-deaf with respect to the desire of the Canadian public to become embroiled in any further military adventures abroad in the aftermath of the Great War. Meighen's call for Canada to cry out 'Ready, Aye, Ready' when Britain asked for Canadian troops proved that he was out of touch with the Canadian electorate. Mackenzie King's refusal to respond to London's call for troops, coming only one year after the Imperial Conference of 1921, publicly marked the end of the principle of a unified foreign policy for the British Empire, although, in reality, it had been Prime Minister Meighen who had ended the diplomatic unity of the empire the year previously, when his intransigence effectively sounded the death knell for the Anglo-Japanese Alliance.

NOTES

[1] Graham, *Fortune Fled*, 82-83

[2] J Bartlet Brebner, *Canada, The Anglo-Japanese Alliance And The Washington Conference*, American Historical Association, Washington, 1934, 52

[3] Brebner, 53

[4] DCER, Vol. III, 171

[5] Graham, *Fortune Fled*, 86

[6] DCER, Vol. III, 173

[7] Graham, *Fortune Fled*, 87

[8] DCER, Vol. III, 172

[9] Brebner, 49

[10] DCER Vol. III, 175

[11] DCER Vol. III, 176

[12] DCER, Vol. III, 180

[13] The same situation had occurred in the Russo-Japanese War when the British Empire had remained neutral but had maintained a benevolent attitude towards its ally in the Far East. After the conclusion of the war, Japan had expressed its appreciation to Great Britain for the moral and other support Britain had offered to it during the war.

[14] Brebner, 55

[15] DCER, Vol. III, 178

[16] DCER, Vol. III, 179

[17] DCER, Vol. III, 182

[18] DCER, Vol. III, 183

[19] DCER, Vol. III, 186

[20] Brebner, 52-53

[21] Brebner, 53

[22] Graham, *Fortune Fled*, 93

[23] Brebner, 54

[24] In 1923, Prime Minister W L Mackenzie King's Liberal Ministry would enact the Chinese Exclusion Act, effectively banning the immigration of Chinese citizens into Canada.

[25] Brebner, 47

[26] DCER, Vol. III, 189

[27] DCER Vol. III, 193

[28] Graham, *Fortune Fled*, 101

[29] Graham, *Fortune Fled*, 103

[30] Allen, 234-35

21. The End of the Alliance

The government of Japan was quite taken aback by the results of the Imperial Conference of 1921. It had not expected that the British Empire would spurn an almost twenty-year alliance between the two island empires. Now, without any significant consultations between Japan and Great Britain, the Japanese found themselves almost side-lined as the British Empire aligned itself with the United States at an international conference the purpose of which was to supplant the Anglo-Japanese Alliance. The alacrity with which Great Britain had moved to set aside the renewal of the Alliance in favour of a multi-lateral approach was unnerving to the Japanese, and they correctly surmised that the attitude of Canada had much to do with the change in British thinking about the Alliance.[1]

The Japanese took particular umbrage at Britain's contacts with China concerning the proposed Pacific Conference. Although the Japanese Government was not unduly concerned about the general naval disarmament conference that President Harding had called for, it was very concerned about the vague proposals concerning the issues for the conference called in respect of the Pacific Ocean, as Tokyo thought that it might represent a plot between the major English-speaking powers to deprive Japan of the dominant position that it was developing in China, and especially in Manchuria.[2] Although the British were generally skilled at diplomacy, they had failed to adequately prepare their Japanese ally for the Pacific Conference proposal because they were rushed into it by the unanticipated intransigence of Prime Minister Meighen at the Imperial Conference. The Japanese, taken unawares, were naturally resentful, and hence suspicious of British intentions.[3]

However, there was never any doubt that the Japanese would attend the Washington Conferences and, as a great power, Japan would be a key player in that forum. As the Japanese delegation arrived in

Washington to begin negotiations word came that Prime Minister Hara had been assassinated in Tokyo. However, the loss of the Prime Minister at such a crucial point in time did not alter Japanese policy. And Japan still hoped to maintain the Anglo-Japanese Alliance, even if a three-party concord might have to be arranged between the United States, Britain, and Japan.

Unlike the Paris Peace Conference, and their prominent position in the League of Nations, Canada and the other dominion governments were only recognized by the United States as members of the British delegation, and therefore they had no separate status at the conferences. That was a diminution of the hard-fought-for international status that Canada had obtained in Paris but Prime Minister Meighen accepted it.[4] The Prime Minister appointed his predecessor, Sir Robert Borden, to represent Canada at the Washington Conferences as a member of the British Empire delegation. It was the last time that Canada would be assigned a subordinate status to Great Britain at an international conference.

From the outset of the Washington Conference, it was clear that the Anglo-Japanese Alliance was on life support. The American opposition to the alliance was as strong as it had ever been and there was little doubt that success at the Washington Conference would spell the end of the Anglo-Japanese Alliance. The British delegation, headed by Arthur Balfour, hoped to achieve three things. Firstly, the British wanted to corral the United States into a treaty arrangement with Britain and Japan concerning Pacific security issues. However, the British recognized that in any such agreement there could be no question of the Americans fulfilling any military commitments to its treaty partners, given the growing isolationism in post-war America. Secondly, the British wanted to bring the Anglo-Japanese Alliance to a respectful and friendly close, and thirdly Britain wanted sufficient flexibility in any multi-lateral approach achieved at Washington to be able to enter into a subsequent defensive military alliance with Japan if German or Soviet strength recovered sufficiently to pose a threat to British interests in the Far East.[5] Balfour passed a draft treaty with these objectives in mind over to US Secretary of State Hughes on November 11th for his consideration. Balfour also asked Hughes for his assent to allow Balfour to approach the Japanese delegation with his draft but Hughes demurred, and thus the discussion relating to a prospective draft treaty remained between Britain and the United States for the time being.[6] That was the clearest sign yet that the formerly close relationship between the British and the Japanese empires was ending.

It was not long before officials in the US State Department leaked knowledge of the draft treaty to the public. The United States was determined to sow enough discord and mistrust in the relations between the British Empire and Japan to ensure that even if the Washington Conference failed there would be little scope for a renewal of the Anglo-Japanese Alliance. When the draft treaty prepared by the British Empire delegation was leaked there was predictable consternation among the Japanese delegation who, as the formal ally of Great Britain, naturally assumed and expected that Japan was entitled to be consulted first about a replacement for their twenty-year alliance. This double-dealing on the part of the British Empire delegation gained Britain and the dominions no favours with the Japanese, and Balfour's lame explanation that he had spoken of Britain's intentions to Prince Tokugawa Iesato, the ceremonial head and chief delegate of Japan did little to mollify them. The Prince mostly handled the ceremonial side of the negotiations and, in any event, Balfour had not given him a copy of the draft treaty that he had supplied to the US Secretary of State. The Japanese delegation finally received a copy of Balfour's proposed draft on November 23rd.[7] The key Japanese delegate, Baron Shidehara Kijuro examined Balfour's work and he quickly realized that it would never obtain the approval of the Americans so he redrafted it and moderated many of its provisions. Shidehara's draft provided that where there was a dispute between states that could not be resolved diplomatically, the issue was to be referred to a conference of the great powers for resolution. It quickly found agreement amongst Secretary of State Hughes and Arthur Balfour, who then withdrew his earlier draft in favour of Shidehara's draft. Secretary Hughes asked that it also be circulated to France and that France's concurrence to its terms be obtained.

On December 10, 1921, the delegates met in conference to exchange their views on the proposed Pacific treaty and it was found to be generally acceptable to the four powers. Three days later, on December 13, 1921, that treaty, known as the Four-Power Treaty, was signed at the US State Department by the United States, Great Britain, France, and Japan. Its text said:

> "Treaty and declaration signed at Washington December 13, 1921
>
> [Names of Plenipotentiaries Omitted]
>
> I. The High Contracting Parties agree as between themselves to respect their rights in relation to their insular possessions and insular dominions in the region of the Pacific Ocean. If there should develop between any of the High Contracting Parties a controversy arising out of any Pacific question and involving their said rights which is not satisfactorily settled by diplomacy and is likely to affect the harmonious accord now happily subsisting between them, they shall invite the other High Contracting Parties to a joint conference to which the whole subject will be referred for consideration and adjustment.
>
> II. If the said rights are threatened by the aggressive action of any other Power, the High Contracting Parties shall communicate with one another fully and frankly in order to arrive at an understanding as to the most efficient measures to be taken, jointly or separately, to meet the exigencies of the particular situation.

III. This Treaty shall remain in force for ten years from the time it shall take effect, and after the expiration of said period it shall continue to be in force subject to the right of any of the High Contracting Parties to terminate it upon twelve months' notice.

IV. This Treaty shall be ratified as soon as possible in accordance with the constitutional methods of the High Contracting Parties and shall take effect on the deposit of ratifications, which shall take place at Washington, and thereupon the agreement between Great Britain and Japan, which was concluded at London on July 13, 1911, shall terminate. The Government of the United States will transmit to all the Signatory Powers a certified copy of the *proces-verbal* of the deposit of ratifications. The present Treaty, in French and in English, shall remain deposited in the Archives of the Government of the United States, and duly certified copies thereof will be transmitted by that Government to each of the Signatory Powers.

In faith whereof the above named Plenipotentiaries have signed the present Treaty.

Done at the City of Washington, the thirteenth day of December, One Thousand Nine Hundred and Twenty-One."[8]

As a replacement for the Anglo-Japanese Alliance, the Four-Power Treaty was shockingly lacking in real substance. For one thing, it was not an alliance but a mere commitment by the parties to arrange for multi-national consultations whenever a dispute arose amongst them that could not be resolved by direct diplomacy. There was no enforcement mechanism and no indication of what could happen if the dispute could not be resolved. But it did provide in clause IV that upon the treaty coming into force the Anglo-Japanese Alliance would lapse. That was the true intention of this treaty and the primary diplomatic objective of the United States. In a multi-lateral context, Great Britain and Japan had agreed to terminate their alliance.

The Four-Power Treaty was a polite way for the British Empire to cast aside Japan, its Pacific alliance partner of twenty years in favour of a new alignment between the British Empire and the United States that came without firm commitments of any kind from either of the two Anglophone powers. The United States was quickly retreating into isolationism, and it wanted no part of foreign military obligations beyond those that solely served its own self-interest. The Japanese were under no illusions about what was happening but Japan realized that Great Britain was now drawing closer to the United States and the strident objections of the United States to the Anglo-Japanese Alliance meant that the British had to choose between its historic relationship with Japan and a new relationship with the United States. Britain, and its dominions, had chosen abandonment of the historic relationship between the two island empires in favour of a hopeful new relationship with the United States. But the vaunted relationship between the British Empire and the United States did not come to pass – it was stillborn due to American isolationism in the years between the two world wars.

As for China, concerning which Prime Minister Meighen had made such an issue at the Imperial Conference, no mention of it was made in the Four-Power Treaty. China was deliberately omitted from the Four-Power Treaty so that the other great powers would not have to invite China into the discussions. All issues relating to China were removed to another treaty, the subsequent Nine-Power Treaty which reaffirmed the Open Door Policy in China. However, the Nine-Power Treaty would prove to be as ineffective as the Four-Power Treaty in maintaining peace in the Asia-Pacific region.

The Washington Naval Conference, held in Washington at the same time as the negotiations that led to the Four-Power Treaty, did succeed in its main objective of limiting naval armaments, and in the straightened financial circumstances of post-war Britain that was an important financial consideration for the British government. For the first time in several centuries Great Britain had opted not to contest a rising power for the supremacy of the world, and Great Britain now contented itself with a slow drift into a subordinate status to the United States. At least in the case of the United States, there was a strong cultural affinity to go along with economic linkages between the two countries. Henceforth, Britain, and especially Canada, would look hopefully to America as their security partner.

Japan reconciled itself to the loss of the Anglo-Japanese Alliance, and its civilian government hoped for the best in terms of its future relations with Great Britain, and the British Commonwealth, but even more so with respect to the United States, which it would increasingly contest with for the mastery of the Pacific-East Asia region. If Great Britain had stood firm against the Canadian pressure at the Imperial Conference, and maintained the Anglo-Japanese Alliance, Japan would have also remained in the alliance because the alliance was the cornerstone of Japanese foreign policy and the one aspect of its relations with other states that had prevented it from becoming internationally isolated. But in the end, the Japanese proved philosophical about the cessation of their ties to the British Empire. Japanese conference attendees told their British counterparts that at Washington the British Empire had provided the alliance with "a splendid funeral."[9] However, former Japanese Foreign Minister Ishii saw it differently, and he said that the alliance had been disposed of like a pair of old worn-out sandals.[10] In certain quarters in Japan, it was considered that Japan had suffered a loss of face and that Great Britain had not treated Japan according to the respect that Japan deserved.[11] Although the Washington Four-Power Treaty was the death knell for the Anglo-Japanese Alliance, the die had already been cast at the

Imperial Conference that preceded it by the adamant insistence of Canada that the alliance should be abandoned.

The formal end of the alliance did not come with the signing of the Four-Power Treaty, however. It was first necessary for the ratifications of the Four-Power Treaty to be exchanged, and deposited in Washington, and that took some time. The ratifications of the Four-Power Treaty were eventually exchanged between the parties, and deposited with the US Government, and the final deposit did not occur until August 17, 1923. On that date, the Anglo-Japanese Alliance was formally terminated.[12] It had lasted 21 years, 6 months, and 17 days.

Its passing went unlamented in Canada, where the government of Prime Minister Mackenzie King had celebrated, on March 2, 1923, the first signing of an international treaty between Canada and another country, in that instance, the United States, without any involvement by Great Britain.[13] It was another milestone on the road to complete *de jure* independence from the British Empire. The year before, in 1922, during the Chanak Crisis in Asia Minor Prime Minister King broke with the Imperial Government over the concept of a unified foreign policy set in London when he refused to commit Canadian troops for the defence of a British garrison facing Kemal Ataturk's armies at the Dardanelles, after the British government called on the dominions, including Canada, to supply military forces to assist the Imperial government. The political evolution of Canada towards full and formal independence from the empire had progressed well beyond the era of a unified foreign policy for Great Britain and its dominions.

NOTES

[1] Nish, *Decline*, 341

[2] Nish, *Decline*, 345-46

[3] Nish, *Decline*, 347

[4] Graham, *Fortune Fled*, 106; Brebner, 57

[5] Nish, *Decline*, 369

[6] Nish, *Decline*, 370

[7] Nish, *Decline*, 372

[8] https://www.loc.gov/law/help/us-treaties/bevans/m-ust000002-0332.pdf [accessed October, 2020]

[9] Nish, *Decline*, 383

[10] Dua, 207

[11] Dua, 208

[12] Nish, *Decline*, 383

[13] Allen, 242

22. The Reckoning of History

There was more than a whiff of ingratitude in Canada's decision to seek the abandonment of the Anglo-Japanese Alliance, given the assistance Japan had provided to Canada, and to Canada's allies, in the Pacific war. Perhaps there was also a dollop of pandering to the racial animosities that were prevalent in British Columbia towards Japan and towards Japanese immigrants to Canada in general. But mainly the abandonment of the alliance by Canada was a policy decision by the Federal government to choose the security interests of Canada in maintaining good relations with the United States over the broader security interests of the British Commonwealth and Empire.

At the time, and afterwards, there were those who considered the outcome of the Imperial Conference of 1921 to have been a significant achievement for Prime Minister Meighen, and the subsequent abandonment of the Anglo-Japanese Alliance to be a desirable foreign policy outcome for Canada. In the reckoning of history, however, it must be seen as a foreign policy debacle of epic proportions. Great Britain and Japan had long ago reached an understanding that the Anglo-Japanese Alliance would not apply if Japan became embroiled in a conflict with the United States, and thus Canada was not at risk of being dragged into a war with the United States through the Anglo-Japanese Alliance. And yet that was the ostensible reason why the Canadian government pressed Britain and the other dominions to abandon the alliance.

A far wiser course would have been for Canada to support the renewal of the Anglo-Japanese Alliance as a means of keeping the friendship of Japan and thus preventing that country from drifting into isolation and becoming a future enemy of the British Commonwealth and Empire. In that way, the broader security interests of the antipodean dominions could have been realized while not harming Canadian security interests in any definite way. Furthermore, the tethering of Japan to an international framework, which the alliance provided, could have allowed the British Commonwealth to exercise a future restraining influence upon Japanese aggrandizement, and adventurism, in East Asia.

Part of the reason for the narrowness of the Canadian foreign policy approach was a lack of deep foreign policy knowledge and experience of the Asia-Pacific region within Canada's small Department of External Affairs. Canada was thus without the capacity to undertake a deep foreign policy analysis of the benefits, as well as the risks, of the non-renewal of the alliance with Japan beyond a continentalist perspective.

Prime Minister Meighen's stance against the alliance was influenced by the US government opinions on the subject, which had been deftly inserted into the formulation of Canadian views by contacts with the Washington foreign policy establishment. Tellingly, Australian Prime Minister Hughes charged that Prime Minister Meighen was only advancing America's position at the 1921 Imperial Conference, rather than Canada's position. Hughes' charge stung because it was a valid criticism of the Canadian foreign policy position on the question of the alliance with Japan.

It was a weakness of the Canadian foreign policy apparatus at the beginning of the 1920's, that too much regard was taken of US foreign policy towards Japan. The foreign policy lens of the United States cast a very jaundiced eye on Japan. American analysts suspected a looming conflict between the United States and Japan for Pacific supremacy, and the firmness of the position that Canada took at the Imperial Conference in 1921 suggests that the foreign policy analysis machinery in Ottawa may have also concurred with that expectation.

Yet, in 1921, it was by no means fated that Japan would subsequently pose a threat to international security in the Pacific. Japan had been a responsible and faithful member of the alliance in the war against the Central Powers. It was a parliamentary democracy, and it had sought recognition and acceptance by the major powers. The American policy of isolating Japan through the sundering the alliance between Japan and the British Empire did nothing to promote a long-term peace in the Pacific during the inter-war years. The failures of British and Canadian foreign policy was compounded by the overall American policy of isolationism during the 1920's and 1930's.

None of this is to deny that Japan's attitude during and after World War One towards China was imperialistic and that Japan posed a potential threat to the territorial integrity of China in Manchuria. However, Japan was not the only power to maintain ambitions in China in the inter-war period. Around the same time that Japan was consolidating its position in Manchuria, the Soviet Union was successfully encouraging Outer Mongolia to break away from China and to establish itself as a separate country under communist rule. In the south-west, the British Indian Empire continued to sustain, if not encourage, the autonomy of theocratic Tibet, which had partially broken away from China at the fall of the Manchu Empire. Tibet exercised a high degree of external autonomy during the interwar years with British encouragement, while acknowledging only a nominal suzerainty over Tibet by republican China.

Although Japan did return the Shantung Peninsula to Chinese sovereignty in 1922, Japan's interests in Manchuria remained and grew. The internationally isolated Japanese civilian governments of the era found it increasingly difficult to control the Japanese Kwantung Army in China, which often acted against orders from Japan's army headquarters. The Kwantung Army became a hotbed of proto-fascist leanings, and it began to favour coups and the assassination of civilian leaders who stood in the way of Japanese militarism. In the 1930's many officers called for an end to democracy, and for the establishment of authoritarian and militaristic rule in Japan.

Over time, a growing gap occurred between the conservative civilian political leadership in Japan and the radical military nationalists. Through the course of the inter-war years, Japan's domestic politics sank towards fascism. One cannot say with any degree of certainty whether the continuation of an alliance with the British Commonwealth and Empire would have arrested Japan's political slide but a continued alliance between the British Commonwealth and the Japanese Empire might well have militated against the growing threat of militarism in Japanese domestic politics. As the world moved once again towards war in the late thirties a politically isolated Japan found new friends in Nazi Germany, with whom Japan signed the Anti-Comintern Pact in 1936, and subsequently with Fascist Italy. By the autumn of 1940 Japan, Nazi Germany, and Fascist Italy, were all allied in the Tripartite, or Axis Pact, and by the autumn of 1941, the militarists under the Japanese Premier, General Hideki Tojo, were preparing for war.

The failure to maintain the Alliance exposed the British Empire to a risk of war, and to the possibility of defeat in the Pacific and the Far East. Lamentably, Winston Churchill, upon whose shoulders responsibility for the defence of the British Empire would fall in the Second World War, stated in his memoirs that the failure of the Anglo-Japanese Alliance led the Japanese to feel that they had been spurned and that the friendship that had existed between the two island empires, a friendship which could have been very useful in the maintenance of peace, was allowed to wither and die.[1]

The failure of the Alliance meant that a renewed consideration had to be given to Imperial defences in the Far East. Great Britain was too constrained financially to support a larger military presence in the Asia-Pacific region, and the Five-Power Treaty that came out of the Washington Conference limited naval armaments worldwide, thus preventing the creation of a large fleet even if London had possessed the financial wherewithal to support a significant increase in naval armaments. The military solution to the disproportionate power of Japan in the Orient was a plan for the passage of the main fleet from home waters to the Far East should British possessions in the Pacific and the Far East become endangered by a hostile Japan. To base a fleet in the Far East, even for a temporary period, required the presence of a large naval base with sufficient distance from Japan. Accordingly, Great Britain, with financial support from the Malay States, New Zealand, and Hong Kong, began the construction of a great naval fortress at Singapore. Much like Imperial Germany had done at Tsingtao, the British constructed, at vast expense, a bastion at Singapore to support a large fleet.

Unfortunately, there were two military fallacies with the British approach to the defence of their eastern empire. In the first place, there would be insufficient naval units available for transfer to the Far East if Britain found itself embroiled in a European war at the same time that hostilities occurred in the Far East. The second fallacy was the expectation that an enemy attack on Singapore would likely come from the sea, and therefore it was at the Singapore seacoast that most of the investment in coastal fortifications was made. The landward side of the island on which Singapore is located was left much less protected because it was thought that the dense Malayan jungles would prevent the movement of a large army capable of investing Singapore from the north. In fact, it was from the landward side that the great Japanese blow against Singapore would fall in 1942.

As the war clouds began to gather in the Far East in 1941, the Admiralty did send two capital ships to Singapore, the new battleship HMS *Prince of Wales*, and the older battlecruiser HMS *Repulse*, as an attempt at deterrence. Both were caught in the open sea without a fighter escort by Japanese warplanes after the Japanese blitzkrieg in the Far East began, and both capital ships were quickly sent to the bottom. Afterwards, the Japanese forces swarmed over the eastern marches of the British Empire. On December 8, 1941, the Japanese attacked Hong Kong, which was partially garrisoned by the Canadian Army. A desperate defence was maintained and Brigadier Lawson, the commander of the Canadian forces, was killed when his headquarters was overrun by Japanese troops. On Christmas Day the British general in command of Hong Kong surrendered the colony to the superior Japanese forces.

All of the other British possessions in the Far East, including Malaya, the Straits Settlements, Singapore, Burma, North Borneo, Brunei, and Sarawak subsequently fell to the Japanese. The Japanese occupied the Treaty Port concessions in China, including the British concession at Shanghai. The Japanese Army penetrated into North-East India after conquering Burma, and the Japanese bombed both the east coast of India and the island of Ceylon. A Japanese carrier task force almost caught and sank the obsolete battleships of the Eastern Fleet of the Royal Navy, which would have been disastrous for the defence of the Indian subcontinent. The Japanese did succeed in sinking the heavy cruiser HMS *Dorchester*, and a small aircraft carrier, HMS *Hermes*. Afterwards, the Admiralty was forced to withdraw the Eastern Fleet to safer waters off the east coast of Africa.

British and Australian possessions were also attacked in the Pacific Ocean and Indian Oceans. The Andaman and Nicobar Islands in the eastern Indian Ocean, part of Britain's Indian Empire, were occupied by Japan, and the northern islands in the Gilbert chain, part of Britain's Gilbert and Ellice Islands colony, were also taken by the Japanese. The eastern islands of the British Solomon Islands were seized and a major campaign was subsequently undertaken by the United States in the Solomon Islands, particularly on Guadalcanal Island, to oust the Japanese. Australia saw the Japanese take Nauru, Bougainville, the Bismarck Archipelago, and North East New Guinea, in the Pacific, as well as Christmas Island in the Indian Ocean. A major bombing attack was made on Port Darwin in the Northern Territory, causing many civilian casualties.

The only domestic attacks on Canada consisted of the shelling of a lighthouse at Estevan Point on Vancouver Island by a Japanese submarine and a flotilla of long-distance balloon bombs that floated across the Pacific Ocean to North America. Neither action resulted in domestic casualties. However, racial discrimination against Japanese-Canadians reached its climax during the war years, as thousands of Japanese-Canadians were rounded up and incarcerated in internment camps in the interior, losing their civil rights in the process, and having much of their property sold off for a pittance. None were disloyal and their only offence was to appear racially and culturally different from other Canadians. It was a national shame and a disgrace that was only ameliorated through a formal apology from Prime Minister Brian Mulroney in 1988, and the payment of compensation to the survivors.

The Japanese occupation of British Commonwealth and Empire territories was not finally terminated until 1945, and it was only through the overwhelming military and economic power of the United States that the final surrender of Japanese forces was obtained, although British and Indian forces did retake Burma, and Australian forces and US forces recovered New Guinea. It was only after the Japanese defeat, and the American occupation of Japan, that the Japanese parliamentary democracy that had been undermined by fascism in the thirties, and forties, was restored. Japan afterwards became closely allied with the United States in the post-war era, as did Canada.

Ironically, a century after Canada played a crucial role in the termination of the Anglo-Japanese Alliance, Canada was once more linked with Japan, through their respective military alliances with the United States, their mutual membership in the Group of Seven countries, and the mutual trading relationships Canada and Japan have maintained in the Comprehensive and Progressive Agreement for Trans-Pacific Partnership ("the TPP Agreement"). Today, Canada and Japan cooperate on many levels diplomatically, economically, and even militarily, and the relationship that was sundered by the abandonment of the alliance has come full circle and been restored, albeit after a great historical cost.

Today, it is unlikely that a failure in Canadian foreign policy, similar to Canada's efforts to terminate the Anglo-Japanese Alliance, would recur. In the century that has passed since the Anglo-Japanese Alliance ended, Canada's foreign policy establishment has grown in depth and complexity, and a simplistic placation of the United States is no longer viewed as the *sine qua non* of Canadian foreign policy. Canada has hopefully learned the lesson that it must apply a broad scope to the formulation of its foreign policies, and to avoid an unduly narrow definition of its national interests.

NOTES

[1] Winston S Churchill, *The Gathering Storm*, Houghton Mifflin Company, Boston, 1948, 14

SOURCES

BOOKS

Ralph Allen, *Ordeal By Fire, Canada 1910 – 1945*, Doubleday Canada Limited, Toronto, 1961

Glen Barclay, *A History of the Pacific, from the Stone Age to the present day*, Sidgwick & Jackson, London, 1978

Geoffrey Bennett, *Coronel and the Falklands*, Pan Books, London, 1967

Pierre Berton, *The Great Railway, Illustrated*, McClelland & Stewart, Toronto, 1972

Winston S Churchill, *The World Crisis*, Charles Scribner's Sons and Maxwell Macmillan Canada, New York/Toronto 1931 (1992)

Winston S Churchill, *The Gathering Storm*, Houghton Mifflin Company, Boston, 1948

Fred Clement, *Guns in Paradise*, McClelland and Stewart Limited, Toronto, 1968

Virginia Cowles, *The Kaiser*, Harper & Row, New York, 1963, 82

Allan Donnell, "The Campaign in Northern Russia" in *Canada in the Great World War, Vol. VI*, United Publishers of Canada, Toronto, 1921

R P Dua, *Anglo-Japanese Relations During the First World War*, S Chand & Co. (Pvt.) Ltd., Ram Nagar, New Delhi (India), 1972

Bryan Elson, *Canada's Bastions of Empire, Halifax, Victoria and the Royal Navy 1749-1918*, Formac Publishing, Halifax, 2014

Imanuel Geiss (ed.) *July 1914, The Outbreak of the First World War, Selected Documents*, Charles Scribner Sons, New York, 1967

Barry Gough, *The Royal Navy and the Northwest Coast of North America, 1810 – 1914*, University of British Columbia Press, Vancouver, 1971 (1974)

Ian T M Gow, "The Royal Navy and Japan, 1900-1920: Strategic Re-evaluation of the IJN", in Chihiro Hosoya, Ian Nish ed., *The History of Anglo-Japanese Relations 1600-2000, vol. 3, The Military Dimension*, Palgrave Macmillan, Houndmills, Basingstoke, Hampshire (UK), 2003

Roger Graham, *Arthur Meighen, Vol. I, The Door of Opportunity*, Clarke, Irwin and Company, Toronto, 1960

Roger Graham, *Arthur Meighen Vol II And Fortune Fled*, Clarke, Irwin and Co., Toronto, 1963

J L Granatstein, "The Right Honourable Arthur Meighen," in Jean Chevrier ed. and Denis Daigneault and Gaétan Jeaurond co-ed., *The Prime Ministers of Canada*, New Federation House, Ottawa, 2005

Eric Grove, *Big Fleet Actions, Tsushima, Jutland, Philippine Sea*, Brockhampton Press, London, 1991

Francis X Hezel SJ, *Strangers In Their Own Land; A Century of Colonial Rule in the Caroline and Marshall Islands*, University of Hawaii Press, Honolulu, 1995

A A Hoehling, *Lonely Command*, Modern Literary Editions, New York, 1957

Rear Admiral (Retd.) Yoichi Hirana, "The Anglo-Japanese Alliance and the First World War" in Ian Gow, Yoichi Hirama and John Chapman (ed.), *The History of Anglo-Japanese Relations, 1600-2000, vol. 3, The Military Dimension*, Palgrave Macmillan, Houndmills, Basingstoke, Hampshire (UK), 2003

William Johnston, William G P Rawling, Richard H Gimblett, John MacFarlane, *The Seabound Coast, The Official History of the Royal Canadian Navy, 1867-1939*, Dundurn Press, Toronto, 2010

Allan Levine, *King, William Lyon Mackenzie King, A Life Guided By The Hand Of Destiny*, Douglas & McIntyre, Vancouver, 2011

Captain A T Mahan, USN, *The Influence of Sea Power Upon History 1660 – 1783*, London, Sampson Low, Marston, Searle & Rivington, 1890

Robert K Massie, *Castles of Steel, Britain, Germany, and the Winning of the Great War at Sea*, Ballantine Books, New York, 2003

Robert K Massie, *Dreadnought, Britain, Germany and the Coming of the Great War*, Ballantine Books, New York, 1991

Robert K Massie, *Nicholas and Alexandra*, Dell Publishing, New York, 1967

Margaret MacMillan, *Paris 1919: Six Months That Changed the World*, Random House, New York, 2002

Margaret MacMillan, *The War That Ended Peace, The Road to 1914*, Allen Lane, Toronto, 2013

J McCombie and F C L Muller, *The Prime Ministers*, Scholastic Publications, Richmond Hill (ON), 1968

Walter A McDougall, *Let the Sea Make a Noise, A History of the North Pacific from Magellan to MacArthur*, Basic Books, New York, 1993

Walter Millis, *Road to War: America 1914 – 1917*, Houghton Mifflin Company, Boston, 1935

Colonel G W L Nicholson, *Canadian Expeditionary Force 1914-1919*, The Queen's Printer, Ottawa, 1962

Ian H Nish, *The Anglo-Japanese Alliance: The Diplomacy of Two Island Empires 1894 – 1907*, University of London/The Athlone Press, London, 1966

Ian H Nish, *Alliance in Decline: A Study In Anglo-Japanese Relations 1908 – 1923*, University of London/The Athlone Press, London, 1972

James Noonan, *Canada's Governors General at Play: Culture and Rideau Hall from Monck to Grey, With an Afterword on their Successors, Connaught to LeBlanc*, Borealis Book Publishers, Ottawa, 2002

Peter W. Noonan, *Peace on the Lakes, Canada and the Rush-Bagot Agreement*, Magistralis, Ottawa, 2016

Peter Pigott, *Sailing Seven Seas, A History of the Canadian Pacific Line*, Dundurn Press, Toronto, 2010

Klaus H Pringsheim, *Neighbors Across the Pacific: The Development of Economic and Political Relations Between Canada and Japan*, Greenwood Press, Westport (CT), 1983

Robert F. Rogers, *Destiny's Landfall: A History of Guam*, University of Hawaii Press, Honolulu, 1995

Roger Sarty, "There will be trouble in the North Pacific: The Defence of British Columbia in the Early Twentieth Century," in BC Studies, *The British Columbian Quarterly*, Vol. 61, Spring, 1984, University of British Columbia, Vancouver, 1984, 3

Charles Seymour, "The Submarine and American Intervention" in Herbert J Bass (ed.), *America's Entry into World War I, Submarines, Sentiment or Security?*, Dryden Press, Hinsdale (IL) 1964

Patrick Fuliang Shan, *Yuan Shikai*, University of British Columbia Press, Vancouver, 2018

John Silverlight, *The Victor's Dilemma: Allied Intervention in the Russian Civil War*, Weybright and Talley, New York, 1970

Charles Stephenson, *The Siege of Tsingtao, The German – Japanese War 1914*, Pen & Sword Books (e-book), United Kingdom, 2017

Richard Storrey, *Japan and the Decline of the West in Asia, 1894 – 1945*, The Macmillan Press, London, 1979

Hew Strachan, *The First World War, Vol. 1 To Arms*, Oxford University Press, Oxford (UK), 2001

Charles Callan Tansill, "War Profits and Unneutrality," in Herbert J Bass (ed.), *America's Entry into World War I, Submarines, Sentiment or Security?*, Dryden Press, Hinsdale (IL) 1964

Merze Tate, *The United States and the Hawaiian Kingdom, A Political History*, Yale University Press, New Haven (CT) 1965

Barbara Tuchman, *The Zimmerman Telegram*, Bantam Books, New York, 1971

Gilbert Norman Tucker, *The Naval Service of Canada, Its Official History*, vol. 1, The King's Printer, Ottawa, 1952

Harmon Tupper, *To the Great Ocean, Siberia and the Trans-Siberian Railway*, Little, Brown & Company, Boston and Toronto, 1965

Allan Villiers, *Men, Ships and the Sea*, National Geographic Society, Washington, 1963

Andrew R Wilson, *Masters of War: History's Greatest Strategic Thinkers*, The Teaching Company, Chantilly (VA)., 2012

SERIALIZED ACCOUNTS

Professor C T Atkinson, "The British at Tsingtao", in *History of the First World War*, Vol. 1, no. 12, BPC/Purnell, Bristol (UK), 1969

Christopher Dowling, "Clearing the Pacific" in *History of the First World War*, Vol. 1, No. 12, BPC/Purnell, Bristol (UK), 1969

Peter Kemp, "The Naval Race, Germany's Bid for Sea Power," in *History of the First World War*, Vol. 1, No. 2, BPC Publishing/Purnell, Bristol (UK), 1969

David Mason, "Converging of the Fleets" in *History of the First World War* Vol. 2, No. 3, BPC/Purnell, Bristol (UK), 1970

David Mason, "Battle of the Falklands" in *History of the First World War*, Vol. 2, No. 3, BPC/Purnell, Bristol (UK), 1970

Ian Nish, "Japan Declares War" in *History of the First World War*, Vol. 1, No. 12, BPC/Purnell, Bristol (UK), 1969

Barrie Pitt, "The Battle of Coronel" in *History of the First World War*, Vol. 2 No. 3, BPC/Purnell, Bristol (UK), 1970

H H Wilson and J A Hamerton, "The Singapore Mutiny" in *History of the First World War*, Vol. 2, No. 14, BPC/Purnell, Bristol (UK), 1970

Terence Wise, "Tsingtao," in *History of the First World War*, Vol. 1, No. 12, BPC/Purnell, Bristol (UK), 1969

Sir Llewleyn Woodward, "Germany's Bid for Sea Power", in *History of the First World War*, Vol. 1, No. 2, BPC /Purnell, Bristol (UK), 1969

JOURNAL ARTICLES

J Bartlet Brebner, *Canada, The Anglo-Japanese Alliance And The Washington Conference*, American Historical Association, Washington, 1934

Donald H Estes, *Asama Gunkan: The Reappraisal of a War Scare*, The Journal of San Diego History, San Diego Historical Society Quarterly, San Diego (CA), Summer 1978, Volume 24, Number 3

Timothy D Saxon, *Anglo-Japanese Naval Cooperation, 1914-1918*, Naval War College Review, Winter 2000, Vol III, No. 1

ACADEMIC PAPERS

Patrick McManus, *Stability and Flexibility: The Rush-Bagot Agreement and the Progressive Modernization of Canadian-American Security Relations*, University of Ottawa (PhD dissertation), Ottawa, 2009

Thomas P Socknat, *Canada, imperial foreign policy and the abrogation of the Anglo-Japanese alliance, 1921*, (PhD Thesis Submission), University of Nebraska, Omaha, 1967

GOVERNMENT PAPERS

Debates of the House of Commons (1921), Vol. III, The King's Printer, Ottawa, 1921

Department of External Affairs, *Documents on Canadian External Relations Vol. 1, 1909-1918*, Ottawa, The Queen"s Printer for Canada, 1967

Department of External Affairs, *Documents on Canadian External Relations, Vol. III, 1919–1925*, edited by Lovell C. Clark, Ottawa, Queen's Printer for Canada, 1970

G P Gooch and Harold Temperley ed., with Lillian M Penson, *British Documents on the Origins of the War, 1898-1914, Vol. 1 The End of British Isolation*, HM Stationary Office, London, 1927

G P Gooch and Harold Temperley ed., with Lillian M Penson, *British Documents on the Origins of the War, 1898-1914, Vol IV, The Anglo-Russian Rapprochement 1903-7*, HM Stationary Office, London, 1929

INTERNET RESOURCES

Leighann C. Neilson, *John Murray Gibbon (1875-1952): The Branding of a Northern Nation*, Sprott School of Business, Carleton University, Ottawa, [ojs.library.carleton.ca E pcharm]

Kirsten Weisenburger and Marc Dinsdale "First Class Warrior Empress, Memories of the luxury liner that once linked Vancouver to Asia", in *Pacific Rim Magazine*, http://langaraprm.com/1998/travel/first-class-warrior-empress/

UK Treaties Online, https://treaties.fco.gov.uk

"Japan's Ultimatum to Germany," at https://wwi.lib.byu.edu/index.php/Japanese_Ultimatum_to_Germany

"Capturing German Outposts," ANZAC Portal, https://anzacportal.dva.gov.au/wars-and-missions/ww1/where-australians-served/captured-german-outposts

"HMCS *Rainbow*," Naval and Military Museum, Ship Histories https://web.archive.org/web/20100819014830/ http://www.navalandmilitarymuseum.org/resource_pages/ships/rainbow.html

Ohrdruf, "SMS Titania – Unlisted German Raider, 1914," *Axis History Forum*, https://forum.axishistory.com/

Four Power Treaty, https://www.loc.gov/law/help/us-treaties/bevans/m-ust000002-0332.pdf

"The Zimmerman Telegram," National Security Agency records, https://www.nsa.gov/Portals/70/documents/news-features/declassified-documents/cryptologic-quarterly/the_zimmermann_telegram.pdf

SHIP INDEX

Australia

HMAS AE-1, 181
    HMAS *Australia*, 142, 144, 145, 156, 159, 179
    HMAS *Melbourne*, 138, 142, 144 fn23, 174, 179, 180
    HMAS *Sydney*, 138, 139, 141 fn23, 142, 174
    HMAS *Una* (ex Ger. New Guinea KGS *Komet*) 180

Austria-Hungary

SMS *Kaiserin Elisabeth*, 122, 134, 151, 192, 193, 194, 195, 197

Canada

Merchant ships

SS *Abyssinia*, 34
    SS *Cetriana*, 128
    RMS *Empress of Asia*, 96, 141 fn23
    RMS *Empress of Britain*, 293
    RMS *Empress of China*, 34
    RMS *Empress of India*, 34
    RMS *Empress of Japan*, 34, 134, 135
    RMS *Empress of Russia*, 96, 139, 141 fn23

Naval Ships

HMCS CC1, 134, 228
    HMCS CC2, 134, 228
    HMCS *Niobe*, 74, 95, 107
    HMCHS *Prince George*, 131
    HMCS *Rainbow*, 74, 95, 107, 108, 109, 127, 128, 129, 130, 131, 132, 134, 144, 215, 216, 228

France

FS *Dupleix*, 96, 142
    FS *Montcalm*, 96, 142, 144 fn23, 175, 179
    FS *Zélée*, 157

Germany

SMS *Dresden*, 131, 135, 136, 137, 138, 145, 146, 157, 158, 161, 162, 163, 168
    SMS *Emden*, 134, 135, 136, 137, 138, 139, 151, 152, 153, 155, 172, 173, 191, 192, 236, 262
    SMS *Geier*, 136, 143, 190, 222-23
    SMS *Gneisenau*, 151, 152, 161, 162, 163, 165, 166, 167, 168
    SMY *Hohenzollern*, 103

SMS Iltis, 192, 195

SMS *Jaguar*, 192, 193, 194, 197, 198

SMS *Karlsruhe*, 135

SMS *Komoran* , 192, 195

SMS *Komoran II*, 136, 137, 155, 191, 192

SMS *Konigsberg*, 172, 173, 176

SMS *Lanting*, 192

SMS *Leipzig*, 109, 126, 127, 128, 130, 131, 133, 136, 139 fn1, 139 fn2, 152, 157, 161, 163, 166

SMS *Luchs*, 137, 192, 195

SMS *Nurnberg*, 109, 126, 127, 128, 129, 131, 132, 152, 155, 156, 161, 163, 165, 166, 168

SMS *Otter*, 192

SMS *Planet*, 182, 201

SMS *Prinz Eitel Friedrich*, 135, 137, 145, 146, 152, 153, 191

SMS *S-90*, 191, 192, 194, 197

SMS *Scharnhorst*, 151, 152, 161, 162, 165, 167, 168

SMS *Seeadler*, 236, 237

SMS *Taku*, 192

SMS *Tiger*, 137, 192, 197

SMS *Titania*, 155, 164

SMS *Tsingtau*, 192

SMS *Vaterland*, 192

SMS *Wolf*, 236

German New Guinea

KGS *Komet* 180

Great Britain

Merchant Ships

SS *Harmattan*, 217, 218 fn14

RMS *Lusitania*, 219

Naval Ships

HMS *Algerine*, 109, 126, 128, 129, 130, 131, 133, 139 fn1

HMS *Apollo*, 74, 127

HMS *Bristol*, 165

HMS *Canopus*, 160, 161, 163, 164, 166

HMS *Carnarvon*, 165, 166, 168

HMS *Condor*, 128

HMS *Cornwall*, 166, 168

HMS *Dorchester*, 330

HMS *Dreadnought*, 24, 68

HMS *Glasgow*, 138, 160, 161, 162, 163, 164, 165, 166, 167, 168

HMS *Gloucester*, 141 fn23

HMS *Good Hope*, 160, 161, 162

HMS *Hampshire*, 95, 141 fn23, 142

HMS *Hermes*, 330

HMS *Inflexible*, 165, 166, 168

HMS *Invincible*, 165, 166, 167, 168

HMS *Kennet*, 191

HMS *Kent*, 137, 138, 166, 168

HMS *Macedonia*, 166

HMS *Minotaur*, 95, 141 fn23, 142, 151, 173, 174, 179, 182

HMS *Monmouth*, 160, 161, 162, 163

HMS *Newcastle*, 95, 132, 133,

134, 142, 144, 179, 182, 216
HMS *Otranto*, 138, 161, 162, 163, 164
HMS *Philomel*, 173, 174
HMS *Pioneer*, 173
HMS *Prince of Wales*, 329
HMS *Psyche*, 173, 174
HMS *Repulse*, 329
HMS *Shearwater*, 109, 126, 128, 129, 130, 131, 133
HMS *Spartiate*, 73
HMS *Suffolk*, 160
HMS *Triumph*, 95, 96, 142, 192, 194, 199
HMS *Usk*, 192, 194
HMS *Weymouth*, 141 fn23
HMS *Yarmouth*, 95, 141 fn23, 142

Japan

Merchant Ships

SS *Kanto*, 147, 148
    SS *Komagata Maru*, 107, 108, 109, 123 fn7, 177

Naval Ships

HIJMS *Akashi*, 235
    HIJMS *Asama*, 136, 143, 144, 145, 146, 147, 148, 184, 223, 236
    HIJMS *Chikuma*, 141 fn23, 172, 235
    HIJMS *Chitose*, 147, 148
    HIJMS *Chiyoda*, 191
    HIJMS *Hirado*, 172

HIJMS *Hizen*, 136, 143, 144
HIJMS *Ibuki*, 138, 141 fn23, 172, 173, 174
HIJMS *Idzumo*, 109, 126, 132, 133, 143, 144, 145, 146, 149, 235
HIJMS *Ikoma*, 172
HIJMS *Iwami*, 191
HIJMS *Iwate*, 191, 236
HIJMS *Kasuga*, 215
HIJMS *Katori*, 185
HIJMS *Kirishima*, 260
HIJMS *Kongo*, 143
HIJMS *Kurama*, 184
HIJMS *Mikasa*, 44
HIJMS *Mishima*, 191
HIJMS *Niitaka*, 235
HIJMS *Nisshin*, 172, 215, 235
HIJMS *Okinoshima*, 191
HIJMS *Otawa*, 175
HIJMS *Satsuma*, 172, 185
HIJMS *Shirotaye*, 193
HIJMS *Suma*, 235
HIJMS *Suwo*, 191
HIJMS *Takachiho*, 191, 197
HIJMS *Tango*, 191
HIJMS *Tokiwa*, 147, 172, 191, 236
HIJMS *Tone*, 191, 235
HIJMS *Tsukuba*, 184
HIJMS *Tsushima*, 175, 235
HIJMS *Wakamiya Maru*, 192, 195
HIJMS *Yahagi*, 141 fn23, 172
HIJMS *Yakumo*, 172, 235
HIJMS *Yodo*, 235

Russia

<u>Merchant Ship</u>

SS *Ryazan*, 134, 136, 155, 192

<u>Naval Ships</u>

HIRMS *Alexander III*, 44, 45
    HIRMS *Askold*, 141 fn 23
    HIRMS *Aurora*, 45
    HIRMS *Borodino*, 44, 45
    HIRMS *Imperator*, 44
    HIRMS *Orel*, 44, 191

HIRMHS *Orel*, 45
HIRMS *Pallada*, 42
HIRMS *Petropavlovsk*, 42
HIRMS *Retvizan*, 42, 144
HIRMS *Suvorov*, 44, 45
HIRMS *Tsarevich*, 42

United States

USS *Milwaukee*, 112
    USS *Raleigh*, 146
    USS *San Diego*, 146
    USS *Saratoga*, 236

GENERAL INDEX

Afghanistan, 25, 54
  Alexander III, (Tsar and Emperor of Russia), 15
  Alexieff, Yevgeny, Admiral (Imperial Russian Navy), (*as Far East Viceroy*) 42
  Allied Expeditionary Force (Siberia) 238, 239, 240, 241, 242; (*allied contingents*) 239, 263
  American Samoa, 237
  Andaman & Nicobar Islands (British Indian Empire), 330
  Angaur (island) (Germany), 180, 185, 186
  Anglo-Egyptian Sudan, 22, 23
  Anglo-Japanese Agreement, 1917 (Pacific Islands), 234
  Anglo-Japanese Alliance (*text of*), 28-31, 57-60, 88-90
  Anti-Comintern Pact (1936), 328
  Armstrong, C. H. A. (Private Secretary to Prime Minister Meighen), 293
  Ashford, Clarence (Attorney-General, Hawaii), 18 fn2
  Ashford, Volney (Lieutenant-Colonel, Hawaii), 18 fn2
  Ataturk, Kemal (Turkish statesman), 323
  Atholstan, Hugh Graham, (Baron), (Canadian Publisher), 310
  Australia (Commonwealth of), 17, 18, 173, 179, 181, 182, 185, 186, 187, 205, 206, 245, 258, 269, 271, 280, 299, 304, 312, 330

Balboa, Vasco Núñez de, (Spanish Explorer), 5
  Balfour, Arthur (British statesman), 225, 227, 317, 318, 319
  Barkley Sound (British Columbia), 144, 215
  Barnardiston, Nathaniel, Brigadier (British Army), 194, 204
  Beatty, David, Lieutenant (Royal Navy), 22
  Belgium, 105, 106, 256 fn4, 270, 302
  Bering Sea Sealing Convention, 129
  Bernstorff, Johann Heinrich von (diplomat, Germany), 224, 225
  Bertie, Francis (diplomat, Great Britain), 27

Bethmann-Hollweg, Theobald von (Chancellor, Germany), 104, 220
Bickford, Andrew, Rear Admiral (Royal Navy), 66
Birkenhead (Earl of), Smith, F. E., (Lord Chancellor, Great Britain), 280, 306, 307, 308
Bismarck Archipelago (Germany), 136, 151, 178, 330
Bismarck, Otto (Prince), (Chancellor, Germany), 41
Bitapaka, Battle of, 180
Bonin Islands (Japan), 11
Bora Bora (French Polynesia), 156, 157
Borden, Sir Robert Laird (Prime Minister, Canada), 70, 74, 75, 95, 106, 107, 113, 116, 117, 126, 214, 227, 228, 238, 240, 241, 244, 245, 246, 248, 251, 254, 255, 267, 276, 283, 284, 286, 287, 288, 291, 303, 317
Borneo (island), 175, 330
Bosnia and Herzegovina (Austria-Hungary), 100, 101
Boxer War (1899-1901), 15, 16, 26, 34
British Columbia (Canada), 6, 32, 33, 108, 109, 111, 112, 113, 116, 126, 133, 149, 156, 177, 210, 211, 221, 222, 228, 325
British New Guinea, 17
British North America Act, 33, 113

British Solomon Islands, 17, 330
Brunner, Helmut, Lieutenant (Imperial German Navy), 197
Byng, Julian, (Viscount of Vimy) (Governor General of Canada), 295

Canadian Northern Railway, 285
Canadian Pacific Railway, 6, 32, 34, 35, 97, 215
Canadian Pacific Steamships, 35, 96, 135
Canadian Siberian Expeditionary Force, 238, 239, 240, 241, 242
Caroline Islands, (Spain/Germany), 10, 132, 136, 151, 178, 179, 184, 185
Carranza, Venustiano, General (Mexican Army) (*as President, Mexico*), 221, 222
Chanak Crisis, 312, 323
Chinese Eastern Railway, 16
China, Empire of (1915-16), 210
Christie, Loring, (diplomat Canada) 288, 293
Christmas Island (Indian Ocean) (Great Britain), 330
Christmas Island (Pacific Ocean) (Great Britain), 155, 156
Churchill, Winston S. (British statesman), 75, 116, 117, 119, 121, 154, 165, 176, 183, 276, 279, 280, 287, 295, 328
Cixi, Dowager Empress of

China (Manchu Empire), 14
Clayton-Bulmer Treaty, 81
Clemenceau, Georges (Premier, France), 245
Cleveland, Grover (US President), 21
Cochin China, (France), 153
Cocos Islands (Great Britain), 138
Confucius, 250
Connaught, (Duke of), H.R.H. Prince Arthur, (Governor General of Canada), 106, 260, 261, 295
Convention of Tientsin, 11
Coronel, Battle of, 144, 161, 162, 163, 164, 165, 205
Cradock, Sir Christopher, Rear Admiral (Royal Navy), 160, 161, 164
Cuba, 9
Curzon, George, (Marquis of Kedleston) (Foreign Minister, Great Britain), 271, 280, 287, 296, 299, 300, 301, 302, 304, 307, 310

Dafoe, John W. (Canadian publisher), 299
Danish Virgin Islands, 256
Declaration of London (1914), 122, 212
Desbarats, J. G., (Deputy Minister of Marine and Fisheries of Canada), 106
Detzner, Hermann, Captain (Imperial German Army), 181
Devonshire (Duke of) Cavendish, Victor (Governor General of Canada), 271, 274, 277, 295
Dewa Shigeto, Admiral (Imperial Japanese Navy) (*as Japanese diplomat*), 145
Dewey, George, Commodore (US Navy), 9
Diaz, Porfirio (President, Mexico), 221
Dual Alliance, 3, 25, 31, 105, 132
Dufferin (Marquis of) Blackwood, Frederick H. T. (Governor General of Canada), 32

Easter Island (Chile), 157, 158, 159, 237
Edward VII, King of Great Britain and Ireland, Emperor of India, 23, 43, 61, 91
Edward, (Prince of Wales) (later Edward VIII), 279, 295
Eki, Hioki (diplomat, Japan), 206
Electric Boat Company, 111
Ellice Islands (Great Britain), 17, 330
Elmsley, J. H., Major General (Canadian Army), 239, 241
Eniwetok Atoll (Germany), 155, 184
Entente Cordiale (1904), 28,

GENERAL INDEX | 347

85
Esquimalt (Royal Canadian
  Navy base), 65, 66, 69, 71, 74,
  95, 109, 110, 111, 112, 113, 126,
  127, 128, 129, 130, 131, 133, 143,
  144, 148, 215, 216, 228
Falkland Islands, Battle of (1914),
  137, 165, 166, 167, 168, 169, 205
Fanning Island (Great Britain),
  155
Fashoda Crisis, 22, 23
Fiji (islands) (Great Britain), 17,
  151, 237
Fisher, John (Jacky) Admiral of
  the Fleet (Royal Navy), 62, 67,
  70, 165
Fitzmaurice, Maurice, Captain
  (Royal Navy), 194, 199
Five-Power Treaty (1922)
  (*also: Washington Naval
  Treaty*), 328
Foch, Ferdinand, Marshal
  (French Army), 4 fn2
Formosa (Japan), 13
Foster, Sir George Eulas
  (Senator, Canada), 21, 70
Four-Power Treaty (1921)
  (text), 319-20; 322, 323
Franz Ferdinand, (Archduke of
  Austria-Hungary) 100, 101,
  102, 134, 152
Franz-Joseph I, Emperor of
  Austria, King of Hungary, 100

Galapagos Islands (Ecuador), 131

Gamo Misao (Viscountess
  Hayashi), 28
Gardiner, William (American
  lobbyist), 289
Geddes, Sir Auckland
  (diplomat Great Britain), 301
Gentleman's Agreement 1908,
  34, 73, 79, 92, 93
George V, King of Great
  Britain and Ireland, Emperor
  of India, 91, 260, 279, 295
George, (Prince of Greece), 15
German East Africa, 136, 143,
  256 fn4
German New Guinea, 17, 151,
  178, 180, 181, 247
German Samoa, 151, 156, 159,
  178, 179, 180, 247
German Solomon Islands, 151,
  178, 247
German South-West Africa,
  246, 256 fn4
Gibson, Walter M., (Premier,
  Hawaii), 8
Gilbert Islands (Great Britain),
  17, 330
Grand Trunk Pacific Railway,
  285
Grand Trunk Railway, 285
Grant, Heathcote, Captain
  (Royal Navy), 164
Great Game, 25, 51, 65
Greene, Sir Conyngham
  (diplomat, Great Britain), 114,
  182, 183, 186, 208, 213

Grey, Albert, (Earl of Grey) (Governor General of Canada), 72, 83
Grey, Sir Edward (Foreign Minister, Great Britain), 62, 91, 92, 98 fn17, 105, 113, 114, 115, 116, 117, 119, 120, 182, 183, 186, 208, 211, 213, 214
Guam (island) (USA), 10, 82, 83
Guangxu Emperor, (China-Manchu Empire), 14
Guthrie, George (diplomat, United States), 119

Haber, Eduard, (Governor of German New Guinea), 180, 186
Hanyehping Iron and Coal Works (China), 206, 209
Hara, Takashi (Prime Minister, Japan), 261, 317
Harcourt, Lewis (Great Britain, Colonial Secretary), 183, 186
Harding, Warren (US President), 289, 309, 316
Hardinge, Sir Charles (diplomat, Great Britain), 37, 39
Harper, Stephen (Prime Minister, Canada), 123 fn7
Harrison, Benjamin, (US President), 8
Haun, Johannes, Captain (Imperial German Navy), 130, 131, 168
Hawaii, Kingdom of/US Territory, 5, 7, 8, 9, 17, 20 fn4, 33, 73, 79, 82, 83, 131, 143, 145, 222, 262, 265
Hayashi, Tadasu, Viscount (diplomat, Japan), 27, 28, 30, 34, 50, 51, 53, 56, 59, 79
Hay-Pauncefote Agreement, 81
Higashifushimi (Prince) Admiral (Imperial Japanese Navy), 260
Hindenburg, Paul von, General (*later Field Marshal*) (Imperial German Army), 221, 262
Hintze, Paul von (diplomat, Germany), 223
Hirohito (Crown Prince of Japan), 279
His Majesty's Dockyard (Esquimalt), 69, 111, 113, 133, 148
Holstein, Friedrich von, (diplomat, Germany), 25
Hong Kong (Great Britain), 9, 34, 62, 95, 96, 107, 134, 135, 142, 174, 183, 191, 192 216, 263, 329, 330
Hongxian Emperor (*also: Yüan Shih-k'ai*) (Chinese Empire), 210
Honolulu (Hawaii), 9, 18 fn2, 131, 136, 143, 156, 190, 222, 236
Hose, Walter, Commander (*later Commodore*), (Royal

GENERAL INDEX | 349

Canadian Navy), 127, 129, 130, 267

House, Edward M., Colonel, 220, 252

Howard, Thomas B., Admiral (United States Navy), 146

Huerta, Victoriano, General (Mexican Army) (*as President, Mexico*), 221

Hughes, Charles Evans (US Secretary of State), 301, 309, 318, 319

Hughes, William (Billy) (Prime Minister, Australia), 83, 246, 247, 251, 279, 293, 303, 304, 305, 306, 308, 326

Hung-Chang Li, (Manchu Empire statesman), 11

Indian Army, 54, 114, 174, 177, 194, 198, 259, 262

    Indian Empire, (Great Britain), 25, 51, 52, , 53, 54, 62, 67, 87, 265, 269, 295, 327, 330

    Indian Ocean, (generally), 117, 138, 143, 172, 173, 175, 176, 211, 212, 213, 214, 235, 261, 262, 269

    Inouye, Katsunosuke, (diplomat, Japan), 115, 261

    Ishii, Kikujiro, Viscount, (diplomat, Japan), (*as ambassador*), 122, (*as Foreign Minister*), 210, 212, 215, 224, 227, 322

    Ito, Hirobumi (Marquis) (Japanese statesman), 40, 84

Ito Sukeyuki, Vice Admiral (Imperial Japanese Navy), 12

Jagow, Gottlieb von, (Foreign Minister, Germany), 110, 220, 221

Jaluit Atoll (Germany), 184

Jellicoe, John (Viscount) Admiral (Royal Navy), 269

Jerram, Sir Thomas M., Vice Admiral (Royal Navy), 95, 96, 132, 142, 151, 179, 191

Jordan, Sir J. (diplomat, Great Britain), 53

Juan Fernandez Islands (Chile), 137, 158, 164

Jutland, Battle of (1916), 169, 269

Kalakaua, David, King of Hawaii, 7, 8

Kamehameha I, King of Hawaii, 7

Kamio, Mitsuomi, Lieutenant General (Imperial Japanese Army) (*as Allied Commander in Chief, Tsingtao*) 193, 194, 196, 197, 198

Kato Sadakichi, Admiral (Imperial Japanese Navy),191, 194, 199

Kato Takaaki (Baron), (Foreign Minister, Japan), 115, 119, 120, 122, 186, 206, 207, 208, 209, 210, 211, 212, 252

Katsura, Taro, General (Prime

Minister, Japan), 27, 54, 91
Khartoum (Anglo-Egyptian Sudan), 22
Kiaochow Bay Concession (Germany/Japan), 116, 122, 151, 153, 178, 187, 188, 189, 190, 191, 193, 194, 195, 196, 197, 198, 199, 206, 207, 209, 233, 234, 246, 249, 250, 253, 254, 262
Kitchener, Sir Herbert, General (British Army), 22, 23
Kolchak, Alexander, Admiral (Imperial Russian Navy) (*as Siberian generalissimo*), 240, 242
Komura Jutaro (Foreign Minister, Japan), 27, 91
Kwantung Army (Japan), 327
Kwantung Peninsula, 82, 206
King, William Lyon Mackenzie (*as Deputy Minister, Labour*) 33, 72, 78, 83 (*as Opposition Leader*) 286, 287, 290, 291 (*as Prime Minister, Canada*) 311, 312, 313, 314 fn24, 323
King, William Lyon Mackenzie, Royal Commission (Japanese Losses) 1907, 83
Kingsmill, Admiral Sir Charles, (Royal Canadian Navy), 71, 73, 74, 267
Korea, Empire of, 11, 12, 16, 28, 31, 38, 39, 40, 45, 47, 50, 52, 53, 61, 80, 82, 84, 92

Korean, Emperors, Gojong, 84; Sujong, 84
Lake Baikal (Russia), 16
Lansdowne Letter, 231
Lansdowne (Marquis of), Petty-Fitzmaurice, Henry, (Foreign Minister, Great Britain), 27, 28, 50, 53, 55, 56, 59, 61, 231 (*as Governor General of Canada*) 27
Lansing, Robert (US Secretary of State), 224, 227, 250
Laurier, Sir Wilfrid (Prime Minister, Canada), 33, 69, 71, 72, 74, 79, 92, 93, 94, 95, 107, 126, 283, 286, 289
Lawson, John K., Brigadier (Canadian Army), 330
League of Nations, 247, 248, 249, 250, 251, 254, 255, 271, 275, 277, 280, 281, 291, 292, 296, 299, 300, 305, 307, 317
Lemieux, Rodolfe, (Minister of Labour and Postmaster-General of Canada), 33, 34 72, 73, 79, 93, 214
Lenin, Vladimir (Russian revolutionary), 237
Lennox, Bertram (lobbyist for China), 289
Liaotung Peninsula (China), 12, 13
Liliuokalani, Queen of Hawaii, 8
Lloyd-George, David, (Prime

Minister, Great Britain), 247, 269, 274, 277, 280, 287, 295, 302, 306, 307, 308

Longyu, Dowager Empress of China (Manchu Empire), 94

Loyalty Islands (France), 17

Luckner, Felix von, (Count) Captain (Imperial German Navy), 236, 237

Lüdecke, Fritz, Captain (Imperial German Navy), 136, 137, 138

Ludendorff, Erich (General, Imperial German Army), 221

MacDonald, Sir Claude (diplomat, Great Britain), 26, 50, 51, 52, 53, 54, 55

Macdonald, Sir John A, (Prime Minister, Canada), 27, 32

Madero, Francisco (President, Mexico), 221

Maerker, Julius, Captain (Imperial German Navy), 168

Magdalena Bay (Mexico), 145, 147, 221, 222

Magellan, Ferdinand, (Spanish Explorer), 5

Mahan, Alfred Thayer, Captain (United States Navy), 154, 160, 178, 187-88

Mahdi (Sudanese mystic), 22

Majuro Atoll (Germany), 155

Makarov, Stephan, Vice Admiral (Imperial Russian Navy), 42

Makovicz, Richard, Captain (Imperial and Royal Austro-Hungarian Navy), 134, 193

Malay States (Great Britain), 329

Manchu Empire (China), 11, 12, 14, 41, 94, 327, (1917 restoration) 235

Manchuria, 12, 13, 15, 16, 38, 40, 46, 47, 62, 80, 81, 82, 92, 205, 206, 207, 209, 300, 316, 327

Manchurian Railway, 38, 46, 47, 80

Manifest Destiny, 6

Marcus Island (Japan), 11

Mariana Islands (Spain/Germany), 135, 137, 151, 153, 158, 178, 185

Marquesas (islands) (French Polynesia), 17, 157

Marshall Islands (Germany), 10, 136, 151, 155 178, 179, 184, 185

Más Afuera (island) (Chile), 158, 164

Mas á Tierra (island) (Chile), 138

Massey, William (Prime Minister, New Zealand), 251, 306, 308

Matsumura, Tatsuo, Rear Admiral (Imperial Japanese Navy) 182, 185

Mazátlan (Mexico), 109, 127,

128, 145, 146
McBride, Sir Richard, (Premier, British Columbia), 110, 111, 112, 113, 116, 117, 133, 134
McKinley, William (US President), 9
Meighen, Arthur, (Prime Minister, Canada) 2, 255, 267, 270, 274 to 281, 283 to 313, 316, 317, 321, 326
Meiji Emperor (Mutsuhito) (Japan), 40, 93, 94
Meiji restoration, 10, 27, 32, 212, 258, 259
Mencius, 250
Mexico, 109, 126, 127, 130, 132, 135, 147, 216, 220, 221, 222, 223, 224, 225, 226, 227
Meyer-Waldeck, Alfred, Captain (Imperial German Navy) (*as Governor of Tsingtao*) 190, 197, 198
Micronesia, 121, 151, 158, 178, 179, 183, 185, 186
Midway Island (US), 143
Mongolia, Inner, 206, 207
Mongolia, Outer, 207, 327
Monroe Doctrine (US), 21, 35 fn1, 304
Moriyama, Keizaburo, Rear Admiral (Imperial Japanese Navy), 143, 144, 145, 146, 147
Mukden, Battle of, 44, 46
Mukden, City of (Manchuria), 40

Muller, Max von, Captain (Imperial German Navy), 134, 135, 136, 137, 138, 139, 141, 152, 153, 155, 191
Mulroney, Brian (Prime Minister, Canada), 331
Mutsu Munemitsu (Count) (Foreign Minister, Japan), 13
Nauru (island) (Germany), 178, 180, 248, (*Australia*) 330
Nebogatov, Nikolai, Rear Admiral (Imperial Russian Navy), 45
Netherlands East Indies, 119, 235
Netherlands New Guinea, 17
Neu Mecklenburg, (island) (Germany) 178, 180, 181
Neu Pommern (island) (Germany), 178, 181
Neutrality Proclamation (US), 111, 112
New Caledonia (France), 17, 179
Newfoundland (Dominion of), 23, 86, 245, 246, 295
New Hebrides (islands) (Great Britain/France), 17
New Zealand, (Dominion of) 2, 17, 78, 79, 83, 86, 91, 114, 121, 156, 158, 159, 170, 173, 174, 176, 179, 180, 181, 184, 186, 187, 205, 206, 232, 234, 235, 236, 245, 246, 247, 248, 251, 256, 258, 259, 264, 269, 271, 275. 276.

279, 295, 299, 304, 305, 306
312, 329
Nicholas II Tsar and Emperor
of Russia, (*as Tsarevich*) 15, 16
(as Tsar) 38, 39, 40, 41, 42, 61,
104, 215, 237
Nine-Power Treaty (1922), 321
Northwest Territories
(Canada), 6
Nuka Hiva (island) (French
Polynesia), 157

Oguri, Kosaburo, Admiral
(Imperial Japanese Navy), 176
Okuma Shigenobu (Prime
Minister, Japan), 115,119, 120
Omdurman, Battle of, 22
Onderdonk, Andrew (railway
contractor), 32
Open Door Policy, 41, 53, 227,
300, 321
Orlando, Vittorio (Prime
Minister, Italy), 253
Otani, Kikuzo, Lieutenant
General (Imperial Japanese
Army) (*as Allied Commander-
in-Chief Siberia*) 239, 241, 242
Ottoman Empire, 123, 177, 232,
244, 247, 312

Pacific Conference 1921 *see
Washington Naval Conference*
Pacific Ocean, (generally) 1, 3,
5, 6, 7, 9, 10, 17, 32, 62, 63, 65,
73, 75, 83, 84, 86, 87, 92, 110,
113, 116, 119, 120, 131, 134, 135,
136, 142, 143, 152, 155, 158, 159,
173, 174, 175, 178, 183, 205, 206,
213, 214, 215, 216, 222, 236,
253, 258, 262, 264, 273, 298,
302, 308, 312, 316, 319, 330,
331
Pagan Island (Spain/
Germany), 153, 155, 158
Page, Walter (diplomat,
United States), 225
Palau (islands) (Germany), 178,
180, 185, 186
Panama Canal, 81, 82, 84, 86,
145, 222
Papeete Battle of, 157
Patey, Sir George, Rear
Admiral (Royal Australian
Navy), 142, 144, 145, 181, 182
Paterson, James (American
businessman), 111, 112
Pearl Harbour (Hawaii), 83,
236, 262
Perry, Commodore Matthew
(US Navy), 10
Pershing, John J., Brigadier
General (US Army), 222
Pescadores Islands (Japan), 13
Philippine Islands (Spain/
USA), 9, 10, 18, 55, 82, 83, 96
Plüschow, Gunther,
Lieutenant (Imperial German
Navy), 194, 195, 198, 203-04
Poincaré, Raymond,
(President, France), 103
Ponape (Caroline Islands,

Germany), 132, 152, 184
Port Arthur (Manchuria), 12, 13, 26, 38, 42, 43, 44, 46, 47, 191
Pope, Sir Alexander (Deputy Minister of External Affairs, Canada), 288
Portugal, 8, 256 fn4
Powlett, F. A., Captain (Royal Navy), 133
Puerto Rico (island) (Spain/USA), 9
Puerto San Bartolome (Mexico), 145, 147, 148
Pu Yi Emperor of China (Manchu Empire), 94
Pyongyang, Battle of, 12

Qing Dynasty (China), 14, 15
Q-Ships, 219

Racial Equality Clause, 245, 248, 249, 250, 251, 252, 253, 259, 265; (text of) 251
Roosevelt, Theodore (US President), 46, 60, 71, 72, 79, 82, 83
Root-Takahira Agreement (1908), 82
Rowell, Newton (Canadian politician), 288, 289, 292
Royal Roads (Esquimalt naval base), 148
Rozhestvensky, Zinovi, Vice Admiral (Imperial Russian Navy), 43, 44, 45, 52
Russian Civil War, 239, 240, 241
Russo-Japanese Agreement (1907) (Manchuria), 80, 81
Russo-Japanese Alliance (1916), 215
Russo-Japanese War, 16, 42, 43, 44, 45, 46, 47, 52, 60, 61, 73, 84, 104, 114, 143, 191, 206, 300, 314
Ryukyu Islands, Kingdom of (later Okinawa Prefecture), 11

Saionji, Kinmochi (Prince) (Japanese statesman), 248, 252
Sakhalin Island, 46
Salisbury (Marquis of), Gascoyne-Cecil, Robert,(Prime Minister, Great Britain), 26, 231
San Diego US Pacific Naval Station, 146, 148
San Francisco (USA), 96, 129, 130, 131, 134, 145, 146, 204
Satow, Sir Ernest (diplomat, Great Britain), 61
Sazonov, Sergey, (Foreign Minister, Russia), 211, 215
Schonberg, Karl von, Captain (Imperial German Navy), 163, 168
Seattle Construction and Drydock Company, 111, 112
Seattle (Washington, USA), 111, 112
Seistan, 54
Selbourne Memoranda, 67

Senegal, 22
Shantung Peninsula (China), 187, 207, 209, 249, 300, 327
Shantung Railway, 193, 199
Shidehara, Kijuro (Baron) (diplomat, Japan), 318
Singapore (island) (Great Britain), 172, 174, 175, 177, 262, 263, 329, 330
Sino-Japanese War (1895), 9, 12, 13, 14, 40, 53, 111
Smuts, Jan (Prime Minister, South Africa), 251, 306, 308
Society Islands (France), 6, 157, 236
Sophie, Duchess of Hoenberg (Austria-Hungary), 100, 101, 102
South Africa (Union of), 86, 245, 246, 251. 256 fn4, 295, 306
Spain, Kingdom of, 9, 10, 17, 221, 272
Spanish-American War (1898), 9
Spee, Maximilian von (Count) Vice Admiral (Imperial German Navy), 1, 109, 132, 134, 135, 136, 137, 138, 143, 144, 145, 151, 152, 153, 154, 155, 156, 157, 158, 159, 160, 161, 163, 164, 165, 166, 167, 168, 169, 173, 174, 175, 181, 182, 183, 187, 211, 261, 262
Stoddart, Archibald, Rear-Admiral (Royal Navy), 137

Sturdee, Sir Frederick Doveton, Vice Admiral (Royal Navy), 165, 166, 167, 169
Sun Yat-sen (Provisional President of China), 94
Suvorov Atoll (Great Britain), 156
Sykes-Picot Agreement (1916), 232
Szögyény, Ladislaus (Count) (diplomat, Austria-Hungary), 102

Taft-Katsura Agreement (1904), 82
Tahiti (French Polynesia), 17, 157
Taisho Emperor (Yoshihito) (Japan), 94, 196, 259, 260
Tasman Sea, 173
Therichens, Max, Captain (Imperial German Navy), 137
Tibet, 25, 54, 327
Ting, Juchang, Admiral (Manchu Empire), 12
Tirpitz, Alfred von, Grand Admiral (Imperial German Navy), 24, 68, 75, 153
Tochinai, Sajiro, Vice Admiral (Imperial Japanese Navy), 147, 172
Togo, Heihachiro, Admiral (Imperial Japanese Navy), 44, 45
Tokugawa, Iesato (Prince) (diplomat, Japan), 318
Tojo, Hideki (General,

Imperial Japanese Army) (as Premier, Japan), 328
Tokugawa Shogunate, 10, 27
Tonga, Kingdom of, 5, 17, 179
Trafalgar, Battle of, 46, 65, 169
Trans-Siberian Railway, 15, 16, 39, 42, 46, 52, 215, 238
Treaty of Commerce and Navigation 1911, 93, 214
Treaty of Portsmouth, 60
Treaty of Shimonoseki, 13, 26
Treaty of Versailles, 244 to 257, 265, 268
Tripartite or Axis Pact (1936), 328
Triple Alliance, 25, 68, 85, 101, 105, 123 fn1, 132, 151
Triple Entente, 105, 211
Triple Intervention, 13 to 14, 16, 38, 110
Trudeau, Justin (Prime Minister, Canada), 123 fn7
Tsingtao (Germany), 13, 122, 129, 134, 135, 137, 151, 152, 153, 175, 178, 187, 188, 189, 190, 207, 209, 212, 223, 253, 259, 261, 262, 329
Tsingtao, Battle of, 191 to 200
Tsushima (Strait), 43, 45
Tsushima, Battle of, 38 to 46
Tuamotu Archipelago (French Polynesia), 17
Turkestan (Russia), 25

Uchida, Kosai, (Foreign Minister, Japan), 273, 274

Valparaiso (Chile), 65
Vancouver, City of (British Columbia), 6, 33, 34, 72, 78, 83, 96, 108, 109, 126, 134, 149, 177, 215, 238
Vancouver Island (British Columbia), 65, 133, 144, 330
Venezuela – British Guiana border dispute, 21, 268
Victoria (British Columbia), 32, 34, 65, 74, 83, 109, 110, 111, 126, 133
Victoria, (Queen of Great Britain and Ireland, Empress of India), 23, 66
Villa, Pancho (Mexican revolutionary), 221, 222
Viviani, René (Premier, France), 103
Vladivostok (Russia), 16, 26, 38, 44, 45, 215, 237, 238, 239, 241
Vogt, Captain Friedrich (Imperial German Navy), 164

Wake Island (USA), 9
Washington Naval Conference 1921 (*includes Pacific Conference*) 281, 302, 308, 309, 310, 316, 321
Weihaiwei (China), 12, 13, 191
Welles, Sumner (diplomat, United States), 198
Wilhelm II Kaiser [*Emperor*] of Germany, 23, 24, 41, 61, 66, 67, 92, 102, 103, 104, 154, 190,

GENERAL INDEX | 357

191, 224, 260

Wilhelmshaven Naval Base (Germany), 154

Wilson, Woodrow (US President), 98 fn17, 111, 112, 220, 221, 222, 225, 226, 227, 230, 245, 246, 249, 252, 256 fn2

Winnipeg General Strike 1919, 285, 286

Witgeft, Wilhelm, Rear Admiral (Imperial Russian Navy), 42

Witte, Sergius, (Russian statesman), 16, 39, 40, 46

Yalu River, Battle of (*also, Battle of the Yellow Sea*), 12

Yamaya, Tanin, Vice Admiral (Imperial Japanese Navy), 184, 185

Yap (Caroline Islands, Germany), 179, 182, 183, 186, 249

Yellow Sea, Battle of the (*also Battle of the Yalu River*), 12

Yokohama (Japan), 34, 96, 132, 134, 135, 216

Yokosuka Naval Station, 148

Yoshioka, Hansaku, Captain (Imperial Japanese Navy), 145, 146, 148

Yüan Shih-k'ai (China, statesman), (*as Manchu general*), 11, 94 (*as President of China*) 206, 207, 208, 209 (*as Emperor*) 210

Yukon, (Canada) 6

Zimmermann, Arthur, (Foreign Minister, Germany), 219, 221, 224, 225, 226, 227

Zimmerman Telegram, (*text of*), 224-25

Zuckschwerdt, Adalbert, Captain (Imperial German Navy), 136, 137

www.ingramcontent.com/pod-product-compliance
Lightning Source LLC
Chambersburg PA
CBHW032025290426
44110CB00012B/673